Fake History

Fake History

101 things that never happened

Jo Hedwig Teeuwisse

WH
ALLEN

2

WH Allen, an imprint of Ebury Publishing
20 Vauxhall Bridge Road
London SW IV 2SA

WH Allen is part of the Penguin Random House group of companies
whose addresses can be found at global.penguinrandomhouse.com

First published by WH Allen in 2023

www.penguin.co.uk

A CIP catalogue record for this book is available from the British Library

Hardback ISBN 9780753559673
Trade Paperback ISBN 9780753559680

Typeset in 12/14.5pt Garamond MT Std by Jouve (UK), Milton Keynes
Printed and bound in Great Britain by Clays Ltd, Elcograf S.p.A.

The authorised representative in the EEA is Penguin Random House Ireland,
Morrison Chambers, 32 Nassau Street, Dublin DO2 YH68

MIX
Paper | Supporting
responsible forestry
FSC
www.fsc.org   FSC® C018179

Penguin Random House is committed to a sustainable
future for our business, our readers and our planet.
This book is made from Forest Stewardship
Council® certified paper.

*For my mother Constance, who had to deal with bringing up a
history-obsessed child, which wasn't easy, but who was nevertheless
always proud of me and who was so excited about this
book but sadly passed away before it was published.*

A note from the author

Nobody knows everything; even people on the internet can be mistaken. On top of that, our ideas about and knowledge of the past change regularly. If you have doubts about something, do your own research, check several sources and never trust anyone blindly – and yes, that includes me.

Contents

Introduction

I've always been obsessed with history.

As a little girl I drove my parents crazy during our holidays by always asking them to take me to castles and ruins while they were trying to relax in the sun on a nice beach. I was also caught several times trying to get people in old paintings in museums to talk to me, and I dreamed of becoming a pirate. I was a bit of a peculiar child.

When I grew up and realised piracy generally no longer involved three-masted ships, cannons and wooden legs, I decided to become a war reporter. Fortunately, my little sister Lotte was then born and I suddenly became a Big Sister and realised this honour was difficult to combine with risking my life for the news.

After working in a less lethal branch of film and television for a while, I discovered my heart wasn't in it and I decided to switch careers. Somehow, I managed to spend the next couple of decades as a historical researcher for authors, museums, documentary, film and television-show makers, and so on. I designed museum exhibits, did research for big international productions, solved mysteries other researchers couldn't figure out and procured items documentary makers thought were impossible to find. I portrayed people from the past as a live historical interpreter at museums, which involved me wearing authentic period clothing and living like our ancestors once did while talking to the public, and I also enjoyed pointing out mistakes and inaccuracies to set dressers and the costume departments of plays and TV shows. History was my bread, my butter, my addictive substance, and it still is.

But one day I decided to escape the city, move to a little farm in the middle of nowhere and slow down a bit, which was when I made the shocking discovery that there are people on the internet who are wrong . . .

It all started with someone sharing a photo from the 1920s on Twitter that I thought wasn't actually from that era. I researched it, proved them wrong and started looking for people who were also sharing things online that weren't quite true.

I had become the Fake History Hunter.

So, these days, after I've walked the dog, have done a bit of work in the garden and answered my emails, I take a long list of keywords, put them through the Twitter search engine and see if anyone has posted any fake history. I sometimes hunt down more benign kinds of fake history – Auntie Doreen posting a fake picture with a fun, but false, caption – but I also focus on powerful and famous people with millions of followers. Some of these people have ulterior motives; they don't just share these things to entertain and get a bit of clout, but to dehumanise their opponents, talk their followers into ignoring medical advice, to fleece others out of their money and to pit one group against another or further some sort of agenda.

This book contains some of the most common and fascinating bits of fake history I've encountered online, which explains why the subjects are so varied and wide-ranging. It also explains why some of the chapters, just like history, are fun, while others are about dark and difficult subjects. There are therefore a couple of images that you may find hard to look at.

Sometimes it's easy to debunk a fake history story, while other times it takes a lot of research and detective work, but that's kind of what my job is, and I love it. I hope you enjoy what I've written and maybe you can even use it to do a bit of fake history hunting yourself.

What is fake history and why is it bad?

Fake history is a lot like fake news, except, well, rather old news.

This book is full of examples, many of which will seem funny or rather harmless (though of course it is annoying for historians and history addicts that people still believe certain long-debunked misconceptions!), but others can actually be harmful and dangerous. Take for instance the myths, misattributed quotations and wrongly described photos that were being shared during the COVID-19 pandemic. People were using stories about the Black Death, the Spanish flu and very poignant and relevant things allegedly said by brilliant minds of the past to either get people to wear masks, follow lockdown rules and take COVID-19 seriously – or to try to convince everybody to do the exact opposite. History is also egregiously abused by people trying to make entire civilisations seem either inferior or superior, for example by claiming that Africans didn't know what the wheel was until European colonisers arrived, or that Europeans didn't know about bathing and soap until the Moors colonised them.

People really like using the past to try to make themselves look better or others look worse. And if you have a historical photo or convincing 'experts' that support things you really want to believe, this can feed hate and resentment and push us further apart. I think, though, that the more you study and understand history, *true* history, the closer together it brings us; our ancestors were more alike than some of us like to believe.

Fake history is, of course, not something that just plagues the internet – there are also myths that are handed down from generation to generation without being questioned. And even the information we learn in museums is not always true. Most of us have

3

memories of museum or castle guides telling some really strange and far-fetched stories that later turned out to be totally untrue.

There are also those who spread fake history for a more basic reason: money. Social media can make you rich; creating popular, widely shared content is big business. There are Twitter accounts that post lots and lots of historical images and claims. They sometimes buy thousands of followers so that they don't look like new irrelevant accounts that appear out of nowhere, and instead seem more legitimate and trustworthy. Once people start sharing their posts those numbers quickly skyrocket. Then, once their account has enough followers, they suddenly start retweeting posts about acrylic stick-on nails, online games, other totally random accounts and, these days, NFTs. Which means they probably made a deal with some sort of marketing company and are just selling retweets. While you technically can't sell your Twitter account (except in rare situations), it still happens quite a lot and it can be very difficult to notice or prove that this has occurred.

So, millions of people end up believing nonsense about something I care a lot about, and fake history can be not only annoying, but dangerous. But for me, as a self-confessed history addict, the worst part about all this fake history is that the myths, misconceptions and claims are often less interesting and exciting than the truth.

History matters. It is a manual that helps us understand the past, figure out the present and sometimes even realise what is ahead of us. I hope the stories in this book show that. We can't stop historians, mercenary Twitter accounts and other powerful people using and abusing history, but we can at least do something about them spreading fake history – all it takes is research and knowledge.

1

Napoleon Bonaparte shot the nose off the Sphinx

A sketch of the Sphinx by Frederic Louis Norden, published 1755

What you may have been told

During his visit to Egypt, Napoleon saw the Sphinx and was furious when he realised that the statue's face looked African. Being a massive racist, Napoleon couldn't stand the idea that the statue didn't depict someone European. So he ordered his troops to shoot the Sphinx's nose off with a cannon. That did the trick.

The debunking

This story probably started as an innocent little myth, a fun story for the tourists, dating back to at least the early twentieth century. But these days, it's shared online for a new, rather unpleasant reason: evidence of racism. I'm not sure when people started to think that Napoleon thought the statue's nose looked too African and therefore had to go, but it's believed by a lot of people.

In 1995, Louis Farrakhan, leader of the Nation of Islam, said in his speech during the Million Man March that 'White supremacy caused Napoleon to blow the nose off of the Sphinx because it reminded you too much of the Black man's majesty.' So the myth is used to make a claim about racism, which of course makes what was once a harmless tale into something a lot more damaging. Ironically, the Nation of Islam and Farrakhan are accused of bigotry towards Jews, LGBTQ+ and white people, and are known for wild conspiracy theories. Although they are not responsible for the claim, they play a big part in its enduring popularity.

Luckily it is quite easy to prove that the myth is nonsense, so take note for when you meet someone who believes the story. Unless they think everything is a massive conspiracy theory, you should be able to convince them with one very simple fact: Napoleon did not have access to a time machine. Napoleon was born in 1769, and went to Egypt in 1798. But we know people were writing about the Sphinx's damaged face and drawing pictures of it BEFORE NAPOLEON WAS EVEN BORN. That should convince any rational person. It would also be really weird for Napoleon to have committed this act of vandalism as he was clearly very interested in Egyptian history and responsible for the first European scientific study of the antiquities there.

Let's look at some of the evidence.

In 1737 (before Napoleon was born . . .), Danish naval captain Frederic Louis Norden travelled to Egypt and made very detailed sketches of the Sphinx, which were published several years later. The statue in these drawings has clearly already lost its nose. You can find these easily online.

In 1759 (before Napoleon was born . . .), Dutchmen Johannes Aegidius van Egmond van der Nyenburg and Johannes Heyman published a book with the catchy title, *Travels through part of Europe, Asia Minor, the islands of the archipelago, Syria, Palestine, Egypt, Mount Sinai, &c. Containing a particular Account of the most remarkable Places, Structures, Ruins, Inscriptions &c. in these Countries. Together with the Customs, Manners, Religion, Trade, Commerce, Tempers and manner of living of the Inhabitants.* It is an amazing book – you can find it online (see the source notes at the back of the book) – and, lucky for us, the adventurers went to check out the Sphinx, describing its nose as 'a little mutilated'.

In 1760 (before Napoleon was born . . .), Dr Siegmund Jakob Baumgarten published *A Supplement to the English Universal History, lately published in London.* In it, he describes the Sphinx as 'very little hurt, except only that his nose is maimed, probably by the Mohammedans, from their bitterness against images'.

There are more examples – those are just a few. But the point is that we have eyewitness accounts and drawings telling us that the Sphinx was damaged before Napoleon was even a glint in his parents' eyes. So anyone who refuses to accept this evidence clearly simply prefers the myth. But if it wasn't Napoleon, who was it?

Dr Baumgarten already gave us a clue – he mentioned the 'Mohammedans', the old-fashioned term for Muslims. In the fifteenth century, historian al-Maqrīzī claimed that Muhammad Sa'im al-Dahr had destroyed the nose in 1378 because he couldn't stand locals making offerings to the Sphinx. This may be the story to which the doctor was referring. But this was of course a story written a while after it happened, and it is only one story, which is not really enough to accept this as the solution to our whodunnit. To make things even more interesting, a couple of decades ago, archaeologist Mark Lehner studied the damage to the Sphinx and came to the conclusion it happened between the third and tenth century AD, in which case it couldn't have been al-Dahr *or* Napoleon.

Many statues in ancient Egypt have been damaged and lost their noses, and this was often done by Egyptians themselves because they believed that a deceased human or deity's soul could inhabit an image and defacing the art would release it.

Besides that, noses also stick out and are more easily damaged than other parts of statues. Lots of old statues have lost their noses or other bits that stick out, like arms, or appendages we dare not mention. It's very common. Greek and Roman statues have also fallen victim to this kind of damage.

In short, there is no evidence whatsoever that the motive behind the Sphinx vandalism is race related. And although there are a few suspects, the truth is that nobody knows for sure who damaged the Sphinx. But we can say without a shadow of a doubt that it wasn't Napoleon or his troops. Not yet existing is a pretty rock-solid alibi.

2

Hugo Boss designed the Nazi uniforms

Rang- und Paradeanzug der Allgem. SS.
Oberscharführer

Trebdienstanzug der SS.
Unterscharführer

Tafel 47

What you may have been told

Say what you want about the Nazis, but they sure did look sharp. Just check out those uniforms! Such a fine cut, so flattering. They looked better than anyone else during the war. But that's not so surprising when you know that Hugo Boss designed all their uniforms. Yes, that Hugo Boss! Strange the brand hasn't been cancelled yet, right?

The debunking

That Hugo Boss designed the Nazi uniforms is almost common knowledge; so many people believe it that every time the brand is in the news you'll find social media posts proliferating online, reminding us of this 'fun fact'. When Formula 1 driver Lewis Hamilton makes statements about racism or political topics he's often called a hypocrite for having Boss as a sponsor. But the thing is, Boss did not design any Nazi uniforms. That's right – not one of those fancy outfits can be credited to him.

Hugo Ferdinand Boss founded a clothes manufacturing company in 1924. He had a small factory with not that many employees and the business mostly specialised in making shirts, jackets and work clothing. One of his first commissions was making brown shirts for a distributor in Munich. Boss probably didn't know at the time that they were then being sold on to the Nazis, though he'd use this later to promote his company, telling people they'd been supplying to the party since 1924.

When Boss joined the Nazi party in 1931 and managed to get a contract to provide the Nazis with uniforms he was still a relatively small, unknown manufacturer, and just one of several companies supplying the Nazis with clothing. His party connections saved his company from bankruptcy, but his name wasn't big or famous at that point. But more importantly, Boss was not a designer but a manufacturer. He was given orders and his employees fulfilled them. There was no creativity or design talent involved; the uniforms had been designed before the orders even arrived at the company. Many other companies in Germany and German-occupied territories made uniforms too. Hugo Boss was only a small player.

Why on earth would the Nazi party ask such a small clothing manufacturer with no real design talent or experience to design their uniforms? There is no evidence whatsoever that Hugo Boss was ever asked to design any Nazi uniforms, and Boss was not given permission to tweak, alter or change the designs of his orders. And seriously, why do people think that manufacturers would be allowed to adapt the uniforms they *did* make – the clue's in the name: 'uniform' – clothing famous for having to be exactly the same.

'Hans, why is your uniform jacket pink with a yellow frilly border?!'

'Oh, you know, Günther, mine was made by some little clothing factory and Hitler decided to just let them do whatever they wanted with the design.'

If companies were allowed to just do as they pleased, half the Wehrmacht would have pranced about like Captain Klenzendorf in the 2019 film *Jojo Rabbit*.

Of course, this doesn't mean Boss is off the hook and was just some innocent factory owner. He was an active supporter of the Nazis who was given and accepted the opportunity to use forced labour as early as April 1940. Although Boss seems to have treated these people relatively well compared to quite a lot of other factories, they were still forced labourers and they were sometimes mistreated and threatened with being sent to concentration camps by Boss employees. And it seems that Boss did nothing to stop this.

After the war, Hugo Boss was heavily fined for having been an early member of the Nazi party, having financially benefited and having been friends with high-ranking Nazis. The company continued to make uniforms but this time for the French and the Red Cross.

The difference between designing and manufacturing may just seem a case of semantics, but there's more at play here. The myth attributes talent to Boss – after all, many people think the Nazi uniforms looked impressive and conclude that he knew how to design very good-looking uniforms. The truth takes this away from him. All that is left is just another enthusiastic Nazi who was also a war profiteer and used forced labour.

If anything, the truth makes him worse.

3

Marie Antoinette said 'Let them eat cake'

What you may have been told

Whenever someone rich or powerful, some politician or billionaire, says something stupid or out of touch, someone will remind them of what happened to Marie Antoinette.

The people of France were starving and yet, as their queen, she was so far removed from reality, she couldn't understand that they couldn't afford food. When she was told the poor couldn't buy bread, she replied, 'Let them eat cake!' Of course, this infuriated the people, who then did that whole French Revolution thing, put the royal family under the guillotine and cut off Marie Antoinette's head.

The debunking

There's no evidence she ever said it, at all – not even as a joke, not even when there was a lot of cake lying about the place. Nobody claimed she did until long after her death. And there is a lot of evidence that it was actually another princess who said it when Marie Antoinette was still a little girl living in Austria.

Yes, Marie Antoinette is the only French person most of us know from that era and yes, she was and still is a symbol of incredibly sickening decadence and wealth, but it wasn't said by her. If anything, she seemed to have cared a lot about the plight of the poor and even wrote about her concerns for the poverty and hunger she witnessed. In a letter to her mother, Empress Maria Theresa of Austria, written on 22 June 1775, she wrote:

> *It is at the same time amazing and wonderful to be so well received two months after the riots and in spite of the high price of bread which unfortunately continues . . . It is certain that when people who are suffering treat us so well, we are even more obligated to work for their happiness.*

Admittedly, the money she spent on just one of her dresses could have fed a starving family for weeks, but in a way she was also just a prisoner of the world she was born into. Antoinette lived in palaces all her life, surrounded by servants and governesses who prepared her for her future role, shielding her from the realities of the real world. Then, at only 14 years old, she found herself married to the king of France, one of the most powerful and richest men on earth. If that happened today, we'd feel sorry for her and we might have teenagers on TikTok telling us she is a victim too and that we should leave her alone.

So if it wasn't Marie Antoinette, what is the origin of this story?

The phrase came from a story written by Jean-Jacques Rousseau in book six of his series *Confessions*, in which he claims that a 'great princess' responded to the news that the peasants had no bread with 'then let them eat brioches' (brioche, by the way, is not really cake but more like a very rich bread, made with a lot of butter and eggs). The princess is not named and may even have just been made up; in fact, the book seems to suggest it was some fable or anecdote Rousseau had heard somewhere. The story was written between 1766 and 1767, and was published in 1782. Marie Antoinette was born in 1755, which means she was about eleven and still living in Austria when the 'great princess' may have made the remark about brioche (assuming it was not a much older story Rousseau was recording). She clearly can't be the princess Rousseau was writing about. And even if it had been her, surely such a response could be forgiven from a child?

The story may have even older origins. It might be one of those things that people have been saying about the rich and powerful for centuries. I can't prove this, but I found an example dating back to the seventh century that is suspiciously similar. In a Jin Dynasty chronicle, it is written that when Emperor Hui was told that his people were starving because there wasn't enough rice, he replied, 'Why don't they eat porridge with meat?'

So this very similar story was circulating almost 1,500 years before Marie Antoinette was born. This of course doesn't prove anything, but it is interesting and maybe one day, when someone finds the time to start looking for other claims just like it throughout history, we'll find out that this is indeed a popular old bit of gossip.

Going back to the French queen, the first time the quote was attributed to her was decades after she died under the guillotine. During her time on the throne she was attacked with tons of propaganda and outright lies: it was claimed she was doing naughty bedroom things with other women and a LOT of men, that she poisoned her own child and was even planning to kill everybody in France . . . but nobody claimed she said the cake thing. So according to the word on the street, she was a pervy foreign child-abusing homicidal maniac, but sure, that's fine, no worries, that's just Marie being Marie. But when she said something silly about bread – *that's* what started the revolution?

Not a chance.

It is interesting to note that the claim became very popular during the Victorian era, and you'll see that this won't be the only time that we can blame the Victorians for messing up our views of the past.

4

That famous person said that smart thing

What you may have been told

You know that really famous smart person? Yeah, he said that really famous smart thing, and I am now going to quote him because it will make me look smart on social media, and you might think I'm smart too and believe whatever I say next.

The debunking

OK, I know, that sounded a bit silly, but that is what happens. People use a quote by some famous, preferably very smart or witty person to appear more learned themselves or to make what they're about to say next seem more impressive. For instance, when yet another lockdown was announced during the COVID-19 pandemic, Einstein's quote, 'Insanity is doing the same thing over and over again and expecting different results', became very popular when people wanted to make a point about the government sticking to a plan that they didn't think was working. But it isn't an Einstein quote.

When someone wants to suggest politicians or the media are lying, Mark Twain's quote, 'It's easier to fool people than to convince them that they've been fooled', often resurfaces. Which is ironic as . . . this quote is not by Mark Twain.

And then there is Marie Antoinette and the cake, of course.

Those who share these quotes are suggesting that they know about history and are very well read. If you're on Twitter, you can even pay for a service that will post a quote on your behalf every day or week. Often, they even come with a nice illustration – a portrait of whomever they think they're quoting or some vague landscape with the quote printed over it, just to give it even more credibility. Sometimes, there will be a link to one of the many quote websites that have pages full of smart, funny, interesting things people have said. The sites look so flashy and impressive that a lot of people assume they wouldn't post nonsense, but I'm afraid they do.

I've got a list of misattributed quotes that I search for on Twitter almost daily but I had to stop correcting everyone who had used them because there were just too many of them. Literally hundreds if not thousands of people share them all the time. Even though I only searched for a few specific ones that were all related to history, I still found more than I could handle.

So when is a quote really someone's quote?

Generally, we attribute a quote to someone when it originated with them: if they were the first to say or write it and we can prove this. When someone says something but they're just repeating what they've read somewhere or are quoting someone else, we can say that they said it, but not that it is their quote.

If you love this sort of thing and want to know more about the research and even detective work that has gone into tracking down the sources of quotes, check out the source notes for this chapter. I can especially recommend the Quote Investigator, who is not only great to follow on Twitter and has a wonderful website, but also published a book on the subject.

Here are some of the most common quotes I regularly spot

on Twitter. I'm pretty sure that at least one or two will surprise you:

Winston Churchill was a famous statesman and sure understood politics, so it is tempting to share his words to make a political point, but the following quotes are NOT his:

'*You have enemies? Good. That means you've stood up for something, sometime in your life.*'

'*If you're going through hell, keep going.*'

'*A lie gets halfway around the world before the truth has a chance to get its pants on.*'

'*The best argument against Democracy is a five-minute conversation with the average voter.*'

'*The fascists of the future will be called anti-fascists.*'

Oscar Wilde may have been the king of sharp wit, and quoting him is always a hit online, but none of the following quotes can be attributed to him:

'*If you want to tell people the truth, you'd better make them laugh or they'll kill you.*'

'*Always forgive your enemies – nothing annoys them so much.*'

'*Be yourself. Everyone else is already taken.*'

'*Some cause happiness wherever they go; others whenever they go.*'

Einstein was a genius, so sharing what he said will possibly make you look smart as well, but these are not his quotes:

'*Insanity is doing the same thing over and over again and expecting different results.*'

'*Everybody is a genius. But if you judge a fish by its ability to climb a tree, it will live its whole life believing that it is stupid.*'

'*If a cluttered desk is a sign of a cluttered mind, we can't help wondering what an empty desk indicates.*'

'*Creativity is contagious.*'

'A clever person solves a problem. A wise person avoids it.'
'Any fool can know. The point is to understand.'

Few people even really know who Voltaire was but he sure did say some smart-sounding things so he's quite popular online. But he didn't say:

'I may disagree with what you have to say, but I shall defend to the death your right to say it.'

'To learn who rules over you, simply find out who you are not allowed to criticise.'

That last one, by the way, was actually written by an American neo-Nazi who was arrested for possessing child pornography. You can imagine how painful it is for some people to realise whose quote they've been really sharing.

This one is especially popular by those who are into that whole business-motivation thing but also with politicians, folks who have sometimes many of thousands, even millions of followers they're trying to inspire. It's a good quote for that but . . .

'If your actions inspire others to dream more, learn more, do more and become more, you are a leader.'

. . . is not a quote by John Quincy Adams, the sixth president of the United States, but singer-songwriter Dolly Parton! Which of course doesn't make the quote any less valuable, but it sure is fun to tell this to the chaps with the sharp suits and overly white teeth who thought they were quoting a statesman.

5

Star Trek showed the first interracial kiss on television in 1968

What you may have been told

Everybody knows that the first ever interracial kiss on television was broadcast in 1968 when Captain James Tiberius Kirk (William Shatner) and translator and communications officer Nyota Uhura (Nichelle Nichols) kissed in the *Star Trek* episode 'Plato's Stepchildren'. It is common knowledge, so every time someone complains about the show being 'woke' these days, people come running to remind them that the show has always been like that, and the kiss proves how far ahead of its time *Star Trek* was.

The debunking

To start with, let's take care of one thing: the first interracial kiss on television was NOT on *Star Trek*. Sorry Trekkies, sorry William Shatner. I guess you didn't like hearing it as you blocked me on Twitter, but it's the truth.

Anyway, now we've got that out of the way, let's technically overanalyse a bunch of kissing scenes in old shows to find out who wins first place for breaking down this barrier. To figure out which kiss was first we have to define the terms 'interracial' but also 'kiss'. Does a peck on the cheek count, or does it have to be a full-on kiss on the mouth? With or without tongues? Should it make you go *awwwww!* or make you feel really awkward if you watch it with your parents in the room? Does it have to be romantic and intentional? Can it be a joke kiss or, as in the case of *Star Trek*, a forced kiss, against one or both of the characters' will?

As Sam sang in *Casablanca*, a kiss is just a kiss – but a kiss is also still a kiss.

But seriously, how precise are we going to be in our definition? If a platonic, innocent peck on the cheek counts, there was an earlier interracial kiss in *Star Trek* when Uhura kisses Nurse Chapel in the episode 'What Are Little Girls Made Of?' Mind you, after watching it a couple of times I thought Uhura seemed quite impressed with that peck, so maybe something more was happening . . . but I'm getting distracted. (Still, if you ever see that episode, you now won't be able to unsee what I thought I saw.)

To keep things manageable, I'm going to say there are two types of kisses: platonic and romantic. (There are of course many more kinds, and I hope you get to experience all the best ones, but let's keep things simple for now.) A platonic kiss is just a peck on the cheek. It doesn't mean much and it can even be part of a joke. A romantic kiss is something more than that. Passion and, if you're lucky, love are involved. There's a relationship of a kind, attraction, perhaps even a hint of hanky-panky. I'll judge the kisses we find during this investigation against these criteria, and we'll look at both kinds of kiss, even though a loving kiss is of course much more important.

But we also have to define the word interracial, and that's a bit more complicated. The whole idea of races is outdated and makes little sense to begin with. It is a social construct and not only have our ideas about what race means changed dramatically over time, but different cultures also have different opinions about what's what. Not to mention that in some countries the whole subject is a lot more sensitive and overloaded with painful history than in others. The first contender makes this obvious right away.

In 1951, Lucille Ball (European ancestry) and Desi Arnaz (Cuban-American) kissed on screen in the TV show *I Love Lucy*. Some people say that this was not interracial as Cuban-American is close enough to European white, or their skin colours are too similar, and so on. But we are talking about 1950s America here; the channel CBS was adamantly opposed to having Lucy married to a Cuban, especially one with such a strong accent – he was 'too ethnic', they decided. Philip Morris cigarettes, a sponsor of the show, said that the American public would not accept Desi as the husband of a red-blooded American girl.

In the 1930s, some official documents described Desi's race as 'Cuban', but on others he was described as white, so it seems even the US government wasn't sure how to categorise him. Of course, both actors (who it's worth pointing out were married in real life at the time) had light skin, which made the kissing less controversial, but back then, a white woman kissing a Latino man was still a touchy subject, especially in the USA. And they didn't just kiss once, and they weren't innocent pecks either – Lucille and Desi did proper kissing. So it's unclear if we can call it interracial but it was absolutely controversial and definitely a romantic kiss, so it should at least be mentioned in this case.

The next contender interestingly enough involves . . . William Shatner! And no, it's not Captain Kirk kissing half the aliens in the galaxy. On 16 November 1958, the cast of the stage play *The World of Suzie Wong* performed a scene on *The Ed Sullivan Show*. The scene ended with William Shatner and France Nuyen kissing each other on the mouth, something that interestingly doesn't appear in Mr Shatner's autobiography while the *Star Trek* kiss gets a lot of attention. Shatner is white and Nuyen's father was of Asian origin, which, again according to some very weird rules, makes their kiss interracial. And it is a proper kiss: mouth to mouth, long and romantic. So if we decide to dismiss the kissing on *I Love Lucy*, this one is the first interracial kiss ever broadcast on television.

In 2015, there was some excitement when the British Film Institute discovered some footage from a televised adaptation of a play called *You in Your Small Corner*, which was broadcast on 5 June 1962 on ITV. It includes a kiss between a Black man and a white woman, and this discovery made news around the world. Even CNN mentioned it, as it of course predates *Star Trek* by several years. Unlike the *Star Trek* one, the kiss was not forced and, goodness me, is it passionate and filmed close up! It's a good and proper kiss – much better than the one on that alien planet.

But there was an earlier one, again on British television. On 1 February 1959, ITV broadcast Ted Willis's play *Hot Summer Night*, which showed a very passionate and romantic kiss between Jamaican actor Lloyd Reckord and white Liverpudlian Andrée Melly. Does that mean Britain can claim the first ever interracial kiss on television between a Black person and a white person?

No, sorry, we cloggies can claim that honour!

On 5 January 1959, at about 8.30pm (prime time), there was a kiss between Donald Jones, a Black actor who was born in the United States, and white actress Roekie Aronds, in the 'Beeldromance' episode of the Dutch TV show *Pension Hommeles*, one of my country's most popular programmes ever. At the time, there were only 100,000 TV sets in the Netherlands. Yet somehow, everybody saw it, as people would visit the neighbours in their street who had a set and watch it together.

Looking at Dutch newspapers of the time, it seems there was no controversy or backlash as a result of the kiss – quite the opposite, reviews were positive. Although the kiss was not as passionate as some of the other contenders, it clearly was romantic and more than just an innocent peck. It would have been problematic on American television back then.

So, which kiss we can consider to be the first interracial kiss on television depends on how we personally or culturally define interracial and if we think some of these kisses count or not. The main contenders are currently:

1951: *I Love Lucy*, Lucille Ball and Desi Arnaz.
1958: *The Ed Sullivan Show*, William Shatner and France Nuyen.
1959: *Pension Hommeles*, Donald Jones and Roekie Aronds
1959: *Hot Summer Night* in the *Armchair Theatre* series, Lloyd Reckord and Andrée Melly

Although we can't really compare the situation in 1960s America and 1950s Britain or the Netherlands when it comes to race relations, these kisses were all ground-breaking in one way or another.

Interestingly enough, Hollywood achieved this milestone long before television did. The oldest interracial kiss on the silver screen I could find was when a white man, played by Gilbert M. Anderson, kissed a Black woman, probably the wonderful Bertha Regustus, as far back as 1903, in the short film *What Happened in the Tunnel*. It is a peck but still a kiss nevertheless, and earlier than other contenders, such as *A Florida Enchantment* (1914) (which also contains women in drag and 'blackface'), *The Greatest Thing in Life* (1918) (an interracial same-sex kiss), *Pinky* (1949) (in which a white man passionately kisses a Black woman) and others.

6

EastEnders showed the first same-sex kiss on television in 1989

What you may have been told

The first time that two people of the same sex kissed on television was in 1989 on the British soap *EastEnders*. It was quite a big story; 20 million people watched it and although it was a wonderful and even life-changing thing for many viewers, others were furious. Members of Parliament demanded that the show be banned and the ever-so-delightful and always tasteful Piers Morgan wrote quite a nasty little piece full of slurs. But he and the others who clutched their pearls were on the wrong side of history, so kudos to the BBC for reaching yet another milestone.

The debunking

Let's rip the Band-Aid off right away: *EastEnders* did not have the first same-sex kiss shown on television. And no, it was not *L.A. Law*, *Dawson's Creek* or *Brookside* either.

It took quite a bit of detective work to find out which kiss was really the first one and eventually I ended up with a kiss that nobody else seems to have found. There are quite a few articles online about this subject and the media mentions it every now and then, but they always give credit to the wrong show.

Just like with the first interracial kiss, I make a distinction between romantic kisses and non-romantic, or platonic, kisses. A same-sex romantic kiss has more meaning, it involves love and/or passion and is part of or alludes to a serious gay relationship. A non-romantic or platonic kiss can have all sorts of meanings; it can just be a peck, a greeting or it can be part of a joke.

There have been same-sex kisses on television almost since they first entered our living rooms, but they were all platonic, and almost always for comedic effect. But when we want to find the first, we can't ignore these kisses altogether.

One of the earliest examples I could find was between famous comedians Dean Martin and Jerry Lewis on the show *The Colgate Comedy Hour*, which aired live on American TV from 1951 to 1955. Although it was platonic and often part of a slapstick joke, their relationship on- and off-screen could be considered as more than just friends. They were showing something rarely portrayed in 1950s America: an intense and loving relationship between two affectionate men who didn't mind showing it. As Jerry Lewis himself described it, 'What we had was a love affair, two men that adored one another, that was the key.' An early version of what some today would call a 'bromance'. So, technically, this could be considered the first kiss between two men broadcast on television, but even though the men clearly loved each other, they were not *in* love with each other, and their kisses were not romantic.

The American drama *Dawson's Creek* had a genuine kiss and is often, like *EastEnders*, credited with broadcasting the first romantic kiss between two men on 24 May 2000. And on 6 December 1998 an episode of *That '70s Show* aired, showing a passionate kiss between two young men. One of the men was gay and the other not, and it was a one-sided unwelcome attempt, so it was technically a (half-) passionate kiss between two men broadcast in the US during prime time.

But neither of these can claim to be first.

On 6 August 1970 at 9.10pm, the BBC broadcast Christopher Marlowe's play *Edward II*. In this adaption, Ian McKellen passionately kissed James Laurenson. This play was also shown in the USA on Ed-TV as part of a CBS broadcast on 27 September 1975 for the first time and repeated on other channels afterwards. Technically, that makes this British recording the first broadcasted romantic and passionate kiss between two men on American television. But, in 1968, on 20 October at 10.20pm in the UK, Granada Television broadcast the episode 'Caligula' from the series *The Caesars*, a big Roman-themed costume drama. In one scene emperor Caligula (played by Ralph Bates) gives Lepidus (played by Sean Arnold) a long, passionate kiss on the mouth. According to some Roman sources, Caligula and Lepidus did actually have an affair in real life. This is the first passionate, meaningful kiss between two men broadcast on television anywhere, as far as I know.

So it seems that British television can be credited with the first gay kiss in the UK and the US!

What about women, though?

Most people think that the first passionate kiss between two women on US television was in an episode of NBC's *L.A. Law* in 1991, but there was also a same-sex kiss in the police drama *21 Jump Street* in the episode 'Change of Heart', broadcast on 15 January 1990 at 8pm. Although it was filmed in extreme close-up, it was still clearly a passionate kiss between two women, one of whom was a lesbian.

But more importantly, unlike some of the other kisses, this was not just some sort of stunt to cause controversy and get publicity; this one was part of a whole episode about homosexuality. It dealt with many issues and tried to explain to its young audience that homosexuality was perfectly normal. This episode was groundbreaking in many ways. But it was not the first passionate kiss between two women on American television either. For that, we once more have to look at a British broadcast.

In 1968, the BBC broadcast an adaptation of Émile Zola's *Nana*, starring Katherine Schofield. In an August 2021 issue of

Prospero, the newspaper for retired BBC Pension Scheme members, the director of this drama, John Davies, claimed that as well as showing a woman's breasts it also contained a scene of Nana, dressed in top hat and tails, kissing another woman. Unfortunately, no footage survives so it is difficult to judge if it was just an innocent peck or something more, but regardless, this makes it the first same-sex kiss on UK television I've found.

It was probably also the first same-sex kiss between women on TV in several other countries as the drama was bought by nations across the world, including the United States, where it was broadcast in 1969.

But . . . it was not the first one ever. That point – as far as we know – goes to Brazil. In 1963, two women were shown kissing in an episode of the show *A Calúnia*. This kiss was not a peck on the cheek, a kiss forced by an alien race, a joke or a misunderstanding; it was a full-blown gay kiss between two women in love. The broadcast was based on the 1934 play *The Children's Hour* by Lillian Hellman, a dramatic story about two women accused of being gay, who find out that they do indeed have feelings for each other. This is the first same-sex and gay kiss I could find in TV history, but because it was broadcast live there is no record of it. Of course, earlier ones may still be found, as many television mysteries are still hidden in archives all over the world.

Some of the kisses I've mentioned here broke barriers and deserve a ton of credit, and often they were the first kiss broadcast before the watershed moment, the first one in a soap (or another first in their own right). A kiss on a late-night documentary is not quite the same as one on a show broadcast on prime-time TV to millions of viewers, but they deserve honour individually for achieving something. Shows like *EastEnders* still did something impressive that should be remembered, and not just to annoy Piers Morgan.

7

Vikings had horns on their helmets

What you may have been told

Vikings had helmets with massive horns on them. Everybody knows that. We've been seeing these Norsemen with their horny hats in films, on television, in books, comics and advertising: everywhere. It is impossible to imagine a Viking without them. In January 2021, some guy with horns on his head participated in that whole insurrection thing at the Capitol in Washington and the entire media called him a Viking!

The debunking

The idea of the Viking helmet with horns is extremely popular, but there is no real evidence of them actually existing, which made it especially annoying when the image of that 'QAnon Shaman' went around the world after Trump supporters broke into the US Capitol building. Pretty much everyone called him a Viking when he was actually wearing a Native American head-dress with buffalo horns.

The Vikings were Scandinavians who from the eighth to the eleventh centuries travelled, traded, raided, invaded and settled all over Europe and far beyond. Technically, the term 'Viking' refers to an act, a profession – so it wasn't a people or nationality, but an activity; it was something you did. Having a helmet with big, pointy, sticky-out bits on top that could easily get stuck, damage things or give an enemy something to hold on to is just not a very good idea, especially when you 'go Viking'. Half your men would have got their helmets stuck in the sail and ripped it to shreds before you were even out of sight of the Kattegat.

It seems like the Vikings may not have worn fancy metal helmets at all often, horns or no horns, because unlike swords, knives, spears and combs, archaeologists just don't find many of them. They've found bits of Viking helmets but only one was ever found that was complete, the Gjermundbu helmet. It did not have any horns.

The idea of Vikings having horns on their helmets is not that far-fetched, though. There are contemporary depictions that show helmets with what could be horns, but it is not clear if that's what they really are or if the people wearing them are even real people. The Oseberg tapestry, for instance, shows a large figure with horns, but some historians think he might be a deity – Odin himself, perhaps – so not a human, not someone who would go Viking around Europe with his pals. And even if it does depict a real human, not a god or other mythical being, we still don't know why he had these horns and what they really looked like.

The horns may have been worn during a sort of ceremonial spear dance, which seems to have been quite popular at the time. Horned figures, waving arms and kicking legs, holding swords and spears, can also be seen on the golden Gallehus horns, the Torslunda plates, the Valsgärde and Sutton Hoo helmets. Although it's not completely clear what is being depicted on these artefacts, it doesn't look like part of a battle and is more like something spiritual or ceremonial – which is always a tempting explanation when we aren't really sure about something, but in this case it is a convincing theory.

We do know there were helmets with horns *before* the Viking age. We're sure of this because some of these have been found, such as the Iron Age Waterloo helmet and the Bronze Age Veksø helmets. Ancient Greeks and Romans described several European tribes as wearing headdresses that looked like animal heads, with horns, antlers, wings and so on. So it is not a huge leap of the imagination to assume Vikings also had horned helmets, but the fact remains that there is still no real convincing evidence of Scandinavians actually having or wearing them, especially during their raids and battles. Even the evidence for them being worn during ceremonial dancing is circumstantial at best.

What makes it even more likely that the whole Viking horned helmet thing isn't based on any real historical evidence is that the idea didn't really pop up till the Victorian era. That's right, it seems the Victorians may be to blame for spreading a myth . . . again.

In the nineteenth century, the Middle Ages were extremely popular. Architects, poets, writers, artists, archaeologists and even politicians were obsessed with the subject. As had happened before and would happen again, a certain view of the Middle Ages was used to promote nationalism, heritage, culture and other ideals. Then, Wagner premiered his successful *Der Ring des Nibelungen* opera (often known simply as *The Ring Cycle*) and his visions, along with those of his costume designer Carl Emil Doepler, spread across the world. He mixed together an awesome but peculiar combination of Norse, Germanic, Bronze Age and Viking history with a massive dose of imagination and unleashed an army of Valkyries and 'barbarians' with horned and winged helmets that marched into our collective consciousness. To thousands and soon millions, the stage costumes became real history. Vikings started being depicted with horned helmets and, to this day, there are many who find it difficult to accept they weren't real.

Historians have been trying very hard to fight this myth but those old horned warriors are not that easy to defeat. The image is just too appealing, but there is a glimmer of hope: the public is no longer being taught at schools, museums and re-enactment events that they had horns, gradually debunking the myth. Now, sharing a picture of a horned Viking on social media will sooner or later result in someone correcting you.

8

People ate potatoes in the Middle Ages

What you may have been told

It's probably not something you've been told directly, but if you watch a film or television drama set in medieval or even ancient Europe, you'll often see people eating potatoes, tomatoes or pumpkins. Or these food items are just lying about on tables, sprinkled around kitchens, market stalls and so on. These must have been staples of a medieval diet!

The debunking

Given how often they crop up, it is no wonder that a lot of people don't realise that these ingredients did not exist in Europe back then. Along with corn (the maize type), peanuts, pineapples, chilli peppers, tobacco, vanilla, rubber, cacao and llamas, they were totally unknown to our medieval, Roman, Celtic, prehistoric and Neanderthal ancestors in Europe, and those in Africa, Asia and the Middle East. People didn't know what any of these things were, had never heard of them, tasted them or learned to enjoy them. Chilli peppers did not hang from kitchen ceilings, there were no tables full of tomatoes and neither were there random pumpkins everywhere either. Yes, I am looking at you, set designers and prop masters.

I know the potato seems so, well . . . medieval. It fits so perfectly with the image we have of that era, but it wasn't till after 1492 that these goods slowly started appearing on the European markets. That was the year Columbus discovered a route to the Americas and that is what all the items on our shopping list have in common – they're native to the 'new world'. They simply didn't grow in the 'old world', and it took sailors and explorers sailing to the Americas, taking these ingredients back to Europe, planting them and getting them to survive, before they became part of the diet of people on that side of the Atlantic Ocean. And even then it would take a while before we got used to these strange, mysterious things from far away. We're so used to them being part of our daily lives that we rarely even think that they once had to be introduced to some continents.

What about those llamas, you're wondering? It's kind of obvious that they weren't really around in ancient Europe, right? Well, perhaps not, because they're walking around in the 2004 blockbuster *Troy*. Next time you meet Brad Pitt, make sure to ask him about those llamas.

9

The word 'hangover' originated from passed-out drunks leaning on a rope

What you may have been told

In documentaries about Victorian times you may hear someone bring up the 'two-penny hangover'. The phrase is either related to the price of getting drunk or to what it would cost to sleep at a dosshouse, the cheapest lodgings available, where the poorest paid tuppence to lean on a horizontally tied rope because they couldn't afford a bed. There are old photos that even suggest there was a standing variant, where people paid to try and sleep while standing half draped over a rope tied across a room. And that's where the word hangover came from that we all use today!

The debunking

It is an appealing story – a poignant origin for a word many of us use regularly – perhaps a bit too regularly. It's the perfect 'did you know' icebreaker at a party or fun fact for the pub (or social media).

But alas, the word has quite a simple and much less exciting background. It is just a literal meaning of something hanging over from earlier – a leftover from the previous night, an after effect, unfinished business.

It isn't till the early twentieth century that we find evidence for it being used in connection with the effects of drinking too much. But yes, there were dosshouses and you could spend a few hours there to rest. The more money you had the more comfortable your stay would be. The cheapest option was the 'penny sit-up', where you'd be allowed to sit on a bench in a warmed room. Just sit, no sleeping, and no lying down. For a penny more, you were allowed to lean on a rope tied across the room so that you could fall asleep without tumbling off the bench. Four pennies would enable you to sleep in a sort of coffin-shaped bed, which is nice. All this is very dramatic and, well, terribly Dickensian and Victorian.

But being forced to stand while sleeping is taking all this suffering to a whole new level.

A non-existent level, because there is no evidence for the standing version of the hangover being a thing. People were already unhappy about having to pay for the very uncomfortable options, but anything would have been preferable to simply draping yourself over a rope without even being able to sit. So how come there are actual old photos of people doing just this, you ask? Well, the only existing photo of this standing-sleeping is not Victorian at all, but a publicity shot from the 1978 film *The First Great Train Robbery*, starring Sean Connery and Donald Sutherland. It's a great film, but not very historically accurate.

There is at least some evidence of the sitting 'hangover' but they're not actual first-hand accounts. It's mentioned in a few sources, such as Honoré de Balzac's *The Magic Skin* (1831), Charles Dickens's *The Pickwick Papers* (1836) and George Orwell's *Down and Out in Paris and London* (1933), in which he writes:

> *The Twopenny Hangover. This comes a little higher than the Embankment. At the Twopenny Hangover, the lodgers sit in a row on a bench; there is a rope in front of them, and they lean on this as though leaning over a fence. A man, humorously called the valet, cuts the rope at five in the morning. I have never been there myself, but Bozo had been there often. I asked him whether anyone could possibly sleep in such an attitude, and he said that it was more comfortable than it sounded – at any rate, better than bare floor. There are similar shelters in Paris, but the charge there is only twenty-five centimes (a halfpenny) instead of twopence.*

We also have a couple of photos showing men sleeping while sitting, hanging over a rope in late 1920s Germany, so we know it was still around in the twentieth century.

So the sitting hangover very likely existed in Victorian Britain, though we have no real contemporary primary evidence for it. But we do know it didn't involve standing and that it is not the origin of the term 'hangover', in the sense of suffering the next day from having drunk too much. You'll have to think of another fun fact for the pub.

10

Santa wears red because of Coca-Cola

What you may have been told

Coca-Cola is the reason Santa Claus is wearing a red and white outfit. Our jolly friend used to be thin and wear green or blue, but then the soda company got involved, redesigned him, made sure his new outfit had the same colours as its brand and turned him into a fun, fat chap. In no time, its version had replaced the original.

The debunking

First things first, Santa is real. Of course he is – tell your kids I said so. But his origin story is quite complicated, and Coca-Cola didn't play a huge role in his makeover.

Santa is the lovechild of the medieval mythical representation of Christmas, called Father Christmas, and Nicholas of Myra, who was born in Turkey in the third century AD and became a very popular saint. Although very little is known about his life, there are many myths and miracles connected to him. One story describes how Nicholas saved the daughters of a poor man from a life of prostitution by secretly throwing a bag with coins for their dowries through an open window, because he was generous but also modest, and didn't need everybody to know that he helped this family out.

It was also claimed that he calmed the sea during a storm and that when he found out that a butcher had kidnapped, killed and pickled three boys, Saint Nicholas resurrected them!

He became very popular and besides seeming to be a rather nice chap, he was also a super Christian. So, of course, it's no wonder, pun intended, that he was sanctified. Nicholas became the much-loved patron saint of children, the poor, sailors, prostitutes, the unmarried and many more. Churches were founded in his name, and in several parts of medieval Europe Saint Nicholas was celebrated yearly with his own holiday, on or around 6 December. He remains popular in many countries such as Belgium, Luxembourg, Aruba, Suriname, northern France and the Netherlands, where Saint Nicholas Day is still one of the biggest holidays in the country. Coins are one of the traditional gifts people give each other on *Sinterklaasavond*, just like the ones he gave the impoverished father with those daughters – although these days, the coins are made of chocolate, unfortunately.

When the first Dutch (and some Germans) emigrated to America, they of course brought their traditions with them and started celebrating Saint Nicholas's Eve in the colonies. In Britain, they had Father Christmas, Germans had their *Weihnachtsmann* and, eventually, traditions and history got mixed together and Santa Claus was born. And as his story changed, so did his appearance.

For a long time, he was depicted in many different ways, wearing all sorts of outfits – sometimes fat, sometimes thin, sometimes in red, sometimes wearing green or a nice jumpsuit, sometimes in a fancy church outfit. So there isn't one person, or organisation, that can be credited with inventing Santa's current look. It evolved over the centuries – although the illustrator Thomas Nast did play a big part in describing Santa and making him very popular in the United States. He drew him wearing a red suit in an 1869 publication titled *Santa and His Works*, 17 years before Coca-Cola was even invented. Still, there were other versions of Santa that were around at that time and even Nast's Santa wasn't quite the same as the one we know today.

By the 1920s, Santa, exactly as he would later be depicted by Coca-Cola, was already a very popular character who regularly appeared on magazine covers and in advertisements, even selling other soda drinks. There are lots of wonderful pictures in old magazines that show us 'our' Santa; any kid today would recognise him right away – except perhaps that he seems rather keen on the pretty Edwardian ladies.

With special thanks to illustrators Norman Rockwell and Joseph Christian Leyendecker, big, round Santa in the red suit with fur trimming, the big white beard, the black boots, the belt and so on, had become a familiar image across the United States. And although the incredibly talented Haddon Sundblom contributed his own individual interpretation of Santa when he was asked to illustrate the 1931 Coca-Cola advertisement campaign, his Santa still looked very similar to several other, earlier Santas.

Of course, one of the biggest brands in the world flooding the media, streets and shops with its Santa played a huge part in making sure that everybody started seeing Santa in this way and forgetting about the ones that looked different. By the time Coca-Cola started using Santa for its advertising campaign, his look was already fully developed and well established in and even outside the US, but the soda brand helped Santa become more famous, eventually making this THE Santa look everywhere.

Of course, in some European countries we're still stuck with a slightly confusing situation, where the original medieval Saint Nicholas visits us on 6 December, only to be followed closely by Santa – both the same person, but also not. They do both wear red, though, and not because of Coca-Cola.

11

Germany invented the concentration camp

What you may have been told

Concentration camps are a German invention. The Nazis were the first to put innocent people in these horrible places during the 1930s. And if it wasn't the Germans, it was the British in South Africa!

The debunking

Before we get started on this stubborn myth that just won't go away, we need to agree on what a concentration camp is, as usual. There are many different types of camp, and in some cases different names have been used for the same kind of place. There have been internment, transit, refugee and extermination camps, and that's just the tip of the iceberg. Incidentally, today there are still camps where people are kept in large groups and in horrible conditions, but modern politicians often put a lot of effort into using names for them that don't immediately evoke the (often equally) horrible camps of the past.

A camp becomes a concentration camp, according to most definitions of the word, when the (usually innocent) people who are imprisoned there, without having had a proper trial, are kept in overcrowded, dirty and inadequate circumstances; where they are abused, not properly taken care of and are allowed to get sick and even die. The particularly inhumane treatment of prisoners is what marks out concentration camps from 'normal' prison camps, internment camps and so on. Transit and internment camps were and are often still terrible places to be imprisoned in, but compared to concentration camps they were generally not as awful. And of course, extermination or death camps were worse than the concentration camps, as people who were taken there were killed. Some extermination camps were also concentration camps, but not all concentration camps were extermination camps. So now we know what we're talking about, we can confidently say that the Nazis were not the first to open concentration camps, as they sadly existed long before the Nazis did.

They also weren't invented by the British (another common misperception), although it is true that the British built and used them in southern Africa during the Boer Wars, in the early twentieth century. They also coined the term 'concentration camp', which is perhaps why so many people wrongly attribute their invention to the Brits. The British Empire was fighting a bitter war with the Boers (the descendants of Dutch immigrants) in southern Africa, and things weren't going very well for the British side. The Boers were fighting a guerrilla war, which is notoriously difficult to deal with if you're a military force.

Lord Kitchener therefore decided to get rid of everything that could support the enemy: farms were burned, crops destroyed, animals killed and Boers, along with native African civilians, were taken away from their homes and put into concentration camps. Entire regions were depopulated in this way, and thousands of people were locked up in camps where they often lived in tents under terrible circumstances. There was a shortage of food, hygiene was bad, and diseases regularly swept through the camps. Thousands died. These camps fit our definition of concentration camp, but they were also not the first.

A possible contender for the title are the camps set up by the Spanish in Cuba in the 1890s. They too were battling guerrilla fighters who were very difficult to defeat with regular army tactics, so the Spanish decided to empty the countryside of the people these fighters depended on for support. Hundreds of thousands of innocent civilians were forced to relocate to towns and camps encircled by barbed wire and guards. If they refused, they'd be shot. Here too, the living conditions were terrible; there was not enough food for all, the shelter was insufficient and hygiene near impossible, which resulted in diseases taking many lives.

Of course, there are earlier times in history when many people, without a fair trial, were kept prisoner and mistreated terribly. Native Americans were put in reservations, prisoners of war throughout history were put in camps where they were terribly mistreated, slaves were often kept under dismal circumstances all over the world and history is full of situations that could be considered concentration-camp like. But finding ones that fit our specific definition gets more difficult the further we go back in time.

One reason that the camps of the nineteenth century are possibly the first we can call concentration camps is because they made use of a then relatively new invention: barbed wire. This allowed a small group of guards to easily and cheaply imprison a very large group of people in a small area, something that was nearly impossible before that time.

In the end, it was all about suffering, and about treating humans like animals or as lesser than animals. We can barely imagine what concentration-camp prisoners went through, but I know from members in my own family that what they saw and experienced there haunted their dreams for the rest of their lives.

12

A narrow doorway stopped monks in Portugal getting fat

What you may have been told

The Alcobaça Monastery in Portugal has a very narrow door in its former dining hall, the so-called 'anti-gluttony door'. Monks who got a bit too rotund found they could no longer squeeze through the 32cm-wide passage (roughly one foot) to collect their food!

Lots of tourists visit the wonderful monastery and many of them, especially jolly dads, seem to take pleasure in posing next to the portal, often showing off their belly, which would have kept them from getting a meal in the kitchen for months.

The debunking

In 2008, a photo of the door was uploaded to Wikimedia Commons with the description: 'Mosteiro de Alcobaça, Refectory, door of unknown usage, said being used for monk's weight-control'.

The picture featured on the page about the monastery on Portuguese Wikipedia, captioned, 'The legendary narrow door of the cafeteria, which was intended to deliver meals to the poor.' In 2014, a user by the name of Daniel Villafruela uploaded a picture of a man unable to fit through the door with the caption, 'I fear to have severely violated the Rule of frugality'. But the myth may have been older and was perhaps already being told by tour guides long before this time.

Many myths are born thanks to a guide who decides to be a bit creative with the truth or who forgets to mention that the story he keeps telling the tourists is nothing more than a fable. I'm sure most of us have been on tours of castles and museums where we've raised our eyebrows at the claims being made by the guide.

Monks have been made fun of and accused of living the good life for centuries. Even in medieval times they were a popular target for mockery and there are countless stories of fat monks who drank, ate and fondled the nuns too much. Although this undoubtedly happened in many monasteries, the men at the Alcobaça Monastery were Cistercian monks, and that particular order was rather strict about what the monks were allowed to eat. Still, even if one of the monks got a bit too large, there surely would have been easier ways to make him eat a bit less than to have an architect plan a special door just in case some of the monks were a bit too greedy. Besides, if a monk was peckish he'd find a way in, especially as there's another door to the kitchen just left of it that is so wide it would fit several monks through it at once. Google Maps has a wonderful virtual tour of the monastery that you can easily find online; there you can see the two doors next to each other. Of course, the bigger door is never in the photo shared alongside the myth!

The real function of the door is that of a serving hatch; plates would be passed through from the kitchen on the other side of the wall. This, of course, isn't a very entertaining story and it is less fun to imagine someone handing out a plate than a sad-looking fat monk trying to fit through the door while his brothers try not to laugh. That is probably why the story is still mentioned at the monastery, even though they also say that it's a myth.

The visitor's guide on the monastery's official website says:

Look at the narrowest door! It's called a "dish-carrier" and was used to pass the dishes and food to the cafeteria. There is a legend regarding to this door, which says that the monks who could not pass through it were considered sinners because they were very fat.

13

The FBI coined the term 'serial killer' in the 1970s

What you may have been told

The term 'serial killer' was coined by FBI agent Robert K. Ressler in the late 1970s. He himself has often repeated this claim, and it was also mentioned in the excellent Netflix drama *Mindhunter* and the documentary *Conversations with a Killer: The Ted Bundy Tapes*. So it must be true, because an FBI agent couldn't be mistaken and Netflix wouldn't lie to us . . . right?

The debunking

OK, I admit, this is a bit of a pedantic one, but it was fun to research and led me to some interesting stories about a gruesome subject, so I'm going to tell you all about it anyway.

A serial killer is a murderer who kills several (generally more than three) people over a period of time (so not all during one event), for no apparent reason or for psychological and/or sadistic sexual motives.

FBI Agent Robert K. Ressler was a very talented and intelligent man who spent a lot of time researching the subject, but, dare I say it, he was also a bit of a serial-exaggerator, because he claimed, several times, that he was the first person to use the phrase, ever, since the dawn of humankind. But he wasn't.

Just so you know, even though it may feel like it's a relatively new thing, serial killers have been with us forever. The further back we go, the trickier it is to know if we're dealing with an actual serial killer or someone falsely accused of being one, but there are cases dating to Roman times where we know of named murderers who apparently didn't stop with 'just' a few corpses. Locusta of Gaul, for instance, may have poisoned as many as seven victims in the first century AD. In 1324, in Ireland, Alice Kyteler was accused of poisoning four husbands (and when she fled, her servant was burned at the stake instead!). In eighteenth-century Netherlands, it was claimed that a family of robbers killed as many as 400 people, and in Victorian England, Amelia Dyer killed at least six babies – though some estimates put the number in the hundreds. Few know her name, yet everybody knows about Jack the Ripper . . .

Anyway, back to the use of the word serial killer. I've decided to make no distinction between serial killer and serial murderer – they mean the same thing after all. But who first coined either term?

Although he wasn't the first to use the phrase, I want to mention Ernst August Ferdinand Gennat, a famous German detective in 1920s and 1930s Berlin. He worked on cases involving infamous serial killers Peter Kürten and Fritz Haarmann, but also revolutionised police detective work, developed what we now call 'profiling' and set up the very first homicide squad. He was like Sherlock Holmes, but real.

In the 1930 article 'Die Düsseldorfer Sexualverbrechen', in which Gennat details his work concerning Peter Kürten, he's quoted as using the term '*Serienmörder*', which directly translates as 'serial murderer' and is often translated to 'serial killer'. And in a way, Gennat popularised it: he was a famous detective, often mentioned in newspapers and magazines. Inspector Karl Lohmann, the detective in one of the best films ever made (*M*, 1931), was based on him. Due to several serial killers getting a lot of media attention in Germany in the 1920s and 1930s, it was a hot topic. (In fact, Gennat deserves his own TV show. I hope you're listening, Netflix executives.)

In a way, this mass focus on serial killers by law enforcement and the public is a lot like what was happening in the US in the 1970s and 1980s when Ressler and the FBI started to look into this phenomenon again and the nation was gripped. Frankly, it would be a bit odd if Ressler had never heard of Gennat or read any of his work. He definitely should have.

Besides Gennat, the term serial killer/murderer was used by others long before the 1970s. But even Gennat's book was not the first time the term serial killer was used. In 1927, an unknown Dutch journalist wrote a review about the film *The Coming of Amos* (1925) in the *Algemeen Handelsblad* newspaper. The film is about an Australian sheep ranger who falls in love with a Russian princess whose admirers keep being murdered. The murderer is described as a '*serie-moordenaar*' (serial murderer) in the article. I do not know who the journalist was, but it is the earliest use of the term I could find. I can't say for sure whether this is the first time this expression was used. I would not be at all surprised if sooner or later an even earlier instance pops up.

14

The word honeymoon comes from giving the married couple a month's supply of mead

What you may have been told

Once upon a time, in a place far, far away, somewhere Babylonian, Viking, pagan or Germanic, you know, in the wild times, it was tradition for newlyweds to be supplied with enough mead for a month. Mead is an alcoholic drink made from fermented honey and the idea was that this would make it a bit easier for the couple to get to know each other, if you know what I mean (nudge, nudge).

The honey relates to the mead that the bride and groom got totally hammered on and the moon is because the drinking and 'getting to know each other' lasted for a month.

Honey + moon = honeymoon.

And that's where the word came from and why this story is told in best-man speeches everywhere.

The debunking

Thinking logically, is it such a good idea to give two young people who barely know each other, who just got married, who have to spend the rest of their lives together, who are supposed to make babies as soon as possible and who are probably very nervous, gallons of very sweet, easy-to-drink mead that will make you fall over in record time? I've drunk mead; it is delicious, even if you're not much of a drinker, and it does a really good job of getting you drunk. In your experience, are people who are way too drunk any good in bed? That is a rhetorical question.

I can just see those youngsters spending the entire month drunk and passed out on the floor, not even half undressed. It sounds like a recipe for disaster and a great way to doom a marriage within days!

For a connection to exist between the words honey and moon, and the period immediately after a wedding, those English words must be the same or very similar to the ones used many centuries or even thousands of years ago. I don't speak ancient Babylonian and my Germanic pagan and medieval Norse are a bit rusty, but I'm pretty sure that their word for honeymoon, if they even had one, probably didn't contain the words honey or even month, which makes the claim of the original meaning of the English word honeymoon a bit suspicious. So the story seems iffy to begin with, but let's check out the history behind the claim anyway.

The first mention of 'honeymoon' does not date back to ancient times or even the Middle Ages; it is actually quite recent. The Victorian writer William Pulleyn wrote in his 1828 book *The Etymological Compendium: Or, Portfolio of Origins and Inventions* the following:

> *It was the custom of the higher order of the Teutones, an ancient people who inhabited the northern parts of Germany, to drink Mead or Metheglin, a beverage made with honey, for thirty days after every wedding. From this comes the expression, 'to spend the honey-moon'.*

Unfortunately, Mr Pulleyn offers no evidence, sources or records for this story and we can only imagine where he got this information from. Nevertheless, the explanation stuck and after this it started showing up everywhere and soon became a popular myth which endures to this day.

If you look at the word before Mr Pulleyn got his hands on it, the word honeymoon always relates to sweetness and how love is like the moon: often changing and sometimes not very long-lasting (which is rather cynical, if you ask me). The oldest mention of the word I could find in English texts was during the Tudor era. Are you ready for a bit of lovely old writing? It's from *A dialogue conteinyng the nomber in effect of all the prouerbes in the englishe tongue compacte in a matter concernyng two maner of mariages, made and set foorth by John Heywood*, from 1546:

> And this yong poore couple shal come fyrst in hande.
> Who, the daie of weddyng and after, a while, could not loke eche on other,
>   but they must smile.
> As a whelpe for wantonnes in and out whipps, so plaied these tweyne, as
>   mery as thre chipps.
> Ye there was god (quoth he) whan all is doone.
> Abyde (quoth I) it was yet but hony moone.
> The blacke oxe had not trode on his nor her foote.
> But er this branche of blys coulde reache any roote,
> The floures so faded, that in fiftene weekes, a man myght espie the chaunge
>   in the cheekes, both of this pore wretch, and his wife this pore wenche.
> Their faces told toies, ye Totnam was turnd frenche and all their light
>   laughyng turnd and translated into sad syghyng, all myrth was
>   amated.

Isn't that gorgeous? I admit, this old grammar is a bit tricky to translate and I'm not going to try. Suffice to say that it describes how a young couple smile and are happy shortly after the marriage, as the 'black ox' has not yet stepped on either of their feet, but soon this would change. The flowers faded, Totnam turned French and light laughing turned into sad sighing. This all describes how feelings can change dramatically soon after the wedding.

So this, the oldest mention known to both me and the *Oxford English Dictionary*, rather cynically describes the honeymoon as the happy but often short romantic time after the wedding. No mention of mead or of this period lasting a month.

When we look at other languages, we get more clues about the origin of the word and tradition. The German word *Flitterwochen* means 'tinsel-weeks', and according to the *Oeconomischen Encyclopädie von Krünitz von 1858* it was a bit of a wry joke in Germany, suggesting that those early weeks when the decorations from the wedding celebrations are still up are wonderful, but that this eventually diminishes. So although 'honeymoon' today has a generally positive meaning that also often involves a holiday, we still say 'the honeymoon is over' to describe the moment when life after a wonderful event gets back to normal.

The mead story is fun but there's not a single shred of evidence to back it up before it appeared in the Victorian books. The Victorians are to blame, again!

But, hey, just because it isn't some ancient tradition doesn't mean we can't make it a new one. Why not bring some mead to give to the happy couple at the next wedding you go to? But please, do me a favour, don't spread fake history.

15

The famous 1920s actress Clara Bow was a Nazi

What you may have been told

One of the most famous actresses of the 1920s and 1930s was Clara Bow – the ultimate 'flapper' and the first 'it girl'. But she was also a massive Nazi who wore a swastika-decorated outfit during a visit to Germany, where she met with Hitler in person, and he even gave her a signed copy of his book!

The debunking

I both hate and love this myth. I hate it because it is nonsense and puts someone whose films I rather like in a bad light, but I love it because scandals and fables like these are often the only reason younger generations hear about the stars of the golden era of cinema. They have no idea who Clara Bow was but become interested when someone shares the picture of her with the swastika clothes, and perhaps this might lead them to watch her films.

I'm a hopeless optimist.

So the photo is real – there she is, one of the most famous women in the world at the time, wearing a lovely hat and dress with swastikas on it; there's no doubt it's her. And yes, she did go to Germany in 1932. According to the biographer David Stenn:

> a starstruck Adolf Hitler presented her with a signed copy of Mein Kampf. 'For my most esteemed friend Clara,' he wrote, 'with the wish that she derives the same pleasure reading this book as I did writing it. Adolf.' 'Madness' was all Clara had to say.

However, any student of the era can see that the photo just doesn't make sense. One of the swastikas is the wrong way round for a Nazi swastika, which would be a bit silly for an outfit meant to impress Nazis. On top of that, the hat Bow is wearing is a typical 1920s cloche hat. These were very fashionable in the twenties but old-fashioned and on their way out by the early thirties. Of course, you'd still see women wearing them, but this is not just any woman, this is Clara Bow, a world-famous star, the original 'it girl', a style icon. It would make absolutely no sense for her to wear this outdated outfit in the 1930s; she'd be a laughing stock. Other pictures of her visit to Germany in 1932 show her wearing the latest fashions.

Logically, it must therefore be a photo from the 1920s. All of a sudden, the swastika makes a lot more sense. To our modern eyes, the swastika is a Nazi icon. Nothing else. But actually, the swastika is an ancient symbol, popular long before the Nazis decided to claim it and ruin its reputation. In the US it was very popular as a good luck symbol in the early twentieth century. If you look, you can find it everywhere – in advertising, on clothes, jewellery, architecture and so on.

I managed to find the first publication of this photo in the *Los Angeles Times* on Friday 13 April 1928 (page 27) with the following description:

ANCIENT CROSS DEFIES JINX DAY
Clara Bow Wearing Swastika

Clara Bow isn't afraid of a jinx. She admits she has had some bad luck in her life, but good luck has far overshadowed it, she says.

Yesterday, however, she admitted she is a bit superstitious, particularly concerning Friday, the thirteenth, which is today. For that reason she is wearing a swastika decoration on her hat and coat lapel to bring her good luck.

The design is an ancient symbol of good luck, consisting of Greek crosses which stand for luck, life, love and light.

The text explains it all and proves that Clara Bow wore the outfit in the 1920s with the swastika as a good luck symbol. She didn't wear it during her visit to Germany and she certainly didn't wear it to tell the world how much she loved those darn Nazis.

16

Coca-Cola used Nazi slogans and symbols in its German adverts

What you may have been told

Coca-Cola is an iffy company, but did you know it also sponsored the infamous 1936 Olympic Games that were held in Nazi Germany? And just like with sponsorship today, Coca-Cola was of course all over the event; it posted its advertisements everywhere. Just check out this original poster. It says *'ein Volk ein Reich ein Getrank Coke ist es'* and over a huge eagle with a swastika there's the logo of our favourite drink and that of the Olympic Games. Amazing, isn't it?!

The debunking

First things first: yes, Coca-Cola has been embroiled in several ethical controversies; yes, it's far from healthy; yes, it is delicious; yes, it was all over the 1936 Olympics; and yes, there are genuine adverts from that time that prove it was doing business in the Third Reich. But this specific poster is not real.

For starters, there are grammatical mistakes in the text. The sentence *'ein Volk ein Reich ein Getrank'* should have started with a capital letter, it's missing commas and the word *'Getrank'* needs an umlaut. Although not completely impossible, it would be very unlikely for such a big brand to make two grammatical mistakes in such an important advertising campaign. But the poster also plays on the famous Nazi slogan, changing *'Ein Volk, ein Reich, ein Führer'* (One people, one empire, one leader) into *'ein Volk ein Reich ein Getrank'* (One people, one empire, one drink). Do you think the Nazis would have approved of an American brand altering their most successful slogan so that their superhero's title is replaced by the name of a soft drink? Insulting Hitler is always a good thing, but not smart when you're trying to sell something in Nazi Germany.

An even bigger clue is that the next line: *'Coke ist es'* is clearly a direct translation of the slogan 'Coke is it', which you may remember from your childhood if you are old enough, because it is from the 1980s. It did not exist in the 1930s. Back then, the Coca-Cola slogan of the day was 'Ice-cold sunshine' and, for the German market, *'Stets Eiskalt'* (Always ice cold).

But we're not done yet!

Coca-Cola didn't have the little registered trademark sign (®) as part of its logo till the 1950s, and even then it still had the words 'Trade-mark' in front of it. The brand didn't change its logo to drop these words till 1991. And finally, using the Nazi eagle as a background image doesn't really fit the style of pre-war advertising. Once more, I reckon the '*Herren*' in brown wouldn't be very pleased with their sacred logo being used as a background picture for an advert.

Now we know it's not real, one question remains: where did it come from?

I knew it was fake the second I saw it, but just knowing it's wrong doesn't convince anyone. I had to trace it to its origin. Through reverse-image searches, I discovered that the picture was first uploaded to an old photo gallery back in 2004. Unfortunately, this gallery is no longer online. So I tried my luck with the Internet Archive's 'wayback machine', a digital archive that allows you to explore over 677 billion(!) web pages it has saved since 1996. Here I found the long-lost pages, and although the pictures were not all there, they did mention that the page belonged to a certain Scott van Looy. I managed to track him down and he confirmed he took the photograph in 2004 at an art show called *Coca-Cola's Nazi Adverts*.

Sometimes fake history hunting is really a lot like detective work. I might only be trying to find out where an old picture came from, I'm not hot on the heels of some serial killer, but it still is very exciting to finally find another lead.

This art show in London was curated by comedian Mark Thomas and artist Tracey Moberly. The goal of the exhibition was to confront people with the truth behind Coca-Cola's role in Nazi Germany, and they also invited artists and members of the public to contribute by making their own fake Nazi-themed Coke adverts. I got in touch with the people behind it and they confirmed that the picture was indeed one of the submissions and a modern Photoshop creation. Unfortunately, it happened so long ago that it's unclear who made the picture. But at least we figured out the truth and another piece of fake history bites the dust.

Case closed.

17

This dog was sent to prison for murdering a cat

What you may have been told

Just look at that mugshot. Yes, that is a dog. Just look at him, that adorable face. All dogs are good boys (yes he's a good boy, yes he is), but . . . perhaps not all the time?

This is Pep, and that is a real prison mugshot. The lovely, adorable Pep was arrested in 1924 and sent to jail after he killed an American governor's cat.

The debunking

On 31 August 1924 a dog called Pep was really taken to the Eastern State Penitentiary in Pennsylvania, but not because he killed a cat, destroyed furniture, ripped apart some cushions or robbed the local butcher. For starters, Pep never had a proper trial, was not officially arrested nor read his *Miranda* rights, did not get decent representation and was never convicted by any judge. So, technically, he was innocent, regardless of what he may or may not have done. This was a miscarriage of justice!

Or was it?

Pennsylvania governor Gifford Pinchot and his wife, who were responsible for Pep being sent to the prison, did not send him there for something he'd done, but to improve morale. In a way, we could say he was an early sort of therapy dog.

When our canine hero arrived at the prison, the guards made him pose for a mugshot and listed him as a committed murderer. They even gave him the alias of 'A dog'. Such jokers.

But this little joke got a bit out of hand when the media got wind of poor old Pep's plight. They loved the story and ran with it. Pep was even invited to be a guest on the radio. A newspaper clipping at the time shows him staring at a microphone surrounded by prison guards. The accompanying article mentions the crime, but it seems like Pep didn't have much to say for himself.

More and more people heard Pep's story and believed it to be true. The idea of Pep really being put in jail, cat murderer or not, caused quite a stir. Animal lovers were getting rather angry with the governor and he started receiving lots of indignant letters from all over the world. The governor's wife, Cornelia Bryce Pinchot, quite an impressive and politically active woman in her own right, seemed truly upset and annoyed by the whole situation – not just because they were attacked for it so often but also because of the dog's reputation. She really wanted to let people know Pep was a lovely dog and absolutely not a criminal. In January 1926, she said in the *New York Times*:

> *'Why, Pep never killed anything or anybody. The report of his crime has circled half around the world, and the governor and I have received volumes of letters, telegrams, resolutions and petitions complaining of the cruelty of cooping the dog up in prison.'*

According to the journalist, Pep's:

> *life work is marked out for him, he likes it and he has the run of the grounds. A dog's happiness consists in devotion to the human family in which he finds himself, and in 'Pep's' case it is a very large family. There must be scores of prisoners in the Eastern Penitentiary to whom a sight of 'Pep' is the great event of the day, to whom his bark is the cheeriest of sounds.*

Talking to the media seems to have worked: according to the article, the stigma of cat murderer was removed from Pep's record. The dog seemed to have felt right at home with his new, large family of wardens and prisoners. He was described as 'unusually intelligent' and 'exceedingly friendly and good-natured'. Pep's presence made the grim lives of the inmates a little more bearable.

What happened to Pep after his time in the spotlight is a bit unclear. In 1935, the *Lake Park News* claimed that Pep was 'pardoned' and adopted by a guard. But according to a 1963 record in the Pennsylvania State Archives, Pep was transferred to Graterford (Eastern State's 'farm branch', about 35 miles northwest of Philadelphia) where he stayed until his death. According to the Eastern State Penitentiary museum website, he passed away there after a long and happy life and was 'buried . . . with a tender reverence in a favourite flower bed on the prison grounds'. Pep seems to have been a remarkable dog.

I'm not crying.

The media at the time couldn't resist Pep's story and more recently he became famous again because of that adorable mugshot being shared online, but he was not the only dog sent to jail to improve morale. There was Nero the St Bernard whose 'death sentence' for biting a doctor's son was commuted to life imprisonment decades before Pep got sent down. Nero's story sounds very similar and it's likely he too was meant to be another mascot and not a real criminal. And then there was Lady, a beagle belonging to Major Brierley, captain of the prison guards, who occasionally took her along to work in the 1950s, and also got an adorable mugshot taken of her.

Correctional institutions, penitentiaries and similar facilities across the world have animal projects to this day. Not only do animals, especially dogs, boost the morale of prisoners, but being taught how to care for them and being given responsibility to look after them are a great distraction and make prisoners' lives a little more bearable. But above all, simply experiencing unconditional love and attention from these animals can make an inmate, and frankly anyone else, a better human being.

Today, the Eastern State Penitentiary is a museum, Pep and the other dogs have their own display and you can buy Pep-themed souvenirs in the gift shop and on the website. According to the museum, Pep is one of their most famous residents. I can't help but wonder how Al Capone's ghost feels about sharing that title.

18

A soldier carried a donkey across a minefield during the Second World War

What you may have been told

When the COVID pandemic began, this photo and the accompanying story were very popular online as many considered it to be a fitting allegory. It depicts an American soldier during the Second World War carrying a donkey on his back because he and his men were walking through a minefield, and if they had let the donkey walk it would have set off the mines and killed everybody. So the GI had to carry the jackass because it was a danger to all, just like those who refused to wear masks or follow lockdown rules. The media also shared the story and even an American governor shared it during a coronavirus briefing on television.

The debunking

I don't want to brag – well, maybe I do a little – but I immediately knew that this photo did not show American soldiers during the Second World War; the uniforms and helmets just looked wrong. But it also didn't make any sense.

If you walk through a minefield you don't scatter, you walk in a line, single file, making sure you step where the soldier before you has stepped. One of the soldiers in the photo is also grinning at the camera instead of paying attention to where he is walking – something else you shouldn't do when there are mines all over the place. The donkey was also very little, a baby donkey. Why would soldiers bring a young donkey along on a mission? It wouldn't be able to carry a heavy load and would be even more stubborn than donkeys already are.

So I knew the story was wrong, but it was a fascinating photo and I wanted to know more about it. I also really wanted to correct a governor. The hunt was on!

It wasn't as easy as I had hoped to find out more. First, I learned that the soldiers involved were members of the French Foreign Legion, who are not the chatty type, plus my French is terrible. Sending the Legion an email involved me filling in a form in French, and at one point I wondered if I had perhaps just signed up by accident. But after a lot of archive searching and talking to several experts and some former French Foreign Legion members, I finally figured out the true story, and it's a gem.

In 1958, the French *13e demi-brigade de Légion étrangère* (13th Demi-Brigade of the Foreign Legion) was active in Algeria when they found a foal that had been abandoned and was dying of hunger. The big, strong, tough, battle-hardened soldiers could not let the creature perish. They decided to take it to their base, but it was so weak that they had to carry it. The photo was taken of them during their march back. It ended up in a French newspaper and soon went around the world.

The *Daily Mirror* wrote:

Here's a soldier who is doing all the donkey work, and enjoying it.

He's a tough French Foreign Legionnaire with a tender heart – a heart that was touched when he and his comrades found this baby donkey abandoned by its mother in a sun-baked Algerian valley.

The troops, on patrol in action against terrorists, decided to adopt the little moke as a mascot.

But the donkey was weak from hunger and could not keep up with the fast-moving Legion men. It looked as if it would have to be left behind.

Then along came a mortar man, already burdened with heavy equipment. Rather than let the donkey die, he hoisted it on top of his pack and carried his 'beast of burden' all the way back to base.

The British Royal Society for the Prevention of Cruelty to Animals (RSPCA) wanted to pay tribute, and on 28 November 1958, they awarded the 13th Demi-Brigade a Bronze Medal 'For their courage and humanity in rescuing a donkey foal from the desert in Algeria'. Unfortunately, but unsurprisingly, the Legion refused to give up the man's identity. A Belgian legionnaire claimed that the man in the photo was Paul Neven, a Belgian man from Antwerp, but I couldn't confirm this, and according to others the men took turns carrying the animal.

Back at the base, the soldiers fed the donkey and named him Bambi because of his appealing eyes, and the men fought over who was allowed to be his keeper. They waited on him hand and foot; they were crazy about Bambi and spoiled him rotten. Soon, he refused to eat animal food, having become used to soldiers' rations, which in turn meant he needed an official rank. It was the only way for the unit to get extra rations instead of having to share theirs with the donkey.

Where there is war, there's paperwork.

Bambi was made the official mascot of the unit and was allowed to go wherever he wanted on base except the bar – he had enjoyed visiting it a bit too much and eventually had to be banned for being an obnoxious drunk.

He saw action a few times but stopped going out on missions in early 1959 as the company was given a helicopter to go into battle with, and stuffing a donkey into a helicopter went a bit too far, even for these men. What happened to Bambi after he retired is unclear. Some say he ended up at a nice farm in France but I couldn't confirm this.

But it is wonderful that an originally nasty pandemic meme about how smart people have to look after the idiots who endanger everybody else is actually based on a story that's more about compassion for the weak and helpless and helping those who need it.

19

This woman made a dramatic dash for freedom at a Berlin border crossing

What you may have been told

A dramatic photo shows a face-off between heavily armed border guards from East and West Berlin on opposing sides of a white line painted across the street, while a young woman kneels on the cobblestones behind them. The woman has just managed to escape after a wild dash for freedom. It so well encapsulates the tension in that part of the world during the 1950s that this picture has been used by newspapers, in documentaries and even in history books on the subject. But apart from its historical value, it's also just a very exciting photo that does well on social media.

The debunking

I've spent literally decades researching the past and analysing images is a big part of what I do. I can't always explain why I think a picture is not as it seems but when I saw this one I had that feeling. Above all, it was just too perfect a photo. When one moment so fantastically illustrates what was going on at the time, and if it is also a rather good photo, you should get a bit suspicious. Of course, that doesn't mean all such photos are not real – they often are. But with this one, if you start thinking about how lucky the photographer was to be there at that moment and how visually pleasing the situation is – with these two sides facing each other, the uniforms, the weapons, that white line, that woman kneeling – then you don't have to be particularly cynical to think there might be a chance that the whole thing is staged. You should never *assume* this, but if that thought pops into your mind, feed it.

To be honest, I hoped my instinct was wrong because if the photo was genuine, there would be an amazing story behind it. Who was the woman? What happened to her afterwards? There were a lot of things I wanted to know. But unfortunately my instinct was right.

Sometimes it takes a lot of detective work to trace an image to its origins: I have to contact archives, retired authors and museums, or get in touch with mysterious characters that I then meet in public places where we exchange briefcases. It can take weeks, months, even years. But this is not one of those cases. It was simply a matter of spending time searching the internet, using reverse-image searches till I found the answer.

East Zone, West Zone is a film that came out in 1962. It was an Italian production with the original title *Oggi a Berlino*, and was directed by Piero Vivarelli. It stars the well-known actor Helmut Griem as the young Hans, who wants to cross the demarcation line to join his family, and Nana Osten as his love interest Rita, the girl sitting on the street in the picture. That explains why the photo looks so perfect: it's staged! What we're looking at is the filming of a scene with actors and extras.

Unfortunately, I didn't manage to get my hands on a copy of the film. Then again, perhaps it's for the best, because according to the reviews it's pretty bad. Dutch newspaper *De Tijd de Maasbode* said, 'Rarely have we seen a movie of which there is so little positive to say,' and called it 'unwatchable'. Ouch.

Still, I guess it is kind of a compliment to those involved in the production that so many people think the photo is genuine. But it does also make you think about how willing people are to believe things without checking.

Finding out that this photo is from a film is something anyone can do. Of course, I don't expect Auntie Doreen who shares this on Facebook to do thorough fact checking, but the story was also shared by history-themed websites and, worse, I've found the photo being used in German newspapers with the claim it shows a genuine event. It's even been on the cover of a book about Berlin during the Cold War!

20

The bird-beak plague doctor mask is medieval

What you may have been told

During the Black Death pandemic in the Middle Ages, doctors wore long coats and a bird-like beak mask that they filled with herbs and other substances to protect them from what they thought of as harmful air. You've seen the masks; they pop up in films, computer games and even documentaries. During the

COVID-19 pandemic, they were all over the media and you could even see them out in public again. Much to the delight of the tabloids.

The debunking

Let me get straight to the point: the plague doctor outfit is real, it really existed – yes, even that freaky bird-beak mask – but it is NOT MEDIEVAL.

I know that may sound a bit pedantic, but it is all part of this very annoying global habit of attaching anything negative, dark and scary to the poor old Middle Ages. In reality, this scary figure is from the seventeenth century. It's almost as silly as people in the future saying tricorn hats were fashionable in the early 2000s. I wish they had been, but alas.

When we talk about 'the plague' we could be talking about lots of diseases. In this case, we mean the bubonic plague, which has been around since at least the Bronze Age but is mostly known for its most deadly outbreak in the fourteenth-century pandemic, better known as the Black Death. Although the bubonic plague returned many times throughout history, the name Black Death is specifically related to that one medieval outbreak. It was one of the deadliest pandemics ever, so it deserves its own name. If someone is talking about the Black Death but they mean an outbreak that happened much later, you can correct them and appear really smart.

Medieval plague doctors existed, and they looked pretty impressive, but they did not wear those amazing masks.

The first account of this specific beaky outfit comes from the writer Michel de Saint-Martin in his 1682 biography of Charles de Lorme, the chief physician of three French kings – Henri IV, Louis XIII and Louis XIV. In his book he writes that during the 1618/19 plague outbreak in Paris, Doctor de Lorme:

never forgot his Morocco [finest goatskin leather] coat of which he was the author, he dressed it from head to toe in the form of trousers, with a mask of the same Morocco where he had a half-foot long nose tied in order to deflect malignancy from the air.

There is no mention of it anywhere else before this time, not even in de Lorme's own papers, nor are there any depictions. But more evidence for the costume starts showing up a couple of decades later.

In 1656, a woodcut was made in Italy showing the plague doctor as we know him and the picture was soon published all over Europe. It seems to have spoken to people's imaginations almost instantly, and even though in some publications the outfit was mocked as a strange Italian custom, there's no denying that the picture struck a chord.

We don't know how often the costumes were actually used; there may have been just a few of them in Italy and France, but because of the popularity of the pictures they seem to have been everywhere when they probably weren't. I've seen a couple of them walking around London in a British historical drama but I can't tell you for sure that the masks were ever actually used in England . . . well, not until 2020 anyway.

As peculiar as it looks, the outfit did work, sort of, a bit. The bubonic plague, especially the septicaemic and pneumonic kinds, is extremely contagious, and although the doctors at the time were talking about 'corrupted air' (miasma) that transmitted diseases, in a way they were not that far off – it was the droplets in the air following coughs and sneezes that spread it, not the air itself. The scary mask would have worked as a sort of filter. The long leather coat and gloves would also make it harder for the infected fleas to bite physicians and would protect them from any bodily fluids they were in contact with when visiting patients.

In a way, they were kind of like early hazmat suits.

There is still a lot we don't know about the plague doctor outfit with the beaked mask, but we *do* know that there's no evidence for it existing during the fourteenth century – it's from a much later, very different time. So leave the poor Middle Ages alone – they've got enough of an image problem already!

21

This Second World War photo shows a German soldier using a mobile phone

What you may have been told

A German soldier during the Second World War is holding a mobile phone. You know they didn't have those in the 1940s, so you know the photo can't be authentic . . . but, what if . . . could it be . . . is this evidence of time travel?!

The debunking

NO. It is not evidence of time travel.

It may sound silly – of course a photo of someone in the 1940s holding what appears to be an iPhone can't be real – but it may surprise you how willing some people are to believe any evidence of time travel. When a photo looks convincing but is not quite detailed enough to exactly make out what's going on, some people let themselves be fooled. I understand the eagerness, I'd love nothing more than to be able to travel back in time. As the poster in the TV show *The X-Files* said: 'I want to believe'.

Still, if you want to convince people that a photo isn't quite what they think it is, you can't just say so, you need to prove it. People are stubborn and don't like being wrong. So I decided to investigate the texting German.

The first copy of this photo that was uploaded to the internet was relatively easy to find – it brought me to Mr Richard Tanton's Flickr account, where the photo had the following description: 'Finally Proof! From deep in the Czech photo archives, finally proof of the rumour that a few German soldiers were issued prototype iPhones in the last years of WWII. However, due to the limited number of repeating towers, "low bars" was a constant problem.'

Was Richard Tanton being serious? The tags used to describe the photo were an obvious clue: film set, Podskalska, Prague.

If this information was accurate and if this was indeed the original upload of the picture, the tags suggested that it was taken during the filming of a Second World War production in the Czech Republic. With a little detective work and Google Maps it wasn't difficult to find the location of the photo: 5 Plavecká in Prague. But as Prague (a gorgeous city) is a very popular location for filming, especially historical dramas, it turned out to be tricky to find out which film was being shot when the photo was taken.

While I was still working on the case, some fact-checking websites researched the picture as well and published their results, coming to many of the same conclusions that I reached, but nothing more. And this is where the quest might have ended, had Mr Tanton not contacted me.

I had sent him a message on Flickr but had not received an answer, and eventually assumed he perhaps had stopped using Flickr and would never reply. But then suddenly I received a message from him! Mr Tanton explained that he had made the Photoshopped image for fun, a joke that wasn't meant to fool anyone. He didn't expect people to actually think it was real. He also confirmed that the photo was taken in Prague on 29 May 2016, but he didn't know which movie was being filmed that day.

There were two movies filmed in Prague in 2016: *The Man with the Iron Heart* and *Anthropoid*.

Most people who have been trying to find out more about the photo got stuck here; it would be very difficult to find out which film set that photo depicted, especially as the films are set in the same era and have similar themes. But after Mr Tanton sent me the original, unedited photo, I spotted a new clue: there was a van parked in the street behind the soldier, which had been carefully Photoshopped out of the version shared online. The text on it was faded and damaged but I could just make out Česká Televize, a public television broadcaster in the Czech Republic.

Just as I was looking into how Česká Televize might have been involved in those movies or re-enactment events, Mr Tanton sent me some photos his wife Jitka had taken that day. In them, I spotted one man in modern clothes giving actors directions. As someone who has spent a lot of time on film sets and who has even done a bit of directing herself, I can spot a director from miles away. But he didn't look like the directors of *The Man with the Iron Heart* or *Anthropoid*.

So, like a police officer, I went around the internet with this man's photo, hoping someone could identify him. I thought that a director who gets to film a big Second World War production in the heart of Prague would have had his face in the media a few times. I was right, and I found him.

The man in charge in those photos turned out to be Robert Sedláček, a director from the Czech Republic who made quite a few big TV series. Having found him it was relatively easy to discover what he was working on that day in 2016. The show is called *Bohéma* and is about the film industry in Czechoslovakia from 1938 to 1953. You can watch the entire series online and because I wanted to be 100 per cent sure, that's just what I did, even though I don't speak Czech. I have no idea if it was any good, but it was about an interesting subject and visually quite pleasing, so I didn't mind checking it out.

I had to look through four episodes before I found what I was looking for at the beginning of episode five. There was a scene in which there's a confrontation between civilians and German soldiers in a street. It involves a German tank (a rather bad replica of the Tiger I) and a German vehicle called a Kübelwagen that I recognised from some of the other photos I'd seen. It clearly was the scene that was being filmed when Mr and Mrs Tanton took their pictures.

So although it was of course already quite clear that the photo was not really from the 1940s and didn't show a time-travelling German soldier sending a text home, now, thanks to Richard and Jitka Tanton and a bit of detective work, we also know exactly what was being filmed.

This kind of detective work is a lot of fun, at least, for me it is. And when you manage to close the case, even if it takes years to get there, it is very satisfying.

22

Toddler François Bertillon was arrested and had a mugshot taken

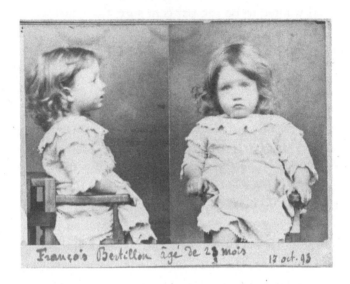

François Bertillon âgé de 2½ mois   17 oct. 93

What you may have been told

A scared-looking toddler, not even two years old, looks back at us from a mugshot taken in 1893. One picture from the front, one from the side. The accompanying text explains that this is 23-month-old François Bertillon's arrest photo, after he was caught nibbling all the pears from a basket. Of course, we're all shocked at the brutality of our barbaric ancestors – how could they put this poor angel in jail?!

The debunking

The photo was taken by the kid's uncle, Alphonse Bertillon, an amazing and very interesting man who can be considered the inventor of the modern mugshot.

After leaving the army, Bertillon got a low-level desk job with the Parisian police but soon got very frustrated with the bureaucratic mess it was in. The police seemed to be powerless to do anything about criminals who kept being arrested over and over again, as it was often difficult to prove they had done the same thing before if their identity could not be confirmed. So, in his spare time, Bertillon tried to figure out a way to do something about this and developed many forensic techniques that soon were adopted by police forces across the world. But he was most obsessed with keeping records, logging details and registering criminals as accurately as possible. He created the Bertillon System, which involved taking a bunch of exact measurements and several photos of criminals. This made it a lot easier to identify every Jean, Pierre or Louis who got arrested, even if they gave a false name.

So what about the kid's mugshot?

It seems that Bertillon experimented on his family, as there are mugshots of him, his brothers, their wives and their kids, and especially little François, who was a popular subject. He seems to have had his mugshot taken very regularly since he was a baby.

It's often claimed that François was Bertillon's son, and I had to do some genealogical research and read the biography written by Bertillon's niece Suzanne to prove that claim wrong as well. Suzanne, by the way, was also an extraordinary person who fought for women's rights, against communism and against Nazism. She got locked up for threatening socialists, joined the Resistance during the Second World War, worked with well-known secret agent Virginia Hall and won several medals.

According to her, Bertillon and his wife Amélie loved and spoiled their nephew and nieces. François seems to have had a wonderful childhood in a great yet eccentric family. There isn't much about him in the archives but he survived the wars and became a doctor. He died in 1963.

So instead of this being the heart-breaking story of a sad little toddler who got nicked for nibbling pears, it's just a photo taken for fun or to help Uncle Alphonse with his continuing development and improvement of mugshots.

23

Members of the media, doctors and nurses were hanged in public in Nuremberg in 1945

What you may have been told

During the COVID-19 pandemic, the hate between those who supported vaccinations and those who opposed them reached extreme levels. At one point, nurses, doctors and journalists were threatened by the mass sharing of a photo of members of the media and medical profession being hanged at Nuremberg after the Second World War. The full text accompanying the gruesome photo was:

Still so sure you want to try to force me to get the experimental vaccination?
Photograph of Hangings at Nuremberg, Germany.

Members of the media who lied and misled the German people were
executed, right along with medical doctors and nurses who participated in
medical experiments using living people as guinea pigs.

Those who forget the past are condemned to relive it.

The debunking

You can imagine how awful it must be when you work day and night and put your life on the line trying to fight the virus, just to then receive messages like this from anonymous trolls. People blindly believed the claim and it was spread in public, even during a busy 'anti-vax' rally in Trafalgar Square, London. It caused quite a stir in the media.

Many of the stories in this book may not seem that harmful – innocent mistakes, misconceptions, myths that harm nobody. But this case shows how fake history can also be used for propaganda, to abuse others, and can turn out to be dangerous, even deadly. When people want to believe conspiracies and are planning to threaten and intimidate others, they generally don't care much about the truth.

Let's look at the text of this 'meme' first. At the International Military Tribunal at Nuremberg in 1946, no doctors or nurses were hanged. Only one person who was executed there, Julius Streicher, could be called a member of the media, as he published a vile Nazi 'newspaper'.

Doctors were hanged at subsequent trials in Nuremberg held by the US military, not an international court. This is not that difficult to look up; the list of those hanged at Nuremberg is not very long and can be found online with just a few clicks. This is not some hidden bit of history you need to dig up in some faraway archive.

So the claim on its own is already iffy. But they didn't even bother to find a real photo of the Nuremberg hangings to illustrate it. For starters, the executions were not performed in public!

But the way everybody is dressed also is a clue. There are a lot of those typical Russian hats and the soldiers are wearing Russian uniforms, which would be odd at a hanging carried out by Americans in front of German civilians. So in other words, this photo was not taken in Nuremberg.

The photo was taken on 29 January 1946 in Kyiv, Ukraine, and shows the hanging of several Nazi war criminals (no doctors, no nurses and no members of the media) who were responsible for some truly horrific crimes, like the massacre of Babi Yar when tens of thousands of Jews and later also prisoners of war, Romani and Ukrainians were slaughtered.

The best way to completely destroy this bit of fake history is by proving that the photo has nothing to do with the claim, so I tracked it down, which was not that difficult. But to get a copy of it and secure permission to print it in this book, I had to get in touch with the archivists at the H.S. Pshenichny Central State Film and Photographic Archives of Ukraine, in Kyiv, who were kind enough to help me with my research while their city was literally being bombed by the Russians and war crimes were once more being committed in their country. I'm much obliged to them.

24

The first depiction of Jesus
is in a museum in Cairo

What you may have been told

What Jesus really looked like has been a popular topic for debate
for centuries – and it's no surprise that the debate has spread to
the internet, too.

A valuable bit of evidence in this debate is, of course, the very
first depiction of him. One picture in particular is often called the
oldest depiction of Christ ever made: it shows the Son of God

surrounded by disciples and is currently in the Coptic Museum in Cairo. And guess what? He looks dark, nothing like the blond, blue-eyed Jesus that's being worshipped in much of the Western world!

The debunking

The debate about what Jesus really looked like has been going on for almost 2,000 years. If you want to get involved, you'll need to examine ancient writings and scientific research papers and, of course, participate in very long complicated debates, as his contemporaries unfortunately didn't bother to write down a detailed description of what he looked like. Even the Bible gives us very few clues.

It is almost as if it didn't really matter to them what colour his skin was . . .

But people who want to make a claim about his skin colour are often tempted to look no further than the first and oldest pictures of Christ. To be fair, this is not a bad place to start – the first people who painted or drew Jesus lived closer to the time when he was alive and often also near to where he lived. But unfortunately, so far, no art has been found that was made while Jesus was still alive or even close to it; nothing has been found that dates from before the second century AD.

Trying to depict someone who has died one or two centuries earlier when you have no photographs, no detailed descriptions and nobody left alive who knew him is going to be quite tricky. But still, something made 200 years after Jesus died and in the Middle East is going to be at least a bit closer to the source than what some artist painted in Texas last week. So let's get to the painting in question.

When it is shared online, the text accompanying the icon usually says something like, 'Earliest known image of Jesus Christ, from the Coptic Museum in Cairo, Egypt. This painting of Jesus is older than the image of the black Jesus Christ in the Church of Rome which is from the sixth century.' That the painting is currently in an Egyptian museum gives the claim extra gravitas.

For some time, it was very popular on social media. It was even shared on Twitter by rapper, actor and film maker Ice Cube, who currently has almost 6 million followers. It was liked by over 170,000 people and shared almost 46,000 times. Of course, I corrected him, but I'm not sure he read my reply.

Although old art often gets a lot darker over time, in this case the figures really do have a dark skin. So if this truly was the earliest known picture of Jesus it would be extremely famous; it would be in all the history books! Of course, some people think that the image was hidden as part of some conspiracy or ignored by historians because they don't like the idea of a dark-skinned Jesus. But if that was the case, someone clearly forgot to tell the Coptic Museum, as it's on public display there and not at all well-hidden. Also, if it really was the oldest picture of Jesus every modern history book on the subject would have mentioned it and it would be seen in every documentary on the subject. Who are we kidding – if it really was what some people are claiming, it would probably have been 'borrowed' and taken to the Vatican. Either way, it would have been very famous and we wouldn't have had to wait for Mr Cube to reveal this secret on Twitter.

If the painting in the Cairo museum was the oldest image of Jesus in the world it would be extremely well protected and you would not be allowed to take a photo, especially not with a flash camera . . . unlike the picture that's being shared online! I can't imagine any museum could resist telling the world about having such an important art piece in its collection – it would increase its visitor numbers and thus its revenue to dizzying heights. No, there is a very simple reason why this painting is not world famous: it is not the oldest depiction of Jesus, not even close.

Unfortunately, this time I can't brag about how I did some first-class detective work; all it took to debunk this claim was for me to send a Facebook message to the Coptic Museum in Egypt and ask its staff about the painting. This was their response:

It shows Saint Thomas touching the wound of Christ with his finger while disciples look on. St Thomas touches the wound of Christ with his finger so he could believe in his Resurrection, while the rest of the disciples look at Thomas or at Christ. Eighteenth century (AD) Greek style.

Just to be sure, I used social media to ask someone to visit the museum in question and that's how I ended up with photos and video footage of the painting, and the museum description next to it.

I also checked with a few experts on Coptic art and read several books on the subject. They all confirmed the age and background of the painting, though the museum telling me when it was made really told me everything I needed to know.

So the painting was made in the eighteenth century, 1,700 years after Jesus lived, and for that reason it is not the first depiction of Jesus ever made, far from it.

Can I resist dipping my toe in the 'what Jesus really looked like' debate and risk alienating some of my readers? Of course not.

Jesus most likely looked like a Jewish man from Galilee who was born in Nazareth. In other words, he looked like someone from the Middle East. So he wouldn't have been what we today would call Black, nor did he look like a tall, blond Norwegian.

The only description of Jesus in the Bible comes from the Book of Revelation in the New Testament, and it doesn't describe his earthly appearance but what he looked like in a vision. The holy texts also tell us of several instances when people who had known Jesus very well when he was among the living failed to recognise him after his resurrection: John 21:4 and Luke 24:16 describe the disciples meeting Jesus but not realising who he was, and in John 20:15, Mary Magdalene confuses Jesus with a gardener. If we take this literally, it suggests Jesus looked, at first sight, very different after he came back to life.

One more valuable clue we get from the Bible is that Jesus did not stand out in first-century Jerusalem – if he had looked very different from any of the people around him or even just his disciples, Judas wouldn't have had to kiss him to identify him. Although Jerusalem at the time had visitors from all over the world, and was full of Romans, Greeks and traders from faraway places, including western Europe, a tall, blond-haired, blue-eyed man would still have stood out, especially in a group of disciples who didn't look like that at all.

So, to conclude, Jesus most likely was neither white nor Black but had light brown skin, along with short hair and no beard, as that was the fashion among men in that part of the world at the time he was alive.

25

Victorian prostitutes used tiny candles to time their clients

What you may have been told

To keep track of the time, Victorian prostitutes would light a tiny candle, slightly bigger than a match, that would burn for seven minutes. When the candle finished burning, time was up and the client had to go.

The debunking

The tiny candles really did exist and they were also a Victorian thing: that much is true. But the whole brothel story is, to put it mildly, dubious. Before we look at the evidence, let's stop and think about this logically for a moment. Why would they not just have used a clock? They had clocks and watches back then; they were already being mass produced and were not that expensive! But even if they couldn't afford a second-hand clock, they could have just used an hourglass.

Technically, seven minutes is also a bit long for a brothel. On the other hand, if a customer wanted something special or, as was often the case, just wanted to talk or be listened to, seven minutes wouldn't be enough. What would the hostess have done when they wanted more time? Light another candle right in the middle of the 'transaction'? Besides, someone working in a brothel would probably have had a madam or pimp waiting outside the room, to keep track of time and make sure the guest was removed or charged extra if he stayed beyond his slot. It makes no sense . . . except when you are trying to get people's attention or sell them something (more on that, later).

The candles were actually called '*bougies de poche*', or pocket candles – tiny wax candles contained in a sort of matchbox, which could be lit and placed in the little hole in the box, providing temporary light when people didn't have a larger candle or lamp nearby. Some of these candles had phosphorus-coated tips, so they could be easily lit like a match. Very handy if you needed to get undressed after coming home from the pub but didn't want to wake anyone up. Also perfect for lighting all the other regular candles or lights in your house without having to waste a match on each of them.

Interestingly enough, these candles were called *bougies de poche anglaises* in the 1867 French book *Le dernier mot de Rocambole*. So in France, they referred to them as English pocket candles, but the book also says that they only burned for three minutes, not seven . . . I can't help but wonder if they gave that name to the candles to take a dig at the English.

But no matter where I looked, no matter which museum or collector I contacted, nobody knew of any historical evidence that connected the pocket candles to brothels or prostitution.

What about their boxes having pictures of pretty ladies on them? Well, many of them did indeed depict gorgeous women and some even had a saucy photo for a label, but not all of them. They also depicted innocent household scenes, knights in shining armour, children playing, and even portraits of royals and important world leaders. Some were clearly made as commemorative souvenirs – mass produced and sold or perhaps handed out at a special event. A brothel-related item at such an occasion would have raised quite a few Victorian eyebrows.

There were some with naughty poems on them, and people sometimes complained about this – which would be odd if the candles were generally accepted as things used in brothels. But this is perhaps why someone once came to the conclusion that there must have been a connection with brothels and decided that the internet had to know.

The first time brothel candles were mentioned online, as far as I know, was on a Reddit post about an online auction in 2016. Now, Etsy is also full of them. Of course, *brothel* candles get a lot more attention than pocket candles, so maybe that's how the fake history began, with someone making up a story to sell something mundane. Or maybe someone simply misunderstood or mistranslated a description they found elsewhere. I doubt we'll ever know how this story was born.

So, to conclude: pocket candles were used when people needed a bit of light for longer than a single match provided but couldn't – or didn't want to – use a lamp or larger candle. And there is no evidence whatsoever of a specific connection between these candles and brothels or prostitution. If you ever find a historical source that does connect them, please do let me know.

26

Medieval people all had terrible teeth

What you may have been told

During the Middle Ages everybody, especially the peasants, had black, green or no teeth. It was, of course, a time when, for some reason, people didn't care about hygiene, health or appearance. We see it in almost every Hollywood film and television series, and many of us were taught this in schools and by museum guides, so surely it's true.

The debunking

Although our world changes all the time, people don't change a lot. Our ancestors may at first appear like strangers with peculiar habits and weird opinions, but if you look beyond that first impression you'll find people who like good food, companionship, comfort, being warm, clean and happy. Since the dawn of time, we also disliked hunger, loneliness, discomfort, being cold, dirty and sad.

When you look at all of history with that in mind, the idea that people during one specific era in one particular part of the world suddenly stopped caring about their teeth or how their breath smelled sounds quite daft. However handsome you are or how drunk your date is, if your teeth are rotting, your gums are bleeding and your breath is stinking, you're not going to be kissed, you're not going to get lucky and you're not going to go home with someone you really like. It does not matter if you're dating someone from the Stone Age (there's evidence that suggests prehistoric ancestors used twigs to clean their teeth!), the Middle Ages, the Victorian era or someone you met last week at the pub.

Don't worry, you can still point at the screen and laugh when you see a knight in some blockbuster film with teeth so straight and bright you have to shield your eyes when he smiles. Nobody in history ever had teeth like the stars in Hollywood do today, but then again, most people in the world still don't have teeth like that. But medieval teeth were also not extremely bad – at least, not as bad as we're often led to believe. In fact, they were pretty good.

Obviously dental care was not as advanced as it is today but – and this is the clincher – medieval people had less need for it as their diets generally didn't contain as much (if any) sugar as ours do today. What we put in our mouths now is in many ways less healthy and more damaging to our teeth than the medieval diet was. Just look at all the soft drinks, sweets and food with dodgy additives we scoff on a daily basis. And, of course, smoking and drinking coffee doesn't help either. The things that threaten our teeth in such an extreme way today were simply not available to medieval people.

Sugar had been present in Europe since ancient times but had to be imported and was very expensive. It remained a luxury till long after the Middle Ages had ended. Coffee and tobacco were not even available in Europe by then. Sad news for our ancestors, good news for their teeth.

But besides their teeth being at a lower risk of damage, medieval people also simply liked to have clean teeth and nice-smelling breath. Although they didn't really have toothbrushes, they did use chewing twigs to clean with, and rags to rub their teeth with, as well as all kinds of homemade pastes or powders. We even have some old recipes for products that were meant to whiten your teeth. The *Glycyrrhiza glabra* plant, for instance, was (and still is!)

especially well-suited to dental care. It is better known as liquorice and contains compounds that prevent and treat tooth decay and gum disease. Many wholefood shops and some chemists still sell these chew sticks.

From the *Regimen sanitatis Salernitanum* (The Salernitan Rule of Health), a long poem that describes daily hygiene practices, probably written in the twelfth or thirteenth centuries, although it could be even older:

> *At early dawn, when first from bed you rise,*
> *Wash, in cold water, both your hands and eyes.*
> *With comb and brush then cleanse your teeth and hair,*
> *And thus refreshed, your limbs outstretch with care.*
> *Such things restore the weary, o'ertasked brain.*
> *And to all parts ensure a wholesome gain.*

And from *Descriptio Cambriae* (Description of Wales), written by Gerald of Wales in the twelfth century:

> *Both sexes take great care of their teeth, more than I have seen in any country. They are constantly cleaning them with green hazel-shoots and then rubbing them with woollen cloths until they shine like ivory.*

But the final nail in the coffin of this myth is that the teeth of many of the medieval skeletons that have been found and examined by archaeologists are in pretty good condition. Our medieval ancestors did suffer more wear, plaque and tartar but fewer cavities, and that's what does a lot of damage to teeth.

Still, we mustn't think that their teeth were all fine and dandy – they had trouble with them too. Many medieval skeletons are missing a few teeth for all sorts of reasons, and what we today would consider a minor infection that can be easily treated could have turned deadly back then. And dentistry was often quite a brutal affair.

Nevertheless, the cliché of medieval folk with black, yellow or almost no teeth just doesn't really match medieval records, archaeological evidence and common sense. We know they cared about their teeth, wanted them to look white and clean, and tried to avoid having bad-smelling breath. They may not have always succeeded, and many of their remedies, recipes and procedures didn't really help much, but they did their best.

27

These windows were made so people could still buy wine during the Black Death

What you may have been told

At the height of the COVID-19 pandemic a story went – pardon the use of the word in this context – viral. Across Italy, a medieval 'plague tradition' was revived when people started selling wine from the *buchette del vino* – the wine windows – like they once did centuries ago. Instead of having to enter a shop or tavern, you could buy your wine from a tiny window just big enough to pass a bottle, jug or glass through. A lovely, quaint little story that made us smile during some very dark times.

The debunking

The *buchettes del vino* are real – there are little hatches in buildings all over Florence that enabled people to buy wine quickly, easily and directly from traders, who didn't need to open and manage a shop or bar, hire staff or pay extra taxes. In a way, it was a sort of drive-through (well, walk-through) off licence.

When the COVID-19 pandemic struck, some Italians started using these windows again, as it allowed them to trade while at the same time still maintain social distancing, sort of. It was the perfect feel-good story for countless newspapers, television shows and websites, so of course everybody started sharing it – without doing any fact checking.

Once more, people seem to be confused about when the Middle Ages were and when they ended because these wine windows originated in the second half of the sixteenth century. Although historians still argue about when exactly the Middle Ages ended they generally all agree that sixteenth-century Italy was not medieval. After all, it's kind of where (and when) the Renaissance began!

The windows were also not really a plague tradition or even plague related, originally. They were created in the 1500s for commercial reasons. It's true that they were used when the bubonic plague came to Italy in the 1630s, as people realised that these windows were also really rather handy for selling stuff without having to get too close to their customers, just like they did in 2020. But this wasn't what they were created for and they certainly weren't medieval. Once more, modern-day journalists got confused and wrote that the Black Death was what drove people to use these wine windows. But as we know, the Black Death was a specific plague outbreak in the fourteenth century, around two hundred years before Florentines had even thought to build their little trading windows.

28

This is a photo of the first Black American female lawyer, Charlotte E. Ray

What you may have been told

Quite regularly, Charlotte E. Ray is honoured online, and rightly so. Against overwhelming odds, she managed to become the first Black female lawyer in the United States. And when you want to share the story of an impressive person online, you of course want to add a picture of them; it makes your social media post more attractive and the odds of people wanting to share it go up. But that's where things get problematic . . .

The debunking

Charlotte E. Ray was a fascinating woman who broke through barriers and deserves the credit and attention people want to give her. Being a Black woman in nineteenth-century America was a whole challenge on its own, but she did not let this stop her. With a lot of support from her family – and by possibly being a bit vague about her gender on her admission papers – in 1872, she became the first woman to graduate from the Howard University School of Law. She was admitted to the District of Columbia Bar in the same year and started her own independent practice.

She was very good at her job but it was difficult for her to find clients because of her gender and skin colour. Eventually, she had to give up being a lawyer and became a teacher. She was impressive and, indeed, she was the first Black, female lawyer in the United States. Which makes her the perfect subject for a social media post, especially for law firms, individuals and companies who care about diversity and feminism, and who want their followers to know how important these subjects are to them. Charlotte sure ticks a lot of boxes . . . but there are no photos of her. I've looked everywhere; I thought that surely there would be a photo of the real Charlotte somewhere, but unfortunately I could not find a single one, which is a bit sad. I so wish I could see what she really looked like and share her image with you and the people who keep sharing the wrong pictures.

So who are the women in the photos that people share while admiring Charlotte? I've found three different women whose portraits have been regularly mistaken for hers, and whose pictures appear at the start of this chapter:

- Lutie A. Lytle (1875–1955), another of the first Black women in America in the legal profession *(left)*;

- Marian Anderson (1897–1993), one of the most celebrated opera singers of the twentieth century and a social reformer *(middle)*;
- Sadie Tanner Mossell Alexander (1898–1989), the first Black woman to receive a PhD in economics in the US in 1921, and the first Black woman to practise law in Pennsylvania, as well as a civil rights activist *(right)*.

It is really embarrassing and a bit painful that people who mean well end up confusing one impressive Black woman for another.

29

A nineteenth-century princess and a countess had a topless duel

What you may have been told

Duels are always a fascinating subject – two men meet at dawn and then fight to defend their honour. And if women duel, it becomes even more interesting, as that didn't happen very often. If one of them is a princess, the other a countess and they get topless . . . then you have the golden formula for one hell of a story.

The tale goes that in 1892, Princess Pauline von Metternich and Countess Anastasia Kielmansegg had a disagreement about a flower arrangement that got so out of hand they decided to solve their problem by having a duel with rapiers. To make sure the fabric of their clothes didn't cause an infection if it was pushed into a wound, they decided to fight topless.

The debunking

The people involved in the story are real: Pauline Clémentine Marie Walburga, Princess of Metternich-Winneburg zu Beilstein, and Countess Anastasia von Kielmansegg were both famous socialites in nineteenth-century Austria. Duels between women also really happened and of course were quite a popular topic of conversation back then, as they were seen as scandalous. Some asked men to duel for them but that was also frowned upon, especially by other women, who sometimes seemed to consider women duelling a sign of emancipation and progress. And then there's the detail about them fighting topless because of the risks of infection. It all sounds very believable.

But the main reason people are falling for it is because it is a very old story. It was all over the newspapers back in 1892 and inspired artists, especially the ones looking for an excuse to paint topless ladies. You can imagine that a modern-day reporter needing a click bait article who does some basic research will not think there's anything suspicious about the story – the people were real, it was in the newspapers and just look at those exciting old paintings. That will surely get people to click on this story!

To be fair, it's not just editors who write for iffy websites who do this. The story has been so generally accepted that it's been mentioned in books, documentaries and so on. It's only when you try to find out if it actually happened that things start to get a little dodgy.

There are no primary sources for the story whatsoever. Nobody directly involved in it ever mentioned it or claimed it happened; there are no eyewitness accounts, no juicy descriptions in biographies written much later and no mention of it happening in Viennese gossip columns. Nothing. At least, not that I could find. Actually, the story is mentioned in some Viennese newspapers, but they appear to consider it some sort of joke.

But the main evidence against it is an alleged telegram, sent by the princess herself and published in the French newspaper *Le Figaro*, that stated:

> *The alleged encounter with the sword which took place between Madame de Metternich and Countess Kielmansegg is definitely denied by the following dispatch:*
>
> *Esztergom, August 22, 8 a. m. 40.*
> *Stupid and ridiculous canard invented by Italian newspapers.*
> *Princess of METTERNICH*

Does this *prove* that the duel never happened? No. But there is no evidence whatsoever that it did, nobody involved in it ever mentioned it and, assuming that the telegram wasn't invented by an over-enthusiastic journalist, the story was publicly denied by at least one of the supposed protagonists.

So all we've got in favour of it having happened is a bunch of gossip in some dodgy non-Viennese newspapers.

30

This beautiful French house was built in 1509

What you may have been told

Photos of a truly wonderful old-looking house are shared online; 'Medieval house built in 1509, Argentan, France', one description says. The building looks really pretty and romantic, as if it came straight from a fairy tale . . . and before you realise it you've shared it! It is so gorgeous, it looks so old, how could it ever be fake history?

The debunking

When I first saw the photos I was immediately suspicious, not because of how the house looked but because it was situated in Argentan, a town that suffered immensely during the Second World War. A large section of it was completely destroyed in 1944. So I wondered how the building survived, and if it was perhaps rebuilt. I looked for higher resolution versions of the photos online so I could look at the details and when I found these I started to suspect that perhaps the house was not as old as people claimed it was.

My first step was to try and find out the origin of the photos, and with a bit of reverse-image searching I soon found one of them had been uploaded to deviantart.com in 2013 by user Hubert61 with the title 'House Argentan Orne France'. Although there was not a lot of extra information on that page, some of the comments there backed up my suspicion that the building was not as old as it seemed.

The next step was tracing the actual location. I digitally wandered around Argentan using Google Maps till I found it. The house is situated on the land behind 72 Rue Aristide Briand. It's on private property, so if you find yourself in Argentan, don't go snooping around the place without permission. But now I could see more of the building, I knew my instinct was correct: there really was something iffy about the building – the side of it didn't look medieval at all!

Once I knew the address, it of course became a bit easier to research the history of this building, but I didn't have much luck. I couldn't just let it go, so after a couple of years I decided to look into it again and fellow fake history hunter Ernst Dommershuijzen mentioned he had found something on Facebook.

A page called 'Ouest France Argentan' had shared the familiar photo but explained that the house was built in 1955 and decorated by a certain Mr Chauvin in the 1960s and 1970s. They also shared a photo taken by François Boscher, a journalist who works for the local newspaper. He was a neighbour – and a good friend – of the Chauvins. His photo also showed the modern side of the building. Mr Roland Chauvin lived there with his wife Rolande. He was quite an impressive gentleman. Like his father before him, he was a saddler, but also an upholsterer and generally a very talented craftsman who kept busy till his death, aged 94. He was born in Argentan and he was so talented he worked on several castles in western Normandy. He was especially proud of the mattress he made for the bed that Queen Elizabeth II slept on during her visit to the Château de Sassy. He loved doing his work and was always busy, but he wasn't a very good business-man: he was too kind and sometimes 'forgot' to send a bill. But he was popular in the town and was even elected to the municipal council.

In 1944, Mr Chauvin and his sister Denise were in their twen-ties. At the start of the heavy bombing of their town, their father rushed the family away from the centre and dug a trench for everybody to hide in, covering it up with earth and logs. They survived but their family home was completely destroyed, and their town turned into what they called 'a butcher's shop' as it was littered with dead soldiers, the sight of which caused Denise to have nightmares for years. They moved into a temporary shelter, constructed from items they found lying around, and eventually the town was rebuilt and they got themselves a new proper home.

We know Mr Chauvin loved making things and was very cre-ative. Unfortunately we can only guess why he decided to make his house look the way it turned out, but it is glorious and I bet he would have been so proud to learn how many people were fooled by it.

31

Thomas Edison invented the lightbulb

What you may have been told

Thomas Edison was a great inventor who provided humanity with many amazing inventions. In 1879, he invented the light bulb and it changed the world forever.

The debunking

Let's get straight to it: Edison did NOT invent the light bulb.

The basic technology behind the light bulb had been tinkered with since before Edison was even born. In sheds across the world, very smart people were trying to use electricity to create light, and they succeeded! Light bulbs already existed and were even patented before Edison decided to put his thinking cap on. Of course, every invention builds on what others have invented before – the first light bulb couldn't have been made if it wasn't for those who paved the way by inventing ways to blow thin glass, generate electricity, develop incandescent lighting and so on. What Edison did was *improve* other people's inventions. Thanks to having access to a lot of funding, a large workshop and employees, he could afford to continue working on things others started but couldn't finish.

So, who should we credit for this invention?

One strong contender is Sir Humphry Davy, a chemist from Penzance, who made a ton of very impressive inventions, one of them being the arc lamp in the early 1800s. It works by having an arc of electricity travel between two carbon electrodes, releasing carbon vapour which creates a very bright light. It was a bit too bright, even. The light worked so well that it was used as street lighting and to light huge spaces like halls and factories, but it was too big, too hot, too noisy and used too much electricity to have any other practical use. But no matter how you look at it, it was the first time electric light was used on a large scale outside of the laboratories and sheds of tinkerers and inventors. And Edison was only born in 1847!

In 1835, Scotsman James Bowman Lindsay gave a demonstration showcasing an electric light that he could read by. Unfortunately the light burned out pretty quickly and Mr Lindsay never made any progress on this project after the demonstration. But it seems to have been the first practical use of an electric light inside a home, and it worked.

My favourite is French-Belgian inventor Jean-Baptiste-Ambroise-Marcellin Jobard, who in 1838 created an actual light bulb that had a carbon filament burning within a vacuum. It was nearly practical and ready for mass use, but Jobard seems to have moved on to other things and let his former student Charles de Changy continue working on it. I think that if he'd had the money and resources that Edison had access to, he may well have been able to make the light bulb a success too . . . but he didn't.

Another close contender is Englishman Sir Joseph Wilson Swan. Although he wasn't the first, he was hot on Edison's heels, and they both patented a working light bulb in 1879. Sir Joseph's house was the first one in the world lit by electric light bulbs. He started installing lights everywhere and in a way was doing in Britain what Edison was doing in the United States – but he did it better and earlier. Edison was not happy and sued Swan for copyright infringement, but Swan won. He had sorted out his patents and could prove he had made his inventions independently from what Edison was doing. The two great inventors later decided to combine forces. Their two companies started working together and eventually merged.

The list of other possible light bulb inventors is long. I could name another 20 people who were tinkering away and making working light bulbs all over the world in the nineteenth century. But there was always something wrong. Sometimes the bulb wasn't good enough or didn't work properly. Sometimes it was too expensive and the inventor couldn't find a way to mass produce it or put all the important components together.

To give credit where it's due, Edison learned from what all those other men had done, combined some of their achievements (and even bought some of their patents) and then created the full package destined for success. Not only did he make a good working light bulb (although the first ones still didn't last very long), he made sure to provide all the other items that were needed to use the lights on a large scale, such as generators, wires and so on. When he started demonstrating his lights he didn't just have a flickering little lamp. No, he lit up his entire laboratory and workshop with lights all over the place. He provided a one-stop shop for an electric light system, not just a single bulb, and he made it very easy for possible investors to imagine how these lights could be used practically. And a few years later he managed to improve the light bulb even more, eventually ending up with the one that would light up the twentieth century and change the world.

So although we can't say he invented the light bulb, his contribution must not be underestimated. Edison didn't make the first light bulb, but he did make the light bulb go big. And to be fair, he himself said:

I never had an idea in my life. I've got no imagination. I never dream. My so-called inventions already existed in the environment – I took them out. I've created nothing. Nobody does. There's no such thing as an idea being brain-born; everything comes from the outside.

Still, I'll never forgive him for the electrocution of Topsy the elephant . . .

32

An angry maharaja used ten Rolls-Royces to clean the streets because of a rude salesman

What you may have been told

During the 1930s, a maharaja visited London and decided to check out a local Rolls-Royce dealer, but when he entered the shop a snooty assistant treated him with disdain. According to the young man, this stranger, this foreigner, looked like someone who couldn't afford these types of cars.

Of course, the mighty ruler became furious and to teach the company a lesson, he decided to buy ten Rollers, had them shipped back home to India and gave an order for them to be used to collect rubbish. The small fleet of luxury cars drove around the busy streets collecting filth, dung and all kinds of waste. Photos of this showed up in the media all over the world and Rolls-Royce was duly embarrassed.

The debunking

When you research this story, alarm bells start ringing almost instantly as you discover that the story is connected to several maharajas! When the internet can't even agree on which person actually plays the main role in an urban legend, you know something is fishy. After all, the name of the person involved surely is the most important detail of the story.

But no, either at least six(!) maharajas have for some reason bought a whole bunch of Rolls-Royce cars to clean the streets of India with or . . . there's something not quite right about the story. Another detail that keeps changing is how many cars in total were bought – five, ten, all the cars in the showroom, all the cars in the region . . . Nobody seems to agree on these rather important parts of the anecdote.

It is, of course, a glorious story: the stuck-up salesman being taken down a peg or two and the fancy company being embarrassed in this way is satisfying. On top of that, it's also a nice David vs Goliath sort of situation; this is an Indian teaching the British Empire a lesson. Which is why some people really don't like you poking holes in this tale.

Maharajas did go to London and they sure loved luxury cars. They definitely bought Rolls-Royces. But that's where the reasonable part of the story ends.

It just makes no sense. In the 1930s, a Rolls- Royce salesman, even a junior one, would have known better: the rich and famous are sometimes an eccentric bunch and wealthy people from all over the world bought these cars. Assuming someone visiting your showroom would not be able to afford a car just because he wasn't wearing expensive clothes or was a foreigner would be rather silly.

Would a maharaja just walk in off the street in common clothing and without any of his entourage? If he did, would he be surprised or angry at someone judging him on how he appeared? The story sounds plausible to modern people as we live in a time when millionaires go around wearing jeans and T-shirts and want to be treated like everybody else, or claim they do. But this was the 1930s and the maharaja himself was part of the class system – he would have grown up with privilege and luxury, way above the level of common people. Surely he would expect or at least understand that a Rolls-Royce showroom assistant would treat him differently if he, for some reason, was walking around dressed like an office clerk or railway engineer?

Of course, these are all just assumptions. Maybe the rich, important ruler did go out in ordinary clothes, maybe he did try to buy a Rolls, maybe the salesman was rude . . . but there's no evidence for it ever happening. I've looked through tons of old newspapers but there's no mention of this anywhere, not till the 1980s when it started appearing in books like Reader's Digest's *Facts and Fallacies* and other publications featuring 'fun facts' and peculiar stories. But there are never any sources given, which is of course a massive red flag. If it was even a tiny bit true, someone, somewhere, would have written about it decades earlier.

But the story comes with a photo! The car has brushes attached to it, but does it really convince anyone? It doesn't really look like a Rolls-Royce and that's because it isn't – it's a common Ford. On top of that, the steering wheel is on the left side, while in Britain and India they are on the right side. And although this isn't an exact science, the people and the background also don't really match the setting of India. Besides, if you're using regular cars to clean the roads, why not tie brushes along the entire bumper?

I found the oldest version of the photo on the internet and it had a big clue written on it:

מתגוננים נגד מסמרים

Which is Hebrew and means: 'protecting against nails'.

In the archives, I found a photo of another car with brushes also covering the tyres. This photo was taken in 1936 during the Arab revolt in Palestine and the idea was that the brushes would help the driver avoid glass, spikes, tacks and other rubble. Which makes a lot more sense than cleaning the streets in India.

So what have we got:

A story with no evidence whatsoever, with details that keep changing, involving several maharajas. And an accompanying photo that has nothing to do with it at all. Which of course doesn't prove it never happened, but you and I know that if there *was* any kind of truth to this urban legend, we'd be able to find evidence.

33

Napoleon was short

What you may have been told

Everybody knows that Napoleon was short – a tiny little petite Frenchman who could barely look over the table and who was so frustrated by this that 'Napoleon complex' came to mean the inferiority complex that suggests short people are aggressive and domineering to make up for their height, or lack thereof.

Yes, he had many victories and made the French Empire huge, but he was still a hot-tempered little fella.

The debunking

I am Dutch; we are among the tallest people in the world. I myself am about six feet tall, so to me Napoleon was short, but then, to me, most people who ever lived and are alive today are short. But for the age and part of the world Napoleon lived in, he was of average height.

The idea that he was short began during his lifetime. His men gave him the nickname '*Le petit caporal*' (the little corporal), but that was a term of affection and meant that he was one of them, one of the lads. But of course some people took the nickname literally. It also didn't help that he insisted on the men in his *Vieille Garde* (Old Guard) being extra tall. Sure, being surrounded by very tall men looks impressive and I wouldn't mind having a group of soldiers even taller than I am to escort me wherever I go, but, well, it is going to make you look short in comparison!

But the main reason many people still think Napoleon was short is thanks to the unique talent of British political cartoonists, especially the well-known caricaturist James Gillray, who really enjoyed portraying 'Little Boney' as tiny and prone to temper tantrums, like a toddler. This portrayal became very popular and soon Napoleon himself heard of it. As he apparently had no sense of humour, he got really annoyed by it. We know this because during a temporary moment of peace, he mentioned it and even tried to get the British government to do something about it – in vain, of course. This inevitably fuelled the fire: there he was, the great powerful emperor, stamping his little feet because of some drawings.

It is a wonderful example of the power of political cartoons, or perhaps even of 'trolling', as hip young people might call it today. Some 200 years ago, someone made a drawing of a 'short' emperor and, to this day, a lot of people still believe it's true. It seems every documentary or book about him these days still has to explain that he was NOT short. So how tall was he?

We have several sources for his height, but just to make things more complicated, the old French and British measuring systems used different standards: the French inch wasn't the same as the British inch and in some cases we don't know which one was used. When Napoleon died he was a prisoner of the British but the doctor who examined his body was French, so which inch did he use?

His doctor, Jean-Nicolas Corvisart-Desmarets, wrote in 1802 that Napoleon was five foot two inches, according to the French system, which would be five foot six inches according to the British system, which was only two inches below the average in France at the time.

One of Napoleon's personal physicians, Dr François Carlo Antommarchi, who performed the autopsy, wrote down that, 'The entire height of the body from the top of the head to the heels was five feet two inches and four lines', which, according to the 1826 English translation of his book, was done according to the French measure and was 'equal to five feet, six inches and twenty two-forty fifths of an inch, the French foot being greater than the English in the proportion of sixteen to fifteen'. That all sounds very convincing, but we can never be completely sure how accurate those measurements were, or if somewhere along the line the numbers got mixed up.

He wasn't tall, but when we look at what we know about his height, it's clear that even if we're a few inches off, he wasn't much shorter than what was the average height for men at the time. And, indeed, no one who met him described him as unusually short, which surely they would have noticed. We're going to have to find something else to annoy the ghost of Napoleon with.

34

Newton came up with his theory of gravity when an apple fell on his head

What you may have been told

The famous astronomer, mathematician, physicist, scientist, theologian and author Sir Isaac Newton was sitting under an apple tree thinking about all sorts of complicated stuff when an apple fell on his head. This helped Newton come up with his theory of gravity.

The debunking

We all like a good story about someone getting slightly hurt; it's one of the cornerstones of comedy. Your teacher in school may even have used this particular one in a lesson – after all, it's a great way to capture children's interest. But it didn't happen and the truth is less entertaining. Sorry, teachers, you're going to have to find another way to make physics interesting.

It might have been an apple but it didn't hit Newton. The person who's probably to blame for the apple falling on his head story is Leonhard Euler, a mathematician, physicist, astronomer and much more, who in 1760 wrote in a letter

> This great English philosopher and mathematician, finding himself one day lying in a garden, under an apple tree, an apple fell on his head, and provided him with the opportunity to make several thoughts.

The book containing Euler's letters became very popular. Then, when the well-known writer Isaac D'Israeli repeated the story in one of his bestsellers, the myth started spreading rapidly.

We only have second- and third-hand accounts of what actually happened between Newton and the fruit but they're pretty solid. For instance, William Stukeley, who was Newton's friend, published *Memoirs of Sir Isaac Newton's Life* in 1752, in which he described the following scene:

> *After dinner, the weather being warm, we went into the garden and drank tea under the shade of some apple trees, only he and myself. Amidst other discourse he told me he was just in the same situation as when formerly the notion of gravitation came into his mind.*

A personal friend writing about how Newton himself recounted the historical moment is as good as it's going to get when it comes to second-hand accounts. Stukeley was not the only one who wrote down the story either; others who had known Newton independently described him telling them the same thing.

So Newton saw an apple fall and this helped him come up with the theory of gravity, or at least, that's the way Newton told it. Mind you, there also wasn't really an instant Eureka sort of moment. After Newton witnessed the apple falling and started thinking about gravity in a new way, it still took him years to develop the theory and put it on paper.

Oh, and by the way, clones/descendants of the tree still stand in several places, including one at the orchard at Woolsthorpe Manor in Lincolnshire. It's a 'Flower of Kent' tree, and produces cooking apples that are green with a hint of red. Another at the Cambridge University Botanic Garden was felled during Storm Eunice in February 2022.

35

Nero fiddled while Rome burned

What you may have been told

Although it's been almost 2,000 years, we still know about Emperor Nero playing a fiddle while Rome burned in AD 64. The phrase has become part of our language and, to this day, you can find people using it on social media, generally to make a statement about politicians. For example, 'Nero' started trending on Twitter in connection with Donald Trump's response to the COVID-19 pandemic.

The debunking

The claim sounds like a typical example of propaganda, something made up by Nero's political opponents to make him look bad. Trying to find out what really happened and how this story came about is of course not easy after almost two millennia. But one part can easily be debunked from the start: he didn't play a violin because this instrument wasn't invented till centuries later.

Nero could have played a lyre or cithara, both heavy string instruments but not bow instruments – they're more like harps than violins. Using the word fiddle for any other instrument than a violin is a bit iffy, but even if we allow that word to describe Nero playing another string instrument, the story still doesn't add up.

Contemporary writers claimed he sang and recited poetry when he saw Rome burn, but these were rumours, not first-hand accounts, and they were often not even written down till decades after the event, in most cases by authors who didn't like him very much. If Nero performed poetry, he probably also played an instrument, as that was often the custom back then, so that sort of makes sense, but there's still no evidence for any of it actually having happened.

The story probably originated with historian Tacitus's description of the fire, written about 50 years later:

> since a rumour had gone forth everywhere that, at the very time when the city was in flames, the emperor appeared on a private stage and sang of the destruction of Troy, comparing present misfortunes with the calamities of antiquity.

At least he made clear that this story was a rumour; later historians 'forgot' to mention this sometimes.

Over a century later, the playing of an instrument was suddenly mentioned by Dio Cassius, and Nero didn't perform on stage but on the roof of his palace.

During the Middle Ages, the type of instrument played in the story started changing, sometimes because of the difficulty of translating words that were no longer familiar. The cithara became a lute, then a fidicula and later a violin. But it was always a symbol of poor leadership in a time of crisis. If we had continued this tradition, by now Nero would have been accused of playing an electric guitar.

In reality, Nero was informed about the fire while he was staying at his villa at Antium (today called Anzio), 35 miles away, and returned immediately. He made himself useful by providing refugees with food and shelter, and even allowing people to stay in his palaces. He offered people financial support to rebuild their houses and put a lot of time and effort into restoring and improving the city. So claiming that he was completely useless, even if he did take a dramatic poetry break, seems a bit unfair.

The fire ruined Nero; his reputation was damaged beyond repair and so was his political career. Not only was he haunted by the cithara/lute/fiddle story, it was even suggested he'd started the fire to get rid of slums to make space for a new palace.

By the time Roman historians started writing about the case, often decades later, they had no way of actually knowing what happened. All they had was hearsay. Still, lots of people then seemed to think he was guilty of the fire, of being a useless leader during a disaster and much, much worse. But he definitely didn't fiddle.

36

The Roman vomitorium was a room for vomiting

What you may have been told

Rich Romans had a special spot in their villas, sometimes even a whole room, just for vomiting. By regularly stepping away from a meal to throw up the food they had just enjoyed, they could continue to keep feasting and bingeing on food. They called these spaces vomitoria and that's where we get the word vomit from!

The debunking

Wealthy Romans loved to party. They had lavish feasts and, like most rich people throughout history, ate and drank way too much. And yes, like most people who overindulge, these posh party animals did a lot of vomiting. And some of them may have vomited on purpose to be able to keep eating or at least to feel a little less bloated.

We do have several contemporary descriptions of emperors and the rich and powerful vomiting in between eating . . . but in those stories the authors may have used a bit of artistic licence in order to make a disapproving point about the elite and their overindulgent lifestyles. Still, at least we know the claim dates back to the Roman era. So far so good.

Specific stories fit some eras especially well because they reinforce the way we think about how people lived back then.

We imagine the Romans having orgies, feasting and generally living a life of luxury, hedonism and excess, whereas we'd raise an eyebrow at claims such things happened in Victorian high society – even though those supposedly very proper gentlemen and ladies were doing lots of naughty things as well. And we have no trouble believing medieval people were filthy and threw their waste in the streets, though we don't think of ancient Rome like that, even though Roman cities had the same problems. So it's no wonder that we're keen to believe the vomiting room story about those gluttonous Romans. Not just because it fits their image, but also because we like stories about disgusting subjects – after all, we're only human.

But no matter how much we like the story and no matter how much the word sounds like it could have been a room for vomiting, there's no evidence for such a room existing. They're not mentioned in Roman records and none has ever been found by archaeologists.

The word vomitorium is real and it does date back to the Roman era but it didn't describe a room for vomiting – it's a passageway meant for groups of people to enter or exit public buildings like amphitheatres. The name comes from the Latin *vomare*, to spew forth – people were spewing forth from these corridors.

The vomiting food claim about the Romans can probably be blamed on the Victorians – again! – as that's when the story about a room just for vomiting first started popping up. It's so often the pesky Victorians who are responsible for fake history . . .

37

Staircases in castles go clockwise so defenders have an advantage during fighting

What you may have been told

I'm pretty sure that during a visit to a castle you've probably heard a guide, teacher or uncle tell you that spiral staircases were designed in a clockwise fashion to give defenders an advantage during sword fighting. You may even have read it in a book, been taught it at school or have had it explained to you in a documentary.

It sounds logical, after all. Such staircases are built around a stone column, which makes it easier for someone who is right-handed, which most people are, fighting from above, to wield a weapon, while the attacker trying to get up the stairs will have to avoid that central column of the stairs. Makes sense, right?

The debunking

For starters, there is no primary evidence, whatsoever, that the people who built, lived and fought in these castles built staircases in that way for that reason. During the Middle Ages, nobody wrote down that you should build staircases like this and why. If it had been common knowledge among castle builders, then why are there still quite a lot of castles with counter-clockwise staircases? If medieval people thought they were an advantage, surely any architect who installed a counter-clockwise staircase into a castle would have been fired on the spot, perhaps pushed down his stupid good-for-nothing steps, and the stairs would be rebuilt. After all, having a defensive advantage is rather important in castles, keeps and gatehouses – it's literally the main reason these buildings exist! But even the Tower of London has counter-clockwise stairs, and if there's any castle where they would want the best of the best, it's that one.

It's almost as if our ancestors knew that it didn't really make a huge difference which way the stairs go; as if they thought that staircases are just meant to take you up or down and are not suitable for fighting at all. Fighting on stairs would be pretty horrible – neither party has a lot of space to wield those long, pointy, sharp weapons. The person below you has the advantage of jabbing at your legs and feet while they can protect their head with their helmet and shield. Frankly, if you find yourself in this position, then the castle is probably already lost.

A better way to stop your enemy might be to block the stairs. You stay and fight those angry, heavily armed men if you really want to, but I'm running upstairs and throwing furniture down. A big chest, a table, some stools and whatever I can find is coming your way. Not only will this hurt whoever is coming up, it will also quite quickly block their way.

I've tried moving furniture up and down those infamously steep Amsterdam stairs and if a closet gets stuck, you get stuck. It will not stop your enemy forever but it will slow them down more than one or two guys. Fighting on the stairs may buy some extra time, but wasting your last defenders on some stupid stairs will probably just result in your men being killed by the attackers below. Or falling down those very narrow, dangerous steps and *then* being killed.

At this point, you may want to consider either surrendering or suicide, unless you're worth a knight's ransom, literally.

So there is no evidence for people during the Middle Ages – or any other period in time anywhere on earth – building stairs in towers going one way or the other for strategic reasons. It seems they just built most spiral staircases clockwise because they were easier to draw, build and use for right-handed people.

This information is particularly fun to keep ready for the next time you visit a castle; you can put money on someone mentioning the myth and you can then debunk it. Spiral staircases may not be a good location for a sword fight but they're perfectly suited for a verbal battle against fake history.

38

The nursery rhyme 'Ring a Ring o' Roses' is about the plague

What you may have been told

Countless children have grown up singing the 'Ring a Ring o' Roses' rhyme on the playground while dancing, often sneezing and eventually falling down.

> Ring-a-ring o' roses,
> A pocket full of posies,
> A-tishoo! A-tishoo!
> We all fall down.

The words of the song date back to the Great Plague outbreak and describes how people get a rash, sneeze and then fall down when they die.

The debunking

Plagues have been part of human life since the dawn of time, but in this case it's claimed that the song relates to the bubonic plague, particularly the Great Plague of 1665–6, or even the Black Death outbreak of the 1340s. However, while the game and the tune may be quite old, there's no mention of the rhyme till the late eighteenth century and the actual connection with any kind of plague was not made till the 1940s. That's right – it wasn't until after the

Second World war, as far as we know, that anybody thought the rhyme had anything to do with the plague.

A theory developed that 'a rosie' rash was a plague symptom; posies were herbs carried as protection, and sneezing or coughing was the last phase of the disease and, well, the falling down speaks for itself. If children had indeed been singing this song since the actual Great Plague, you'd expect someone, somewhere, to have mentioned it during the 280 years between then and the late 1940s. The symptoms described in the rhyme also don't really fit the ones that are part of the bubonic plague – it doesn't make you sneeze.

Songs and rhymes tend to change a lot over the centuries, and we know that this one has altered quite a bit over time. For instance, this is how it was recorded in one source in 1881:

> *Ring-a-ring o' roses,*
> *A pocket full of posies,*
> *Hush! Hush! Hush! Hush!*
> *We're all tumbled down.*

There's no sneezing and tumbling sounds less ominous than falling. And who would tell someone dying of the plague to be quiet?

Here's another even older version, supposedly from the late 1800s:

> *Ring a ring a rosie,*
> *A bottle full of posie,*
> *All the girls in our town*
> *Ring for little Josie.*

What? Who is Josie? Posie in a bottle? Nobody falling down?! And this one is from the 1790s:

> *Round the ring of roses,*
> *Pots full of posies,*
> *The one who stoops last,*
> *Shall tell whom she loves best.*

Same song! Same game! But nobody is dying – quite the opposite, it's all about love!

The oldest one I could find dates back to the late 1700s and is in German. It's very similar and it also involves ending the song by all sitting down.

> *Ringel ringel reihen,*
> *Wir sind der Kinder dreien,*
> *Sitzen unter'm Hollerbusch*
> *Und machen alle Husch husch husch!*

No mention of any disease.

There are many different versions of the song and many of them have no obvious connection to any kind of disease.

Have you ever tried making sense of the games children play and the songs and rhymes they sing? It is a lot of fun to try to trace the origin of the lyrics that played such a big part in our childhood, but it's also quite frustrating because they rarely make much sense.

It is quite amazing that a story that has become so generally accepted as truth appears to have been totally made up long after the epidemics it supposedly is all about, but everything suggests that this is the case.

39

The two-finger gesture dates back to medieval archers at Agincourt

What you may have been told

The rude two fingers in the air gesture that generally means something along the lines of 'up yours' goes back all the way to the Middle Ages and specifically the Battle of Agincourt in 1415, when the French were defeated by the English, thanks in part to the longbow. After this humiliation, the French soldiers threatened that they would cut the index and middle fingers off any English archer they'd catch to make sure they'd never be able to shoot arrows again. This led to the English mockingly showing those fingers to their enemy in defiance every time they faced each other on the battlefield. Thus the V-gesture was born.

The debunking

There may be some truth to the story as there are contemporary records that claim the French did indeed make that threat. Jean de Wavrin, a fifteenth-century chronicler, wrote that Henry V addressed his men before the battle and told them that:

> the French were boasting that they would cut off three fingers of the right hand of all the archers that should be taken prisoners to the end that neither man nor horse should ever again be killed with their arrows.

Yes, three fingers, not two!

So although the threat may have been real, it involved three fingers, which makes the connection with the V-gesture a bit iffy . . . It does make more sense though, as those old longbows, especially the war-bows, are very difficult to handle with just two fingers. Many archers, then and now, prefer using three fingers.

Wavrin was present at the battle and so, even though he was on the French side and probably didn't hear the speech himself, he is still a pretty valuable source, especially for an event so long ago. But he does not mention the gesture. Which of course doesn't mean that it didn't happen, but it would be peculiar if the one writer who thought the threat was noteworthy did not then mention gestures being made that are supposedly related to it. Other people present there, such as the heralds whose job it was to record the battle, also did not write about anyone sticking one, two or three fingers in the air.

We also don't know for sure whether what Henry (probably) said was based on something that really happened – it could have just been a rumour – or a bit of propaganda to motivate his men to fight even harder. It sure would convince me to fight to the bitter end. There is no real evidence of the French doing this to captured archers, and I'm yet to hear about archers' skeletons being found with their fingers cut off. You can tell by looking at a skeleton if it was a medieval archer as archery leaves its marks on your bones. And you'd notice if missing fingers were cut off with a sharp tool. If this was a punishment that happened a lot you'd expect at least a couple of fingerless archer skeletons to have been found by now.

It's also unlikely that archers got any special treatment. Taking them prisoner would be a hassle and it's also a lot of work having to cut the fingers off every captured archer. Cutting the entire hand off would be much easier and faster. In fact, in that case, why not just go and cut the hands off everyone you capture? Pikemen were a pain in the *derrière* as well, and everybody hates the guys with the drums. Or you could also just kill the lot. Murdering your prisoners was frowned upon and was not as common as you may perhaps think but still, why bother going to the effort of mutilating just a specific group of them, however annoyed you were by their accuracy with an arrow? It would have been impractical and there's no evidence for it.

But what about the gesture?

It probably was rude during the Middle Ages to stick two fingers up at someone. The first clear description of the V-gesture as an insult comes from the book *Pantagruel*, written by François Rabelais in 1532. In the chapter 'How Panurge put to a nonplus the Englishman that argued by signs', the author describes an argument fought with gestures: 'Then stretched he out the forefinger and middle finger or medical of his right hand, holding them asunder as much as he could, and thrusting them towards Thaumast.'

The story (it's very funny) contains many gestures that are so clearly described that you can't help but try them as you read, and some of the others are very familiar to us to this day as well. This is very convincing evidence that at least some sixteenth-century people saw the gesture as rude and it is interesting that it is an Englishman who uses it. But after just a couple of mentions the gesture appears to vanish from recorded history and doesn't show up again till the twentieth century!

Film footage shot by the Mitchell and Kenyon film company shows men standing in line outside the Parkgate Iron and Steel Company works in Rotherham in 1901. One of the men, clearly not too pleased about being filmed, makes the gesture at the camera, and in a way at us, the viewer, as if to say: 'Take that, future people.' You can find it on YouTube, it's glorious.

It is odd, though, that the gesture managed to avoid being depicted or even described for several centuries. That, I'm afraid, I can't explain. But we do know that there is no evidence whatsoever that the gesture came about because of the threat French soldiers made towards the English archers at Agincourt.

40

Lady Godiva rode a horse in the nude because of taxes

What you may have been told

When the people of medieval Coventry were upset about their high taxes, Godiva, the wife of Leofric, Earl of Mercia, asked him to reduce them. He told her that he would if she would ride through the town naked. To everybody's surprise, she called his bluff. Out of respect, everybody looked away as she rode past, except one cheeky chap called Tom, later known as Peeping Tom. Luckily, most of her body was covered by her long hair. The earl kept his word and lowered the taxes. How nice.

The debunking

A story always becomes a bit suspicious when there are no contemporary records – after all, if something this incredible happens you'd expect someone to make a note of it at the time. In medieval times, not that many people could read or write, but towns, nobles and the local clergy often kept records in one way or another, and several chroniclers were busy collecting all sorts of stories and news. But we have nothing about Lady Godiva being a nudist.

There really was a Leofric, who really had a wife called Godiva (or Godgifu, which means God's gift), and they were in charge of Coventry in the eleventh century AD. Chroniclers write about how they ruled: how kind, generous and respectable she was; how they made donations to the church but . . . no naked horse ride. For over a century since it supposedly happened, there's not a trace of the event anywhere. Then, in the thirteenth century, chroniclers of the abbey of St Albans wrote down the whole naked horse-ride story and it understandably became very popular.

Perhaps there were earlier records that later vanished – it happens – but we need to stick with what we can prove. On top of that, there's also just too much about the story that doesn't quite add up.

Coventry at the time wasn't much of a town. In fact, it was barely even a village – the Domesday Book records 50 villagers, 12 smallholders and 7 slaves living there in 1086 and it belonged to Godiva. It was her possession, so raising taxes was her privilege, not her husband's. You may think that, as a woman, she would be subservient to her husband and so, although legally the owner, she wouldn't have much real power. But that was not necessarily the case back then; medieval women rulers often had power and influence of their own.

Godiva was rich and powerful even before her marriage. She owned land given to her directly from the king, so the idea of her having to appeal to her husband, humble herself, even beg him on behalf of the villagers, fits in the era when the myth first appeared but *not* the time when it supposedly happened. This small village was hers, and so were any taxes.

The size of Coventry then also doesn't quite fit the image later depicted of a crowded city with streets and marketplaces. This is much more like Coventry a century later. So the audience for any nudey ride would have been fairly small, and made of up Lady Godiva's own peasants. What is also interesting is that the tax most likely related to ownership of horses, and most of the inhabitants of Coventry back then wouldn't have owned a horse so the number of people helped by her sacrifice would have been even smaller.

Medieval chroniclers often had the unpleasant habit of using their imagination and adding fun little details to what they were writing about. Come to think of it, that's an urge some historians to this day can't resist.

If you look at all the later descriptions you'll find more and more details being added or changed. Some even include the dialogue between Godiva and her husband. It is extremely unlikely that someone was close enough to overhear them, noted down their exchange, kept it safe for a century or so and then quoted it to the cleric so he could write it down.

And if you were wondering about Peeping Tom, the only person in Coventry to take a peek at the naked lady, and who was struck with blindness or paid for it with his life, there's no mention of him anywhere till the seventeenth century.

There are similarities with other stories that some of our medieval clerics probably knew about, and pagan fables and ceremonies sometimes involved naked women on horses. Add to that local folklore, rumours, gossip and the unreliability of the oral tradition and very little is left that we can rely on. It wouldn't be the first time several different stories got mixed up and combined into a new one.

Who knows, it may have started with Lady Godiva riding into the village telling people she was going to lower their taxes, but she forgot to wear a cloak and didn't cover her hair, and people started talking about how she was so eager to give them the good news that she didn't even get dressed properly . . .

Or maybe she did penance for something completely different, riding through the village wearing just her chemise, an underdress, which would have been quite something back then. So even if someone had written down that she rode through the village 'undressed', we'd still not know what they exactly meant.

41

The Victorians had vampire hunting kits

What you may have been told

The Victorians were so afraid of vampires that they had special hunting kits made: boxes filled with revolvers, bibles, crucifixes, hammers and, of course, wooden stakes. All very handy if you found yourself visiting a suspicious castle in Transylvania and your host suddenly developed a peculiar fascination with your neck.

If you're worried about vampires or are considering becoming a vampire hunter, you're in luck because you can still buy the kits. These totally authentic and original nineteenth-century kits regularly show up at auctions across the world, but you'll have to bring a lot of money with you as they often sell for thousands.

The debunking

I can understand people being tempted to buy these kits – they are fantastic. Wonderful, mysterious wooden boxes filled with crazy props – so gothic, so Victorian, what a conversation piece! If you really like them you should totally get one. You can buy them online on websites like Etsy, where they're often not too expensive, though of course they're not original nineteenth-century kits . . . But neither are the expensive ones being sold by the auction houses – they're all modern creations.

They are well made and they look old, but what's sneaky about them is that although they're made with old bits and bobs, none are original sets. Sellers find an antique box, stuff it with all sorts of flea-market trinkets, add some homemade knick-knacks and then try and pass it off as if it had all always belonged together. Honest people explain this when they sell them, but others only hint at it in the fine print or describe a kit in such a way that avoids clearly explaining it was all put together recently. Yes, it IS a Victorian box, that IS Victorian stuff in it, so we can call it a Victorian vampire hunting kit. Sure, we made it last month, the complete set isn't Victorian, but we never said it was . . . You get the picture. It's technically not a scam, but it kinda is.

The main giveaway that there's something fishy about these objects is that there is no mention of them anywhere, ever, before the 1950s. No adverts in old newspapers, nobody writing about using or seeing them, no mention of someone finding one – not a bill, no manufacturer's paperwork, nothing. It is likely that the Hammer horror films (you know, the ones with the reddest blood ever) of the 1950s inspired the first creators of these kits.

People did once really believe in vampires – some still do. And people used to do horrible stuff to dead bodies to make sure they wouldn't come back to life and start biting folks. But the tools used for making sure alleged vampires were (extra) dead or to actually kill them were very basic. Even if vampires were real, you wouldn't need a luxurious and fancy kit – unless perhaps the vampire was in high society and you wanted to make a good impression before killing them. And you really don't need a gun with silver bullets unless you're hunting werewolves on the side. Everybody knows you just need a crucifix, a couple of wooden stakes and a mallet.

So, buy a vampire hunting kit if you like them, but don't assume it really is a Victorian kit just because the auction house says so, no matter how renowned it is. When they sell a Victorian vampire hunting kit, what they may mean is: 'An old box with Victorian stuff in it'. But that doesn't appeal as much, does it?

If you want a real Victorian one, ask the seller if the kit has been authenticated – make them prove the set existed *as a set* over a century ago. If they can prove this, contact the newspapers because you've just found the very first actual antique vampire hunting kit. But I wouldn't hold my breath if I were you.

42

Einstein flunked maths

What you may have been told

It's such a comforting thought: Albert Einstein, a man about whom most of us know very little, except that he was really smart, was also a bit of a dummy, because he failed maths in school.

If you, like me, are a complete idiot when it comes to doing simple calculations, or are just not very good at studying, the idea that someone who later became a genius was once a nitwit like us gives us hope for the future. If you are currently desperately trying to keep motivated or encourage your kids by convincing yourself or them that this story is true, it's probably best to stop reading here and skip to the next story.

The debunking

Sorry, my fellow idiots, Einstein did not fail maths.

So where does this myth come from? According to a *Time* magazine article in 1935, a Princeton rabbi showed Einstein a 'Ripley's Believe It or Not!' newspaper column with the title 'Greatest Living Mathematician Failed in Mathematics' and Einstein (who, by the way, was not even a mathematician) told the rabbi that he never failed maths – in fact, he had mastered differential and integral calculus before he was fifteen . . . what a swot.

I don't even know what any of those words mean.

So not only did he not fail maths, he excelled. I'm not sure if the journalist who wrote that article just made it up or was confused by the fact that the school Einstein went to flipped their grading system, from one being the best and six being the worst, to six being the best and one the worst. Which meant that Einstein had a lot of ones one year and then suddenly a lot of sixes the next year. Or maybe it's because Einstein often asked mathematicians to check his work – but that's just smart.

When little Albert was only seven, his mum bragged in a letter about how he was top of his class, and when the media kept suggesting he'd received poor grades, the school's principal decided to publish a letter pointing out that Einstein actually had rather good grades. It's true that he did fail an entrance exam once – but he was two years younger than the other students and he succeeded when he did the exam again.

Oh, and he was also a talented violin player.

Yes, I know, it's all getting a bit annoying; we've gone from a myth that made us feel better about ourselves to a truth that makes us feel even worse. If you're struggling with French at school, you can find some solace in the fact that Einstein's grades in that subject were not very good.

Ha, what a dummy Einstein was! He was *rubbish* at French grammar.

43

Ancient and medieval statues and buildings were always white or unpainted

What you may have been told

Our ancestors didn't care much for colour. We know that because all the ancient Greek and Roman statues and buildings are white, and medieval castles are all just grey stone or white plaster. We see it in films and television dramas all the time and when we visit museums or very old cities we can see it with our own eyes!

The debunking

It is of course true that when we look at the remnants of old civilisations today that they're not painted, and so we tend to assume that is what everything must have looked like back then. The view we have of the past is a world without bright and vibrant colours. But thanks to modern scientific research, we can now find the tiniest, microscopical remains of paint on almost everything!

It seems that throughout history humans have been crazy about colour and patterns, and that's a bit of an understatement. Historians had read the old records in which people mentioned that statues were colourful but it was still a bit of a shock when it became clear how these statues and castle walls actually looked. For a lot of people, perhaps even most, the idea of ancient buildings featuring more and brighter colours than a 1970s hippy living room is still difficult to imagine.

The explanation is quite simple – after centuries of being exposed to the elements, the original paint faded and vanished. The stone underneath was all that was seen for many generations.

Some historians even thought that this was done on purpose – that the Romans, for instance, wanted statues to be white, that white bodies were the nicest-looking . . . Some people will use anything to claim supremacy over others. To be fair, some of these masterpieces do look amazing just in white marble. Colour can distract from the details, the craftsmanship of the sculptor – after all, paint covers up a lot, literally.

Everything changed in the 1980s when new techniques were developed to not only test the old statues but also to reconstruct them. German researchers, scientists and archaeologists studied the traces of colours and then created replicas of mostly ancient Greek and Roman statues and buildings as they once looked, in vibrant Technicolor.

It does take getting used to, as the colourless, stone versions are so familiar to us. And even though we've known about the colours for decades, every time they're shared on social media people are still astonished. But once you get used to them, suddenly it makes sense – of course our ancestors loved colours, why wouldn't they have?

The painting of classical works of art in multiple colours is called polychromy, and it remained popular into the Middle Ages. All those dingy, dark, grey stone castles and majestic solemn churches and cathedrals? Many of them were also covered in colours, sometimes as gaudy as a 1950s jukebox.

44

In the Middle Ages millions of women were accused of witchcraft and burned at the stake

What you may have been told

During the Middle Ages everybody was terrified of witches. Innocent women were hunted down and tortured, and millions of them were burned at the stake.

The debunking

We've all grown up with stories about witches and the image of the woman with her pointy hat, a hairy wart on her nose, flying through the sky on a broomstick. They're part of Western culture, and we've all been told about how the witch trials resulted in terrible suffering for many, but this wasn't really a thing during the Middle Ages.

I can understand why people might think it was – after all, medieval society was one of superstition, cruelty, violent punishments, misogyny and so on. The Middle Ages weren't a fun, lovely, peaceful time of equal rights and tolerance, but the medieval era doesn't deserve the reputation we've given it. And that's also the case when it comes to the hunting and treatment of assumed witches.

For most of the Middle Ages, believing in witches was considered a silly superstition. Even the church said that witches didn't exist – not in the way we imagine them today, anyway. If you thought someone was a witch and was placing curses on you, giving your sheep pox and going into the woods at night to do naughty things with the Devil, the church would call you a fool. Sometimes literally! You would be told that you were being fooled and that the witch was innocent – but you, the person *accusing* her, were perhaps guilty because you allowed the Devil to make you believe in nonsense. When you think of it, this was quite a rational perspective, which in a way defended those accused of witchcraft.

It was also progress compared to how things were earlier in time. The ancient Greeks and Romans believed in witches and persecuted and executed, sometimes by fire, those suspected of witchcraft. Yet somehow in the collective mind those eras are seen as advanced, cultured and better than the Middle Ages.

I'm not saying that medieval people didn't believe in witches at all – in fact, many of them did. But superstition rarely leads to mass suffering if it's not supported by the state, the church or a large group of powerful people. So, for most of the Middle Ages, the men and women accused of being witches were relatively safe. Things could get dangerous if someone's behaviour was perceived as being that of a heretic, which was a risk if you were doing something that looked a bit pagan; that could get you killed. But heresy was usually the charge, not being a witch doing magic.

It's fair to say that there were some witch trials in medieval Europe, but they were relatively rare and if you had accused someone of a crime and they turned out to be innocent, you could sometimes get punished yourself and even accused of being a heretic. This made people think twice about accusing someone. But even if someone *was* found guilty of witchcraft, the punishments would generally be mild. They were very rarely burned to death at the stake.

I know, you've seen it in films and on TV, you may even have read about it in your schoolbooks or were told about in a museum, but during the Middle Ages the punishment for being a witch would not be death by fire. And even *after* the Middle Ages, when witch hunting reached its height (ironically, the most barbaric witch hunts were in the Renaissance, the period of so-called rationality and enlightenment), in most cases witches were hanged, drowned, buried or boiled alive, and so on. And in many cases, even if a witch was burned, they were first strangled.

In the late fifteenth century, interest in witchcraft started to increase. It was everywhere. Lots of writings were published on the matter, and thanks in part to the newly invented printing press, they were easily distributed. This had an impact on those who were educated and they became fascinated with the whole subject. Leaflets and books, like the infamous *Malleus Maleficarum* (The Hammer of Witches), spread like wildfire. Witchcraft went from a common superstition to a serious matter, and this fake news started to reach those with power, both in the church and on the throne. The church started to change its mind on the subject, and heresy and witchcraft became more and more linked. Extra tension because of the Reformation didn't help. A witch-panic broke out and the hunt for witches and warlocks was on.

Originally, the ones being persecuted were mostly educated men. After all, you had to be able to read magic books and the people who could read such texts were usually men. But then the story changed and the 'experts' claimed that you didn't need to be able to read to memorise spells. So people turned on women. This was easily rationalised: women were weak, they were closer to evil because Eve had talked Adam into eating an apple, and women were sex mad and completely insatiable. They had lustful thoughts they couldn't control and the Devil could help them with that.

Just as with any mass panic, some used this as an opportunity to get rid of powerful women – not just rich important ladies but also widows who inherited their husband's business, successful

brewsters and midwives who had a highly respected and important role in many small communities. But before we judge those
who became scared and believed all the stories they were being
told, it might be good to remember that today millions still easily
fall for totally ridiculous conspiracy theories.

On a sidenote, in the Dutch city of Oudewater they decided
that the best scientific way to find out if someone was a witch
was by weighing them. They believed that a witch wouldn't have
a soul so they'd weigh a lot less than a normal person their size.
Although it was not used very often, anyone who was weighed
and considered too heavy to be a witch was given an official certificate. You can still be weighed there today and, if you're not a
witch, you'll get a certificate that proves it.

So, during the Middle Ages, not everybody was afraid of
witches and millions were not burned to death at the stake,
but when the witch-hunt madness truly gripped Europe, many,
mostly women, suffered immensely and died gruesome deaths.
But not millions. It is of course difficult to get a reliable and
exact number of victims. Not all deaths were recorded and, even
if they were, many records haven't survived. Although the witch
hunts ruined millions of lives, current estimates are that between
30,000 and 80,000 people were murdered. Some claim the number
is much higher, maybe 200,000, but as horrific as this number is,
it's nowhere near the claim of millions.

45

The Nazi salute has Roman origins

What you may have been told

Whenever the Nazis and Italian Fascists were saluting each other, they would stick their right arm in the air with extended fingers. This salute originated in ancient Rome and was called *il saluto romano*.

The debunking

This is one of those bits of history that is a very common misconception; it's been generally accepted to be true for such a long time that the idea that it may be nonsense messes with our minds a bit the first time we hear it. Whatever next? Is the thumb gesture not connected to people deciding over the life of a gladiator? Well . . . I'll talk about that in another chapter.

For once, we can't blame the Nazis and Fascists for this myth. We can blame them for not doing proper research, but it's no surprise that they weren't really into facts and preferred to ignore or alter history if it didn't fit the story they wanted to tell. This is a typical example of people choosing to believe a fantasy version of history over reality because it fits well with their ideals.

Fascists, especially the Italian ones of course, were very much into using Roman history and symbols to give their movement more credibility and a connection back to when their ancestors ruled much of the known world. Saluting is important, especially if you're in a military, uniform-wearing, flag-waving and marching sort of club, so they were delighted when they found a salute they thought had a direct link to their heroes, the Romans.

So Mussolini's *Partito Nazionale Fascista* adopted the salute as it was commonly believed to have Roman origins, and the Nazis, well, they just copied their friends' work, although they later claimed it had old Germanic roots . . . which they would, wouldn't they? And even Mussolini nicked it from other Italian extreme nationalists, like Gabriele D'Annunzio.

But where does the salute being Roman idea come from?

Although there were both salutes and gestures in ancient Greece and Rome, nothing we know is convincing enough to say 'the Roman salute' was a real thing with a specific meaning. But in 1784, Jacques-Louis David painted *The Oath of the Horatii*, which depicts a legendary story about Romans promising to fight for their cities and taking this oath with their hands outstretched and flat – yes, 'the Roman salute'. This painting was a huge hit and, of course, the subject was very appealing to later Fascists and Nazis.

I'm not sure if anybody depicted Romans making the salute before this painting, but it is clear that *after* it was made we start seeing it everywhere, long before the Fascists got their hands on it, pun intended. It fitted with the idea people had of the Romans, or maybe it was just what theatre directors, writers and painters were looking for.

Relatively recently, the fact that there's no historical evidence at all for the salute having Roman origins has started to take root, and we're starting to see less and less of it in films and on TV. Progress!

46

Vikings were 'buried' at sea on a burning ship

What you may have been told

When an important Viking died their body was placed on a ship that was then pushed out to sea. And as it floated away, archers let loose flaming arrows that set the ship on fire. Thus our hero sailed to Valhalla on a burning ship.

What a sight! How glorious, how amazing, how irresistible a vision for authors, film and television makers. From *The Vikings*, the 1958 film starring Kirk Douglas, to the very recent hit TV series *Vikings*, millions have seen this scene played out.

The debunking

We want to believe this is true because it fits our vision of the Vikings so perfectly. Ships meant a lot to Vikings; they were raiders, warriors, so this is the way to go! And if we're honest, quite a few of us are so taken by the burning ship funeral that we'd like one for ourselves when we die, even though few of us will be allowed into Valhalla.

But alas, it's most likely a myth.

The idea probably originated in the saga *Gylfaginning*, part of the Prose Edda. In the story, Baldr, the son of Norse gods Odin and Frigg and the brother of Thor, was murdered by Loki. According to the tale, Baldr's body was placed on his ship and it was set on fire and then a giantess pushed it out to sea. Vikings may have dreamed of a funeral like this but unfortunately there's no evidence whatsoever of any of them ever having had one.

Vikings did have ship funerals, but on land. They dragged a ship to a nice spot, put the dead Viking (and often lots of valuable items and a couple of slaves and animals) on the ship and then buried it. Sometimes they even set fire to it first – cremation was very popular – but they still buried it afterwards. We know they did this because we have eyewitness accounts, like the one by the Arab writer Ahmad ibn Fadlān, but archaeologists have also found ship burials and some of these show signs of having been set on fire. The Sutton Hoo ship burial, although not Viking, also gives us a good idea of what one may have looked like.

Ships were and are really quite expensive so they were generally only buried and/or burned on special occasions; it was something you had to earn. When the dead person wasn't important or wealthy enough to be buried in an actual boat, they sometimes were given a boat-shaped grave, with stones outlining the shape of a boat, which is rather nice.

So we have the Saga and we know they buried ships and cremated the bodies of their dead, which makes it quite easy to understand how someone once put all of that together and assumed setting the ships on fire while it was sailing was also a real funeral tradition.

For argument's sake, let's say the Vikings tried it. Why wouldn't they have, after all? It's in the Saga! First, you need to take the ship to a spot where it can safely reach the sea, away from your harbour, your village or the fjord you live in. You wouldn't want the ship to get stuck and not sink properly, ending up blocking the route you regularly use.

Then you need to push the ship away from the shore and hope it keeps moving along for a while. It would be really embarrassing if it just floated a few feet from the shore or perhaps started floating back to where the entire village was watching. Or drifted across to the rest of your fleet.

On top of that, just because a boat is on fire doesn't mean it will burn up completely and sink. Imagine the fire going out and this burned floating raft with, pardon the expression, a barbecue of several humans and animals still smouldering and eventually starting to smell, just bobbing around the harbour.

And what if the weather was just too bad? Are you going to wait, with a corpse that's starting to stink and Odin becoming impatient for the warrior to join him in the afterlife? There is so much potential for things to go wrong.

But if you buried the ship you'd end up with a wonderfully impressive mound you could visit regularly and where, according to some sagas, you could sometimes see the dead having a great old time.

There are thousands of Viking graves but still no evidence at all for the sea funerals. Of course, if it did happen, we'd not find much evidence of it, would we? But still, you'd think that by now we should have found some burned remains of a ship surrounded by grave goods near some Scandinavian shores. So until we find some evidence, we're going to stick with it probably never having happened.

That of course doesn't mean you can't have one yourself. Just make sure it's legal and try not to bring grave goods that pollute the air when they burn or the sea when you sink.

47

The Bayeux Tapestry is a tapestry (and Harold was shot in the eye by an arrow)

What you may have been told

The Bayeux Tapestry is a tapestry. Clue's in the name, right?

The debunking

It's not a tapestry, it's embroidery. A tapestry has patterns woven into the cloth; the Bayeux 'tapestry' is cloth with decorations stitched to it. The end. You're welcome.

I know, that was a bit childish, but I did give you a nice little fact to go annoy people with!

OK, you want more. What if I told you that the Bayeux embroidery IS FAKE HISTORY?! I know, sit down, take a deep breath.

But it's true: the whole story of the arrow in the eye is fake. Where to start with this? At the beginning, of course.

This representation of the Battle of Hastings in 1066 was made a few years afterwards and it tells the story of this battle according to the Normans. So it's a good example of 'the victors write history'. Nobody really knows who made it, and whoever did was probably not at the battle, making quick sketches or even some snap-embroideries. They likely created the story based on what they were told, maybe by someone who wasn't even there themselves, either.

Now here comes another shocker: the 'fact' that Harold God-winson, the English king, was killed by an arrow to the eye is something historians don't agree on – it may not have happened. Some contemporary sources say that he was hacked to bits. Very shortly after the battle there are songs and writings about Harold being pierced with a lance, his head cut off with a sword, his entrails removed with a spear, and finally his thigh cut off and taken away . . . that'll do it. There are only a few mentions of him dying because of an arrow to the face.

It's not even certain that the man in the embroidery every-body calls Harold was actually Harold; after all, there are a couple of men depicted underneath where it says '*Harold Rex interfectus est*' (King Harold was killed) – is he perhaps the one being run over by a horse, or is he the man on a horse with a sword?

Many historians agree that the man falling down while hold-ing an axe is actually Harold. On the left, we see an Anglo-Saxon shield wall and a horseman who appears to be Norman crash-ing through it, hitting a man, probably also striking him with his sword. This man falls right under the words 'is killed' and the scene fits the other stories about his death, about Normans rush-ing forward and slaughtering the king. Then again, the names of other figures in the embroidery are not always directly above the person they're supposed to be.

To make things even worse, restorers, specifically VICTORIAN ones (well, not quite Victorians as they were French, but still) were a bit too eager and creative during their work. In the eighteenth century, a certain Antoine Benoît made a detailed sketch of the embroidery and, guess what? The man we thought was Harold appears to be holding what could be a spear in his right hand – it's not an arrow and it's not stuck in his eye! But then again, maybe Benoît got it wrong.

To complicate matters even more, maybe both of the men in the scene are Harold and it shows, like a comic strip, how he's first hit by an arrow and then dies by the sword.

In essence, what exactly is happening in the scene on the embroidery and how Harold really died are still up for debate. And annoyingly, the last part of the artwork is missing. Yes, there originally was more! So things may not have been as they appear, even though we've been told the story of Harold with the arrow in the eye as fact for a very long time.

On a side note, it's a miracle the embroidery survived at all. During the French Revolution, it was confiscated and was going to be used to cover wagons, but someone saved and hid it at home. And during the Second World War, the Nazis spent a lot of time studying it. They liked it because it showed the invasion of England, and they also tried to use it to prove their nonsense ideas about Nordic people being superior to everybody else. When Heinrich Himmler realised things were going badly for his side, he ordered the embroidery to be taken to Paris where it was stored in the basement of the Louvre museum. While the Resistance was literally fighting in and around the Louvre during the battle for the city, SS officers wanted to take the embroidery to Berlin, but the sound of machine-gun fire emanating from the museum made them reconsider; they didn't want to risk their lives for art.

48

Nelson's last words were 'Kiss me, Hardy'

What you may have been told

As Vice Admiral Horatio Nelson lay dying from a French sniper's bullet at the battle of Trafalgar, surrounded by his brothers in arms and good friend Thomas Hardy, his last words were 'Kiss me, Hardy.'

The debunking

There are several accounts of Nelson's death with differing claims about what his last words were, but the one about him asking Hardy to kiss him has proved the most popular. Which is odd, as the other possible last words were much more heroic and poignant. But maybe it's because it's a bit unexpected and perhaps even funny, especially to sniggering school kids during a boring history lesson. Or maybe because it's a very human way to die and for that reason more familiar and endearing to us than the patriotic farewell others described.

It took Nelson hours to die of his horrific wounds and he knew or at least assumed he was dying. During most of that time, he was surrounded by several men who later shared their eyewitness accounts of that moment. This is why we know that Nelson did indeed ask Hardy to kiss him and Hardy obliged – a kiss on the cheek and one on the forehead. Yet these were not Nelson's last words, not even his last words to his old friend Hardy. His parting words to him were 'God bless you, Hardy.'

Witnesses Surgeon William Beatty, Chaplain Alexander Scott and Purser Walter Burke all mention the emotional scene happening, so there's no real doubt that it did. But it's not quite clear what Nelson's actual last words were.

It seems that Nelson had thought about what his last words should be and I think he tried really hard to make sure that they would be 'Thank God I have done my duty,' because, according to Dr Beatty, he kept repeating it. But the doctor was not there when Nelson lost the ability to speak.

According to the chaplain, Nelson's last words were 'God and my country,' which are also very impressive last words. But during this time he also kept asking for something to drink, and for someone to fan him and rub his chest as that alleviated his pain a little bit, so his last words could also have been 'Drink drink, fan fan, rub rub.' The eyewitnesses do describe Nelson uttering these words but of course they're not that impressive as the last words of a dying hero. Those who were there respected him deeply and probably realised what Nelson wanted his last words to be.

Then again, all of this was happening as a sea battle was still raging on around these men, huddled in a dark noisy corner of a ship's deck as others ran past, and cannons and rifles were being fired, so it is not surprising that the accounts differ in some areas.

Regardless, the one thing they do agree on is that 'Kiss me, Hardy' were not Nelson's last words.

49

Hundreds of books were left floating in the street after the Paris flood of 1910

What you may have been told

The photo of a flooded street full of floating books has been horrifying book lovers for a long time. In 1910, there was a huge flood in Paris and on the Rue Jacob the contents of a library floated out of the building. Countless precious books soaking up the water is a heart-breaking sight for every bibliophile.

The debunking

Take a deep breath, calm down, count to ten. I know books are wonderful and just the idea of so many of them slowly being destroyed by filthy water is very upsetting, but there is nothing to worry about. They're not books.

There was a huge flood in Paris in January 1910, that much is true. It was a catastrophe during which the water level of the Seine rose 8 metres above its regular level, causing, in today's money, over 1 billion pounds of damage. The flooding lasted almost a week, in which time thousands of Parisians lost their homes, electricity stopped working and public transport became almost impossible. The photos of this event are quite sobering.

However, what we have here is a modern person looking at an old photo with something in it they don't understand or recognise, assuming it's something it isn't. The shapes in the water may look like books but they are in fact wooden blocks, which were used at the time for paving.

I hope that is as much a relief to you as it was to me.

Wooden blocks have been used as pavement for centuries and by the nineteenth century they were quite common. They were relatively cheap, easy to install and didn't cause as much noise as stone did when horses and carts rode over them. In Victorian London, for a while they were even more common than cobble-stones. So yes, whenever Sherlock Holmes and Dr Watson rush off through the foggy streets of London in a hansom cab, the sound of horseshoes and wheels on wood would probably be more historically accurate than on stone, which is what we hear in many TV shows and films.

The downside to these blocks was that unless they were treated with creosote they started to rot and decay quite quickly. They were also tricky to keep clean and absorbed all sorts of horrid fluids, making them rather smelly. And if a street became submerged under water, they may well have started floating away . . .

When carts and horses started being replaced by cars with rubber tyres, the plus sides of wooden blocks no longer outweighed those of the alternatives. But in some spots in London you can still see traces of them, like on Belvedere Road, behind the old County Hall near Waterloo.

50

Carrots were made orange by the Dutch in homage to their royal family

What you may have been told

The only reason carrots are orange is because of the Dutch!

Before the sixteenth century, carrots came in several different colours, but then Dutch farmers started cultivating the orange variant as a tribute to William of Orange, who led the revolt against the Spanish, made the Netherlands independent and sort of started the Dutch royal family. These orange carrots became so popular that they replaced all the other coloured carrots across the world.

The debunking

This is one of those popular 'fun facts' that keeps popping up. Who doesn't like a did-you-know story for the dinner table, to impress your guests with while impaling a carrot with your fork? To this day, the myth is widely believed and also regularly shared online, where I have to correct it, again . . . and again . . . and again!

Let's start with the basics. Yes, carrots came and still come in many different colours. The most common ones were white, yellow and purple. Orange carrots did then become extremely popular and pretty much pushed the other coloured ones aside, to the extent that a lot of people don't even know carrots also come in not-orange. It is also true that the Dutch royal family's colour is orange and that it's therefore the Netherlands national colour, which you may have noticed during football matches, or if you've found yourself in the Netherlands on our King's Day national holiday. I apologise on behalf of all Dutch people to anybody who has got stuck in that mad orange chaos, unless of course you had the time of your life, in which case you're welcome.

William of Orange did indeed lead the Dutch revolt against the Spanish in the sixteenth century. He was very popular and is still seen as a national hero, who, in a way, was the founding father of the Netherlands.

But orange carrots were already being cultivated in medieval Spain in the fourteenth century, perhaps by using carrots or their seeds brought there from Arab regions by traders using the Silk Roads. We know orange carrots existed at least as far back as the fifth century AD, when a helpful artist drew a lovely and very orange carrot in the Anicia Juliana Codex. This may be a copy of an even earlier book, but that one sadly didn't survive. So, the Dutch definitely did not make the carrot orange but they did make it more popular – a bit like Coca-Cola did with Santa. It was the Dutch who, when they got their hands on orange-ish carrots, went wild with them.

The little country was an agricultural and trading powerhouse at the time and its people managed to tweak, grow, develop, stabilise and trade orange carrots all over the world in huge quantities, which resulted in them becoming very popular. The orange carrot went from something that existed but was not very common, to the cool, must-have carrot of the day. It wasn't just down to their colour but because they were also a bit sweeter and 'fleshier' than the alternatives. Unlike purple ones, which can make your pottage, soup or stew look a bit of a mucky brown colour, orange carrots don't dye food, which was probably another reason people preferred the new, hip orange carrot. They also were very easy to grow in the western European climate.

So, we can credit the Dutch with developing and stabilising the already existing orange carrot further and making it more popular but they didn't 'invent' it and it didn't have anything to do with the House of Orange, originally. The carrot probably got its connection to the royal family much later. During politically unstable times the colour orange was sometimes banned from public view, including carrots, which of course made them only more popular among royalists.

There's no need to be sad about the white and purple carrots, though; they've been making a comeback and not being orange is now seen as a bonus as it allows them to be sold as 'heritage' carrots, something fancy and, ironically, 'new' while being old.

So every time you see a big pile of orange carrots in a computer game, film or TV drama set in pre-seventeenth- century Europe, you can still point, laugh and annoy your family and friends, or complain about it on the internet. A historically accurate carrot-related scene should have white, purple and reddish carrots, and perhaps one orange carrot, but a bunch of exclusively orange carrots is just wrong.

51

Carl Benz invented the car

What you may have been told

In 1885, Carl Benz invented the car!

The debunking

To decide who we credit with inventing the car, first we have to decide when a car can be called a car. There were many 'almost-cars', some going back to the fifteenth century, before Carl put his Patent-Motorwagen together.

In 1479, a man called Gilles de Dom sold a carriage that moved forward only by mechanical means to the city of Antwerp . . . but that's all we know. To be fair, we don't even know if that's true, I just found the claim in an American magazine from 1901, but it sounds intriguing, doesn't it?

But another 'car' from the same era that we do know a bit about was the one designed by Leonardo da Vinci himself. He thought of a fun little wind-up vehicle that, through a system of springs, would drive around. It really worked but may not have been meant to be used for transporting humans.

So let's agree that when we talk about cars, we mean a motorised vehicle, a motor car that humans can actually use to drive with, so no miniature test models or any old vehicle that can move without a horse, pushed or powered by some sort of spring. (Sorry, Leonardo.) This definition also rules out the steam-operated vehicles, like the vehicle Ferdinand Verbiest designed in 1672, the military tractor Nicolas-Joseph Cugnot invented in 1769, the electric carriage the Scot Robert Anderson built in the 1830s and the one the Dutch professor Sibrandus Stratingh built around the same time. I think you could make a good point defending some of these vehicles as the original car; after all, why would an electric car not count? But while these inventions were all extremely impressive and in some ways can be considered cars, seeing how we define cars today, they're probably better described as the ancestors of the car; they're not quite motorised vehicles that work on fuel and are meant to transport humans.

People were experimenting with many different types of vehicles all over the place back then, and in the early 1800s there were already cars running on hydrogen and coal gas.

The gasoline-guzzling motor car with a combustion engine is what most people mean when they honour Benz with the car's invention and, to be fair, it was this type of car that eventually led to a breakthrough, resulting in a vehicle that could be mass produced and used by most people. That's what started the age of the car, so there we are. But even when we limit ourselves to just that type of motor car, Benz still wasn't the first . . .

Édouard Delamare-Deboutteville built a four-wheeled (one more than Benz's three-wheeler) vehicle in France that was powered by a combustion engine. It was tested in 1884 and patented in the same year, predating Benz. But some of his cars had a nasty habit of exploding and the invention's practical use couldn't be proven, so it didn't become a success.

Benz created his car in 1885, patenting it in 1886. It was an impressive invention, a proper automobile, and it became the first commercially available automobile ever, which, thanks to his wife Bertha, soon became very famous. We really can credit him with pushing the car from obscure test subject to the transport vehicle that would change our world forever.

But there's one man whose name is always forgotten when it comes to this topic: Austrian inventor Siegfried Marcus. His contributions were literally covered up.

Marcus probably built his first car in the late 1860s, at least 15 years before Benz built his. It was a vehicle with an internal combustion engine, a carburettor and four wheels. (On a totally unrelated note, he also invented the T-handle plunger igniter – official name the 'Wiener Zünder' – used to blow up dynamite, and the type often used by Wile E. Coyote.) He wasn't just some amateur tinkering in his shed, he was very well known and during his lifetime was widely considered to be the inventor of the motor car.

But Marcus was Jewish.

He died long before the Nazis came to power, but they were still very embarrassed by his accomplishments and literally tried to erase him from history. His monument was taken away, evidence of his inventions was destroyed and they even removed his name from encyclopaedias, replacing it with Benz and Daimler as the inventors of the modern automobile. Which unfortunately makes the truth about his contribution difficult to confirm.

Were his cars experimental and impractical? Perhaps, probably, but it was a car, it worked, and the machines and the man who invented them deserve the credit the Nazis tried to take away.

So although it remains difficult to agree on who we should credit with inventing the very first car, I think it is clear that it's not Carl Benz. There are too many other contenders and vehicles that we can absolutely call cars that came earlier. Benz is a name that's easy to remember, but I think Monsieur Delamare-Deboutteville and Herr Marcus deserve to be at least mentioned in the same breath.

52

This is a photo of Bertha Benz and her sons during the first ever car trip in 1888

What you may have been told

In 1885 Carl Benz built the very first automobile, practically inventing the car, but it was his wife Bertha Benz who three years later decided to take the vehicle for a proper spin, thus inventing the car trip and possibly also committing the first car theft.

Yes, the very first car trip ever was made by a woman. And amazingly, there is a photo showing Bertha and her two sons with the car during that very first trip!

The debunking

It is such an interesting story: the inventor of the car having doubts about the feasibility of his invention, lacking confidence to promote it, his wife then deciding to take matters into her own hands and driving the car through fields and towns, terrifying the locals and upsetting the cows, but by doing so proving to the world that the car was here to stay. We can almost envision the scene. And you don't have to worry, I'm not going to debunk it, it really happened.

Yes, Carl may not have been the inventor of the car, as I explained in the previous chapter, but Bertha really did borrow the one he built and took it for a joyride. Although technically, legally, I guess it was also her car as she was married to the owner, had invested her own money into its creation and, well, I doubt there were any laws regarding stealing cars at the time.

Anyway, Bertha was quite amazing. Besides investing her money into her husband's work and being a test driver for his first horse-less carriage designs, she also made contributions to the design and suggested important improvements. She was as much involved with inventing the 'first' car as he was and deserves shared credit, I reckon.

Carl had sold a couple of his cars, but he wasn't doing a very good job of marketing their invention and he also didn't seem very confident in his invention's future. Bertha knew better, so one day she decided to borrow the car and, without telling her husband, took it for a trip from the workshop in Mannheim to Pforzheim where her mother lived, 66 miles away. In a way, she also invented the first ever petrol station when she stopped at a pharmacy to buy fuel. It was not an easy journey, but her plan worked. It generated a lot of publicity and it boosted the development and popularity of the automobile.

But she didn't think to bring a camera along.

So when I saw there was a photo floating around the internet accompanied by the claim that it shows Bertha and her sons on that historical day, I just knew something was suspicious about it. And when I looked a little closer I spotted something very few people seemed to have noticed – Bertha's sons are wearing modern shoes with thick rubber soles. But for some reason, that was not enough to completely convince everybody that the photo they were sharing online was not genuine. I guess people really wanted to believe it was real.

Stock photography websites are always a good place to start when you're trying to find out more about a picture, but not in this case, because even they seemed to think the photo was real. And even official Mercedes websites, books, newspapers and magazines have used the photo without knowing or mentioning that it doesn't show the real Bertha in 1888. But by trying several reverse-image search engines, trawling through countless car websites and long-abandoned forums and blogs, I eventually hit pay dirt.

I found the photo but in colour instead of black and white, which made it even more obvious that this photo was modern. More detective work and searching through the Daimler and Mercedes archives eventually led me to the original – a photo that was taken during the hundredth anniversary celebration of the first trip, in 1988.

Another clue was that the car in the photo is not the 1888 Model III version Bertha used but another model, and that the location in the picture is nowhere near where the trip was, but in the rather pretty town of Ladenburg, just around the corner from the Dr Carl Benz Automuseum . . .

An amusing detail is that when I contacted the Daimler archive in Germany in connection to the photo they responded: 'You will not believe how many asked for these pictures [or the right to use them] believing that they show Bertha and sons.'

53

In the Middle Ages, nobody except the clergy could read

What you may have been told

In the Middle Ages, nobody could read or write. Even kings had to sign documents with an X. Only members of the clergy were literate and all written sources from the era come from them. Everybody else was too busy barely surviving so had no need or reason to learn how to read and write.

The debunking

It is true that most written material that survives came from the clergy. You can probably imagine the scene of monks in monasteries, carefully making the most amazing books with superb illustrations, writing just a few lines a day.

Technically, literacy originally related to the ability to read and write Latin, which I guess makes most of us alive today illiterate, including me. But just for clarity, I'll use the word as it's generally used now: the ability to read and write in general. Common people who may not have been able to read or write Latin did sometimes know how to write in their regional languages.

It is tricky to make any statement on literacy in medieval Europe; after all, it's a pretty big place with cultures and habits that widely differed from region to region, sometimes even from one village to the next. The Middle Ages also lasted rather a long time; a lot of things changed rather dramatically during those 1,000 years. On top of that, nobody, as far as I know, went door to door with a clipboard and quill to ask people who in their household could read and/or write, unfortunately. (What I wouldn't give for there having been a detailed census about everything going back to the Stone Age.) Any claim on this subject for the whole of Europe during the entire Middle Ages has to be taken with a few very big grains of salt.

It's also important to remember that those few precious books that survived are not representative of all the writing that once may have existed. After all, what kind of writing do you take good enough care of so that it survives for many centuries? Expensive books are going to get different treatment than some homework or a shopping list. They were also written on expensive vellum (parchment) with high-quality ink, protected by a hard cover and safely locked away. Whereas more everyday writing was done on little wooden planks covered in wax, a sort of tablet, that medieval people scratched their notes on to with a stylus. They also used wood, bone and even bits of tree bark to write messages on. These rarely lasted for a couple of months, let alone centuries. So simply looking at what has survived gives us a skewed idea of the kinds of writing that existed back then.

You can imagine that a message written on tree bark wouldn't last, as it's fragile to begin with and it wouldn't take long for it to rot away. But in the 1950s, over 1,000 messages on bark were found in Russia. The special soil in the region of Novgorod somehow preserved tree-bark messages dating from the eleventh to the fifteenth centuries. Interestingly, a lot of them appear to have been written by common people, and contain many different glimpses into daily life centuries ago. They're not religious masterpieces or important political documents, but business deals, very private messages, naughty stories and even school exercises and drawings made by children.

The writings left by seven-year-old Onfim are especially lovely. He practised his alphabet and asked God for help but he also made drawings of humans with rakes for hands, just like children still do today. After all, hands are difficult to draw.

Mikita wrote to Anna: 'Marry me, I want you, and you me.' Boris wanted Nastasya to send him his shirt that he'd forgotten and a son asked his dad for trousers and fabric, promising to pay for it if he's still alive.

This suggests that either there was a small area of the world where literacy was a lot higher than anywhere else, or that literacy was higher than we think in many places but, because the people there weren't obliging enough to lose their writings in special soil, very little of that writing remains. The climate often makes a difference – cold weather, bogs and peat allow materials that often rot away elsewhere to survive.

In Norway, hundreds of medieval texts scratched into wood and bone, the so-called Bryggen inscriptions, have been found. Many have religious subjects but some are . . . well, too cheeky for me to share here. And just like the bark messages from Russia, many appear to have been written by common people.

And then there's the graffiti in regional languages all over Europe, from Vikings scratching naughty things on the walls of Neolithic monuments to someone scratching 'God help me' on a wall at St Mary's in Steeple Bumpstead in fourteenth-century England, possibly in the middle of the Black Death pandemic. All of this is clearly evidence of people being able to write (but not in Latin) during the Middle Ages in different places in Europe.

On top of that, archaeologists almost drown in the styluses people once used to scratch messages into wax, they turn up so regularly.

We know that some books were not written in Latin: the twelfth-century *Peterborough Chronicle*, Geoffrey Chaucer's famous *The Canterbury Tales* and the popular *Wycliffe's Bible* from the fourteenth century were all written in Middle English. Who were these books written for if only the clergy could read and they only read Latin?

None of these examples prove that literacy numbers were high in medieval Europe, but they do suggest they may have been higher than we've assumed for a very long time. Any claim regarding literacy in medieval Europe or medieval anywhere is usually a very rough estimate but some historians have come to the (in my view, cautious) conclusion that by AD 1200 everyone probably knew at least someone who could read and write.

We are finding new things all the time, records are (re)discovered, new studies made, perspectives change. Until relatively recently, there was little interest in the lives of common people, but that has changed quite a lot in the last couple of decades, so who knows what else we'll learn in years to come.

54

The first ever video or computer game was Pong

What you may have been told

Back in 1972, a bunch of clever chaps created the world's first computer game in which you moved a white rectangle up and down, trying to hit a small cube back to your opponent's rectangle. With a bit of imagination, this could be considered a game of tennis.

The debunking

It may seem like it was just yesterday that computer games became part of our lives, so finding this subject in a book about fake history may have made you feel really old. Sorry to be responsible for this realisation, but if you remember those first computer games and if you, like me, like to tell those pesky young people that you've been a gamer since *Pong* and they don't know what it's like to have to load a game from an audio cassette tape . . . it means you're old. And, like most old people, we think everything started when we remember it starting. So *Pong* has stuck in our collective memories as the first computer game. But it wasn't.

Computer Space (the one with the tiny spaceship in the centre of your screen that you could rotate to shoot at asteroids) was created in 1971, a year earlier than *Pong*, and both games were the first that were commercially available to the public, appearing in arcades, which probably explains the origin of this myth.

But much of the pre-history of gaming happened away from public view. For instance, another tennis game was only seen by those who happened to attend Brookhaven National Laboratory's visitor days in 1958. This game, later called *Tennis for Two*, was often used as the smart corrective response to people who claimed *Pong* was first. Created by physicist William Higinbotham, it used an oscilloscope connected to electronic analogue computer Donner Model 30 and a display. But this was also not the first video game.

As with everything, it all depends on your definition of a video game. And to make things even trickier, the definition seems to have changed over the decades and continues to evolve today. I'm working with a definition of a video game as something that is played with a computer and involves manipulating images on a video display for the purpose of entertainment.

There were, of course, computer games back when computers didn't even have screens.

We may never know who invented the first computer game; it was perhaps someone working in a lab somewhere, messing with really big serious computers, killing time while calculations were being made; a simple game that vanished forever the second the professor returned with his cup of tea.

Or maybe it was some of the code breakers at Bletchley Park, taking a break from winning the war and having a bit of fun using Alan Turing's bombe code-breaking machine when he wasn't looking. At least, that's how I like to imagine it.

Of course that's a bit silly, but not as far-fetched as it sounds because Turing himself, together with David Champernowne, developed a chess-playing program called *Turochamp* in 1948! In some ways, this could be considered one of the first computer games ever developed – although unfortunately Turing never managed to run it on a computer as they just weren't powerful enough at the time.

Not all early computer gaming happened behind closed doors, though. At the 1939 New York World's Fair (season two of which took place, confusingly, in 1940), a huge machine weighing a metric ton called the Nimatron was exhibited. Its only function was the game *Nim*. Technically it was a computer and you could play a game with it – so you could say that makes it a computer game – but it didn't really have a screen, just a bunch of light bulbs. The device got a lot of publicity, though, and the game was played by many thousands of visitors. It may have been the first 'computer game' the public heard about, so it deserves a mention. And I also really like the idea of a granny somewhere being able to tell her pesky grandchildren she's been a gamer since 1940.

In 1949, cinema visitors in Britain watched D.W. Davies play noughts and crosses on a machine that thought for itself. It did use a display, though this too was just a glorified set of lightbulbs. But in a way it was still a computer game. Mr Davies's later inventions are considered key to the creation of the internet. You can find this footage on YouTube with the title 'Noughts And Crosses Machine (1949)'. It's brilliant.

Another early contender is Bertie the Brain, built in 1950 by Dr Josef Kates for the Canadian National Exhibition. This was another massive machine (4 metres, or 13 feet, tall) that allowed visitors to play a game of noughts and crosses on a screen. But it too used a display that worked with lightbulbs, which means that while it sort of was a computer game, it was not really a video game. Again, it depends on which definition you use.

In 1952, several games were created that not only used computers, but involved direct manipulation by their players and also used a proper electronic display instead of lights switching on and off. These finally fit our definition of a video game. So one of these was probably the first video game ever, that we know about anyway.

In spring 1952, Christopher Strachey, a pal of Alan Turing, managed to get a game of draughts (aka checkers), which he started work on in the previous year, to work on the Manchester Mark 1 computer at the Victoria University of Manchester. Although the exact date of it first running is unknown, and it may have worked as a test as early as the beginning of 1951, there is no doubt that it existed and worked by 9 July 1952 at the latest. Strachey gets my vote for being the inventor of the video game, and for his draughts being the first ever (known) video game.

Around the same time, Massachusetts Institute of Technology (MIT) student Oliver Aberth created a game that involved bouncing a ball into a hole on the Whirlwind I computer. This happened somewhere between early 1952 and February 1953 – probably later, as a demonstration in early 1953 only mentioned the bouncing ball, not it being a game. There is also only anecdotal evidence for it.

Near the end of 1952, Alexander S. Douglas managed to get a game of noughts and crosses (later named *OXO*) to work on the EDSAC computer at the University of Cambridge. In November, Stanley Gill created a game involving opening gates for sheep on the same computer. Also at the end of 1952, Arthur Samuel managed to program the game draughts for the IBM 701, and chess followed soon afterwards.

Whether any of these games qualify depends a bit on how strictly you're sticking to the definition of video game, but it is still clear that neither *Pong*, *Computer Space* nor *Tennis for Two* can be called the first video game. By the time they arrived on the scene people had been gaming for decades.

55

The Great Wall of China is the only human-made object visible from space

What you may have been told

Although it is centuries old, the gigantic, amazing Great Wall of China is so impressive, it is the only human-made structure you can see from space!

The debunking

We humans like to think we're pretty special, which we are of course, but we like to have that confirmed as often as possible. We're a needy bunch. Perhaps that's why we find it comforting to believe that what we do does not only have an impact on the Earth but also far beyond it. And why we like to think that what we create on our little planet can be seen from space. And much of what we're responsible for can indeed be seen from space – but not the Great Wall of China.

It is one of humankind's most impressive architectural achievements. Over 21,000 kilometres long, it goes through valleys and over hills and mountains, cutting a line through nature, and it took centuries to build . . . but you won't find it while peering out the window of a spaceship.

Interestingly enough, the claim has been around since before space travel was a thing. As far back as 1754, an Anglican clergyman, historian and physician from Lincolnshire by the name of William Stukeley (Newton's old pal – see chapter 34) thought the wall might be visible from the moon. We don't know if that was how the myth began but it didn't take long before it stuck.

First of all, being able to see anything on Earth depends on where in space you are: space is, famously, pretty big. When we depart Earth in our spaceship, we first enter what's called low Earth orbit, LEO for short. This is where some of our space stations and artificial satellites end up hanging out. It begins at an altitude of about 160 kilometres, which technically makes it space. But that doesn't sound very far, does it? It's less than half the distance between Amsterdam and London. But from LEO, under perfect weather conditions, you can see the Great Wall of China.

Wait, did I just debunk my own debunking?

Sort of, yes. You can see the Great Wall of China from space – low orbit space, just outside Earth's backdoor . . . If you squint, there's sort of a line where the wall should be, on a good day, sometimes, if you're lucky . . . according to some astronauts. If you use binoculars you can see it a lot better, but with really good binoculars you can also see things as tiny as planes and ships!

But the International Space Station orbits the Earth at a much higher altitude, at about 420 kilometres. Good luck seeing the wall from up there.

The claim I'm debunking here also says that it is the only human-made object visible from space, and that's just not true, especially not from LEO. For instance, ladies and gentlemen, if you look out the window on the left side of our craft, you'll see, 180 kilometres below us, the Great Pyramids of Giza. And some of the other human-made things we'll be able to see during our scenic route around the globe include: desert roads, the greenhouses of Almería in Spain, huge bridges, the cooling pond of Chernobyl and yes, of course, on the dark side of the Earth we can see a lot of evidence of human life, like the billions of lights that are switched on every night.

But perhaps the most impressive human-made object visible from space is the Netherlands, parts of which were created by the Dutch, as they turned sea into land.

56

Medieval people thought the world was flat

What you may have been told

Up until the 1500s, people always believed the world was flat – especially those dumb medieval folks who didn't know anything and had no education and no interest in science. When, during the Renaissance, people first claimed the world was round, they were burned at the stake. Thanks to good old Columbus discovering the Americas instead of falling off the edge of the world, people finally realised the Earth was round.

The debunking

Somehow it is comforting to believe that our ancestors were idiots. But there is no evidence to suggest that believing the Earth was flat was very common in medieval times.

Of course, that doesn't mean *nobody* believed it was flat. I could find a few cases of people thinking the world was flat, or being accused of it and being mocked for it, but we have lots of sources showing that people knew the Earth was round and that saying so wasn't considered some sort of controversial statement.

The ancient Greeks already thought the Earth was spherical by the sixth century BC, and medieval scholars agreed and were supporting their claim since at least the seventh century AD. The ancient Greeks had studied the subject and Aristotle had proven it with pretty accurate calculations. He even provided an impressive estimate of the Earth's circumference. By the first century AD, the famous historian Pliny the Elder claimed that everybody agreed on the Earth being a sphere.

In the seventh century in the Visigoth kingdom of Hispania, there was a renaissance – not 'the' Renaissance, but the first of several 'little' renaissances in medieval Europe. The sciences flourished in this part of the world and the renaissance is called the Isidorian Renaissance, after Isidore, the bishop of Seville. He described the world as a wheel and in his work *De Natura Rerum* he even claimed that the Sun orbited the Earth, and that this was why one side of the Earth was dark when the other side was light.

Yes, he wrote that in the seventh century. That doesn't sound very 'dark ages' does it?

Another impressive example of how people were thinking about the Earth back then is what Thomas Aquinas wrote in his *Summa Theologiae* in the thirteenth century:

> *The physicist proves the Earth to be round by one means, the astronomer by another: for the latter proves this by means of mathematics, e. g. by the shapes of eclipses, or something of the sort; while the former proves it by means of physics, e. g. by the movement of heavy bodies towards the centre.*

And a little later, Dante Alighieri wrote about a spherical earth and even described the shift of gravity when he passed through the centre of the Earth and ended up near Jerusalem in his fourteenth-century epic poem *Inferno*, something he didn't figure out by literally going through the Earth, as that's impossible.

Of course, none of this tells us very much about what the common people thought on the subject. They weren't generally asked and they rarely had the chance to leave their opinions and ideas behind for us. But as long as we have no evidence telling us their opinions, we have to stick with what we do have.

Victorian anti-religious propaganda and the Romantic movement of the era are guilty of misinterpreting a few sources, and they incorrectly assumed that the tensions between the church and science that existed during the Victorian era must have been even worse in medieval times. Yes, when it comes to history myths, once more, it's the pesky Victorians we can blame. I couldn't find much evidence of people claiming our ancestors thought the world was flat till a history book about Columbus written by Washington Irving in 1830 mentioned it.

In medieval times, the church assumed science would only help them understand God and the world he created better, which is why the church so often supported scientific research, progress and education. This attitude only changed a bit later on, when scientists started to make discoveries that clashed with what the church wanted the truth to be.

So there is no evidence that suggests that most people thought the Earth was flat before the Renaissance. In today's world, on the other hand . . .

57

In the Middle Ages, everyone emptied chamber pots into the street, often from windows

What you may have been told

During the Middle Ages, our dirty, filthy, disgusting ancestors would open their windows and empty buckets full of waste into the street below; even the contents of their chamber pots went the same way. And this often would hit passers-by, who ended up being covered in that muck, but they didn't care as everybody was always dirty anyway. As a warning, some of the better brought-up folks would at least shout 'Gardyloo!' before chucking a pile of vileness out the window.

The debunking

Of course, I am not saying it *never* happened, but the idea that this was common, happened all the time and people tolerated it is a myth.

Overpopulation wasn't a problem in most cities and towns till the Renaissance and Early Modern era. The majority still had an agricultural character and most houses were not that different from farms – residents had their own plot of land or yard with space for an outhouse and dung heap or cess pit; they kept animals, had a vegetable patch and a herb garden. What they rarely had was a first floor with windows to throw stuff from. They had no real reason to empty a chamber pot out of their window, as they could just chuck it in the yard. Even if someone wanted to be a filthy Freddy, this would happen on the ground floor – the awfulness would not come from above.

We have to also remember that people would never, ever have been fine with being showered with someone's urine or, you know, something worse. If anything, our ancestors would have been even angrier than we would be – after all, we can throw our clothes in the washing machine and take a shower while we let the police take care of the person who threw the contents of their chamber pot on us. A medieval person would have had to handwash their clothes and perhaps, if they could, have a quick bath by jumping into a canal or pond – all actions that took a lot more time and effort back then.

Getting the law to deal with this person would also not be that easy, mind you. As most medieval people carried a knife, you might be tempted to deal with this scoundrel yourself, causing even more trouble for everyone involved. So why would you risk a fine or even being stabbed by whoever happened to be walking underneath your window if you could just as easily dump it on your compost heap at the end of your garden? Or save it and then sell it, as it had value! Urine and faeces could be used in many ways, including as compost or as an ingredient as part of an industrial process – like tanning, laundering, cloth making and so on. Being able to sell your waste was another reason not to throw it out.

When cities and towns started growing and getting overcrowded at the end of the Middle Ages, land became more valuable because more people wanted to live there, so people started to build higher houses, with gardens and yards getting smaller and eventually disappearing when someone decided to build a house there. Of course, when there are more people there is going to be more waste, and when there are fewer places to get rid of that waste, you're going to have problems.

You can imagine that when you suddenly have to carry your waste to a special dumping area or wait for it to be collected, the temptation to throw it somewhere where you're not supposed to would be strong. City records show people complaining and getting very angry with neighbours who made a mess or caused discomfort. In fourteenth-century London, fines could be levied against anyone living near the place where filth was found, so if you saw your neighbour dumping waste in the street you knew you'd be at risk of a fine for what he did! On the other hand, if you told on someone who was being mucky, in some places you could receive a portion of the fine they had to pay, so it was lucrative and you helped keep your neighbourhood clean.

We have records that show that a chap caught merely urinating in the street was almost beaten up by locals for doing something so filthy, and a man who threw just a bit of fish skin on the street caused the owner of the house to be fined for it, who then got so angry he attacked the litterer. If anything, old records seem to suggest that medieval Europeans tried really hard to keep cities and towns clean, and most examples of things getting rather filthy come from much later.

During the sixteenth century (so technically just after what we generally consider to be the Middle Ages), we see several new laws popping up regarding the handling of waste. For instance, in Belgium there was a very specific law stating that windows overlooking a neighbour's yard or garden needed bars so a 'piss pot' could not be emptied out of this window. This shows that this dirty habit did happen in that region at that time, at least often enough for this law to be thought necessary.

So although it clearly happened often enough for specific laws to be created in one small part of medieval Europe, it still was not something that, at least in Antwerp, seems to have turned the streets into one massive cesspit, according to what other records suggest. And even when it did happen, it would normally take place in side alleys and backstreets; people weren't just dumping it out of windows on to people in busy streets below.

At the same time, we shouldn't look at laws and assume they were always made because something was a huge problem: some laws are about things that are minor inconveniences, or they're only meant for a small section of society. And some laws were about something problematic at the time but are still around even though the problem no longer exists.

Of course, things often went wrong, and there were plenty of incidents where people ended up complaining about a filthy stench or waste everywhere. But the idea that this was a fact of daily life for all of medieval Europe is the myth we're debunking. The reason we have all these records is because problems were noticed and people complained because they didn't accept what was going on; they insisted on things changing.

During the Middle Ages, people connected smell with health. Bad air was assumed to be unhealthy. So besides just not liking bad smells, like all humans who have noses do, our ancestors had an extra reason to want to try to fight unhygienic situations. But still, every time people write about medieval hygiene they depict it as being non-existent. Films and TV shows wallow gleefully in the filth.

There's a famous medieval illustration of a topless woman literally emptying her chamber pot from a window over some musicians. Surely that's a convincing bit of evidence to show that it happened . . . or is it?

In actual fact, it comes from the book *Das Narrenschiff* ('The Ship of Fools'), which is all about bad behaviour and ridiculous and strange situations. The woman empties her pot over a bunch of annoying idiots, who are playing loud music under her window at night. Which is icky and disgusting but clearly isn't meant to be a depiction of some common daily occurrence. Imagine if, one day, future generations base how they think we all lived on some footage of drunk people misbehaving on a Saturday night in any UK city centre . . .

So waste was not hurled willy-nilly from windows. It was mostly dumped in one's own yard, given to a collector or taken to a communal dump or designated river, stream or gutter meant for this purpose, which would have flowing water in it, thus not causing much of a stink (unless it got clogged; that would be horrible). It was only when cities became overpopulated that this relatively well-functioning system started to break down every now and then.

The Middle Ages always get blamed for these horrible situations while Roman cities had the same problems, and quite a few medieval towns were a lot cleaner than the slums of Victorian London.

58

Queen Elizabeth I bathed once a year 'whether she needed it or not'

What you may have been told

Everybody in Tudor England was filthy. Nobody ever washed and they even feared water. Queen Elizabeth I was the exception; she bathed once a year – 'whether she needed it or not'! If even the richest and most powerful people bathed so rarely, surely the common people bathed even less?!

The debunking

Many of us are obsessed by or at least fascinated with the royals. This has been a thing since the first person ever decided to put on a crown. Strange and unusual behaviour by royalty or rumours about them get a lot of attention, and are used to judge everybody who was alive back then.

That's especially the case with this myth: Queen Elizabeth I only bathed once a year 'whether she needed it or not'.

You've probably heard this claim before, especially if you're British (one variant of the myth is that she only bathed once a month, which is also false). It's taught in schools, mentioned in museums – even serious historians write it in history books. I'm going to deal with the claim in two parts: first the bathing claim, then the quote.

The bathing claim

So how often did Queen Elizabeth I bathe, and where does the idea that she did it so rarely come from?

Researching how often the Tudor royals bathed is tricky – after all, what do we mean today by bathing and what did the Tudors mean when they talked about a bath? When the Tudors speak about bathing do they mean a full immersion in a big tub with hot water, or do they mean a quick jump in a lake, washing themselves in a small tub with warm water, washing themselves with water from a basin or having servants scrub them clean? We don't always know for sure what they meant.

For instance, when some (not all) doctors and members of the church warned people about baths, they didn't necessarily mean literal bathtubs but bath houses, where sometimes naughty things happened and certain diseases flourished. Luckily, there were more ways to get clean than visiting a bath house.

Another important thing to remember is that sometimes when a bath is mentioned, our ancestors meant a medical bath – so not just to clean yourself or to enjoy soaking in for a bit, but a bath for medical reasons. Although some doctors warned against hot baths, others encouraged them.

Let's get one thing straight: having a full hot bath was indeed a lot of work back then – it was a luxury. BUT . . . literally any other way of washing and bathing required relatively little effort.

We know that the Tudor royals liked their baths; after all, they had bathrooms installed in many of their palaces – very luxurious bathrooms like the one at Whitehall that had a steam chamber, running hot and cold water (yes, really) piped in from a freshwater spring, a 'sweat bath' and a water feature with oyster shells and rocks that the water poured from. They had special bathing clothes made and the water was filled with cinnamon, cumin, mint, liquorice and all sorts of other herbs and flowers that made the water smell nice and had alleged health benefits. They may even have used oils to rub on themselves before a bath, thinking this would close their pores (some people thought that hot water opened the pores, and that this was dangerous and would let illnesses enter through your skin).

We know that the royals hated people stinking and that it was not tolerated at court – from records and palace rules it's clear they were pretty much obsessed with it. So besides bathing and washing, people also used nice scents (such as rose oil). Some chose to bathe less frequently and instead focused on making sure their clothes were clean, especially their underclothes. This actually works better than the opposite option: bathing regularly but not washing one's clothes – at least when it comes to how one smells. It was put to the test by historian Ruth Goodman (read about it in her book *How to Be a Tudor*). You may find it hard to believe, but not washing for months does not make you stink as long as you keep your clothes clean. Linen does a pretty good job of cleaning the skin and absorbing any unpleasant odours, such as sweat. Which also explains why rubbing yourself clean with a linen cloth, even without water, would work rather well. Of course, the cloth would need to be washed before it was used again.

The royal family employed a legion of laundresses and seamstresses that continuously cleaned, washed and repaired the many clothes being used. So although we may frown at that idea and think it's dirty, at least they wouldn't stink much – and even if they did, you'd have to do some pretty serious stinking to smell so strong that it would overpower the smell of smoke coming from all the open fires everywhere.

But even with this popular focus on just washing underclothes, the Tudors, including common people, bathed. There were still bath houses and people jumped in canals and lakes for a wash, which we know from town records that documented those who drowned while bathing.

Back to Elizabeth.

We know she had several extremely luxurious bathrooms that made bathing a joy. A LOT of effort and money was put into allowing the Tudor royals easy and regular access to very comfortable and pleasurable bathing. And this was not just at her palaces – she even had a 'hip bath' (the ones you can sit in but not lie down in) that she would take with her on trips. Yes, she wanted to be able to bathe in between palaces.

So even if she did only have a full bath every now and then, she also washed herself and was washed a lot more often than that. Of course, when she was washed by her ladies with wet cloths she would end up being very clean, but I doubt many people today would describe such a rub-down as having a bath or bathing, even though it might be more effective than a modern-day shower. On top of that, Elizabeth seems to have cared a lot about her personal hygiene, appearance and health. When she in 1562 felt unwell, the first thing she did was take a bath (unfortunately it didn't help, as she turned out to have smallpox).

So where could this idea of her never bathing have come from? It is not totally unfounded. During the last phase of her life, things changed. Her health started to fail, she became depressed and she started losing her best friends. That included some of the ladies who had been with her since childhood and were involved in washing and bathing her. She was a frail, sick 70-year-old woman who had lived a very stressful and demanding life, full of regrets, like giving orders to execute people she cared about. Her health was deteriorating and she was melancholic. Having used a lot of unhealthy lead-based make-up may have made things worse. She was lonely and plagued by visions of ghosts, she was no longer herself. She refused to be bathed and washed, and she also refused to let doctors examine her, which of course is not too surprising for someone in her condition.

Maybe this is where the myth originated that she rarely bathed, perhaps in combination with generally misunderstanding Tudor era hygiene. It's unfair and ridiculous to claim Elizabeth never bathed and was dirty based on her life just before she died. Regardless, we can safely say that she bathed more than once a year and was probably washing herself or being washed daily.

The quote claim

When the claim is made that Elizabeth only bathed once a year it is often suggested she did so 'whether she needed it or not'. The quote is very popular. It is even mentioned in many well-researched books, but none of them provides a contemporary source for it. Who said it? Did Elizabeth say it herself? Did someone else say it about her? If so, who was it and how did they know?

For us to even consider that the quote really did come from Elizabeth or someone who knew her, we'd need to be able to trace it back to when the queen was alive, shortly after that time or as close as possible. But so far I've not even managed to come close, which makes the entire quote highly suspicious. I can't find ANY mention of the quote in connection to Elizabeth I before the 1920s.

According to the October 1927 issue of the *Two Bells* magazine for employees of the Los Angeles Railway, at a conference in London, Dame Beatrix Lyall claimed she was quoting the following from an Elizabethan 'gossip sheet': 'The queen hath built herself a bath, where she doth bathe herself once a month, whether she require it or no.' In other publications there's mention of this taking place at the Mothers' Union Housing Conference, possibly a few years earlier, but I have no access to those archives. To make things even more suspicious, the publication then also mentions an infamous hoax.

In 1917, journalist H.L. Mencken published an article in the *New York Evening Mail* claiming that the bathtub had been invented in 1828 and the first bath was introduced to the US in 1842. Although this is obviously nonsense and was debunked almost immediately, the story refused to die and was mentioned on television unironically as recently as 2008.

In the 1930s, the Elizabeth quote was published in the US in a book called *The Body Taboo: Its Origin, Effect, and Modern Denial*, by Elton Raymond Shaw, and the story went on to lead its own life. The quote and its supposed source often changes a bit. Some claim the information comes from court papers or a diarist, others mention letters from an ambassador and so on. But trying to find those is fruitless and I always come back to the 1920s conference. Until an earlier mention is found it might be Dame Beatrix Margaret Lyall who's to blame for implying Elizabeth I did not wash often.

Interestingly enough, the quote seems to have existed earlier without the connection to Queen Elizabeth. In the 15 April 1893 issue of *Timber and Wood Working Machinery*, a suspiciously similar sentence is said by an entertainer from the States, known as the Yankee Entertainer. In the course of his lecture he remarked: 'I take a bath once a year whether I need it or not.'

And in 1905 we find the following mentioned in Sigmund Freud's book *Jokes and Their Relation to the Unconscious*:

Two Jewish jokes, though they are of a coarse type, are even clearer, since they are free from any trace of displacement:

'Two Jews were discussing baths. "I have a bath every year," said one of them, "whether I need one or not."'

It is obvious that this boastful insistence on his cleanliness only serves to convict him of uncleanliness.

So it seems to have been a commonly known joke. This of course makes it even unlikelier that there ever was a genuine connection to Elizabeth.

My conclusion so far, based on what I've found, is that Elizabeth did not bathe just once or twice a year – and bathed more than once a month, too. She most likely bathed several times a month, was washed and rubbed clean quite regularly, probably daily, except for the last weeks or months of her life. And there's no evidence whatsoever that the famous quote has any connection to her. The quote is most likely an old, well-known joke that was connected to Elizabeth in the 1920s just to get a cheap laugh at a conference, and it has stuck with her ever since.

If you know of an earlier mention of the joke or can provide me with a link to a contemporary record proving Elizabeth indeed only bathed once/twice a year/month and that she said something similar to the quote, or if you know of someone living at roughly the same time who said something like that about her, please let me know.

59

The phrase 'Upper crust' comes from the rich getting the top of the bread (the poor got the bottom)

What you may have been told

In the 1500s, bread was sliced and handed out according to status. As it was baked on the floor of wood-burning ovens, the bottom of the loaf often had ash and even little bits of burned wood stuck to it, so this went to the poor who often also used the bread as a plate. The middle bit of bread went to those who were above them in status and the top of the bread, the 'upper crust', would go to those who had money, or it was reserved for guests or whoever had the highest rank at the dinner table. Ever since then, the term 'upper crust' has been used to refer to the higher classes.

The debunking

We love little stories like these. The origins of phrases and words are fascinating, and when they make sense and we think we've learned something we can almost feel ourselves get a little smarter. These 'fun facts' and 'did you knows?' are gold dust for social media. If you share a good one you're almost guaranteed a bunch of clicks and interaction, but you also risk quite a few people showing up who want to correct you.

But surely if it is mentioned in documentaries, by teachers and an army of castle guides, it has to be true?!

No, it does not. It is not a completely crazy idea though.

Many years ago I worked in the archaeological open-air museum Archeon where I portrayed a fourteenth-century baker. I got to dress like a medieval woman and spend all day in a perfect replica of a medieval house, making bread in a medieval oven using medieval techniques. It was an amazing experience – no matter how much you read and study, there's nothing quite like actually trying it yourself.

Medieval bread ovens worked by first burning wood inside a brick or clay oven, not underneath it. Once the chamber in the oven was really hot, you'd remove the remains of the fire, clean the floor of the chamber and then place the dough on the same floor. You'd close the door and then wait; the heat of the bricks and air in the chamber would bake the bread. This means that the bread would indeed have some ash and tiny bits of burned wood on the bottom. But unless you had a really sloppy baker, that really wasn't a big deal; you didn't taste it. I've eaten a lot of bread baked that way and it never bothered me at all. In fact, it was the best bread I've ever eaten.

People did use bread as plates – called trenchers – but they would generally use bread that was a couple of days old for that, or bread specially made for the purpose. After all, it needed to be sturdy and not fall apart as soon as a bit of grease or pottage soaked into it. This bread, full of food juices, could be given to the poor or to animals, but sometimes, depending on what's eaten on it, it can be rather tasty, so I bet sometimes the plates got eaten by the ladies and gentlemen themselves, when nobody was looking.

It may have been considered good manners to give your fancy guest the top of the bread but we only have a few sources for this practice, and they say roughly the same thing, like here in John Russell's *The boke of nurture, folowyng Englondis gise* (1460s):

first pare the quarters of the loaf round all about, and cut the upper crust for your lord, and bow to him; and suffer the other part to remain still at the bottom, and so nigh spent out, and lay him of the crumbs a quarter of the loaf.

These are instructions for a servant written by an usher, so are rather specific instructions for how to serve bread to someone fancy. The servant has to cut the upper or outer crust for the guest or his lord. Which makes sense, as it is quite nice if someone cuts your bread for you. The upper crust may have been considered the best part of the bread and the bottom the least appealing, but the sources we have don't mention that only the top was given to the guest or that the rest was given to the poor, just that the bread was sliced.

The story as we know it didn't appear till the nineteenth century. ARGH! I hear you scream, it's the Victorians AGAIN who have given us a history myth we can't seem to get rid of. Probably the earliest use of the phrase we know about comes from a book with the glorious title *Slang, a Dictionary of the Turf, the Ring, the Chase, the Pit, of Bon-Ton, and the Varieties of Life*, published by John Badcock in 1823. It claims, 'Upper-crust – one who lords it over others, is Mister Upper-crust'. So although we can't say for sure that there's no direct connection, it is very odd that the phrase managed to escape being written down anywhere for centuries.

It's more likely that at a time when the Middle Ages were very popular someone did a bit of reading and then combined the crust-cutting bit with the story of using bread plates and giving those to the poor, and came out with the whole loaf being cut in pieces and allocated depending on which class you were. 1+1=3.

60

A long beard killed its owner

What you may have been told

A very peculiar photo that regularly appears on social media shows us a gentleman with an extremely long beard. The man is Hans Staininger, the *Stadhauptmann* (governor) of the Austrian town Braunau am Inn. He was very proud of his beard that was about 2 metres long. But the beard led to his downfall when he tripped over it trying to escape a fire in 1567 and broke his neck.

The debunking

If you haven't already figured out that the story can't be true, read it again.

Think about it. There is a photo of a man who died in 1567? Exactly. In the sixteenth century, photography had not yet been invented, so that can't be right. It seems like this is another instance of someone wanting to share a cool story they read somewhere but as they couldn't find a picture they just used whatever they could find to accompany it. Or maybe someone read a story about long beards and assumed the photo related to Herr Staininger, when it wasn't supposed to. One case of sloppy sharing on social media and a whole new fake history myth is born.

So what is the real story?

Hans Staininger was a real person. He really was the governor of Braunau in the sixteenth century and, yes, he did have a massive beard that was about 2 metres long! It was so long he used to keep it rolled up in a little bag. He was quite famous for it at the time. The story goes – which of course means there's no real evidence for it – that when he spotted a prince he rushed to show his devotion to him, stepped on his beard, fell and died.

If you ever find yourself in Braunau am Inn, have a look around. You can find wonderful and impressive depictions of the man and in the local Museum Herzogsburg you can even see his beard . . . yes, really! After his death, the beard was cut off and kept by his family, who centuries later donated it to the town of Braunau, which then put it in the museum.

One thing the museum doesn't have though is – you've guessed it – a photo of him. Because photography was not yet invented.

So who is the man in the photo with that glorious and very long beard? His name is Hans Nilson Langseth. He was born on 14 July 1846 in Norway and he holds the record for the world's longest beard. When he died in 1927 (not because he tripped), his beard was measured at 5.33 metres (17 feet and 6 inches) after it was cut off.

If you look on YouTube for a video called 'The End of the Chase (1923)' you can even see Mr Langseth in action, showing off his beard on film (another medium that didn't exist in the sixteenth century, by the way). Mr Langseth's beard ended up in a museum too; it was presented to the Smithsonian Institution in 1967.

61

Queen Elizabeth II bowed to Emperor Haile Selassie

What you may have been told

Two old photos show Queen Elizabeth II and Prince Philip bowing down to Haile Selassie, emperor of Ethiopia, and Menen Asfaw, empress consort. The British monarch usually wouldn't bow down to anybody but because Selassie was ancient African royalty and an emperor, he outranked the queen, so she had to.

The debunking

This is an old story that has been debunked many times but it keeps coming back. People love sharing it on social media. To some, it is a wonderful moment of a representative of the British Empire having to show respect to a Black man. It is a charged photo; it has a political meaning but also involves national pride.

But the photo doesn't show what people think it shows. For starters, the queen and her husband are not even in it. The photos were taken in Ethiopia in late October or early November 1955 by photographer Alfred Eisenstaedt, probably on 2 November during the twenty-fifth anniversary of Selassie's coronation. It was a great celebration with many important guests, but the British monarch was not among them. If she had been it would have been big news. The many reporters and guests would have all mentioned it, it would have been in the newspapers, the cinema newsreels and so on. Many photos were taken and published; the event was not a private one and there was nothing secretive about it. Elizabeth and Philip were just not there – they were not even in the country.

Where the queen went and what she did was generally not a state secret, at least not after the fact, especially trips abroad. These trips involved a lot of paperwork and dozens if not hundreds of people who had to take care of transport, documentation, protection and so on. The idea that she and her husband could have somehow visited an emperor in Africa during a huge public celebration without anyone noticing is ridiculous.

It's not a perfect alibi but the queen was rather busy at the time. During the celebrations in Ethiopia she was touring towns and cities all over England, as reported in many newspapers.

From the *New York Times* we learn that Queen Elizabeth sent a silver cigar box as a gift – another sign that she wasn't there herself.

Elizabeth did visit Ethiopia but that was a decade later, in 1965, a trip described by the media as the monarch's first formal visit to the country. The empress who is in the photos in question died in 1962, before Elizabeth's visit. And Selassie had visited Britain the year before the anniversary, in 1954. Both those events also got a lot of publicity. But during neither of those visits did the queen bow for the emperor. After all, neither one outranked the other – they were equals. The couple bowing in the photo have not been identified, but they are likely members of the diplomatic corps.

62

Medieval Europeans were filthy and had to be taught about basic hygiene and soap by the Moors

What you may have been told

When the Moors from Africa invaded Europe in AD 711, they found a backwards people who were dirty and never bathed. And not only did medieval Europeans never bathe, they also didn't know what soap was.

The debunking

You may frown at this claim and wonder if people seriously believe it, but yes, I'm afraid they do. If you start looking around social media or the internet in general you'll easily find people repeating this claim. If an expert dares to suggest we should perhaps shower a little less, or some American celebrity says something about not using lotion, or a silly person on TikTok claims they very rarely shower, then people start bringing up the Moors. Often combined with the claim that white people are still all very dirty and don't wash their legs, along with a whole bunch of other strange misconceptions and ideas.

But when people make claims about history, we can at least do our research and relatively easily prove they're wrong.

Sometimes these myths are connected to the Nation of Islam, an organisation founded in the United States in 1930 which is considered by many, including the Anti-Defamation League, to be a Black supremacist group that has issues with Jewish people and LGBTQ folks, and promotes racial prejudice towards white people and so on.

But anyway, let's get back to the basic claim.

The idea is that Europeans, all of them, were living like cavemen, literally, till the Moors arrived and civilised them. Of course, the idea of invaders making native people 'civilised' is one that belongs firmly in the past. Interaction between different cultures always leads to an exchange of ideas and knowledge but claiming that people were uncivilised till others taught them basic things is simply outdated. Just like Europeans didn't civilise the Africans they colonised, the Moors didn't civilise the Europeans; there were civilisations on all continents long before any of these things happened.

It is understandable that people sometimes want to believe that stories like this one are true; after all, if you're a minority that has been called backwards, uncivilised and dirty by Europeans for a very long time, it's brilliant to then turn around and tell them your ancestors taught theirs everything they know about hygiene, and that it is their ancestors who were dirty instead.

The Moors from northern Africa, mostly from the region where Morocco is today, did indeed invade and take over a part of Europe in the eighth century AD, and yes, they brought knowledge and introduced new goods. But they didn't introduce either soap or bath houses, nor did they teach anyone how to bathe. Bathing and washing had been a popular habit in much of Europe long before that time. The Romans were rather keen on it and, as they invaded much of the then-known world, they built bath houses wherever they went. They're quite famous for it, to this day. But in a way, they continued the habits of the Greeks before them, who also had bath houses, bathtubs and even showers, thousands of years ago. And even the 'barbaric' tribes of western Europe were into bathing and washing. It was actually the Celts, and specifically the Gauls, who introduced soap to the Romans. The Romans fell in love with the product and soon started transporting it all over the Roman Empire.

Pliny, Julius Caesar, Tacitus and Aretaeus of Cappadocia all wrote about European tribes using soap, bathing and generally caring about their hygiene. And they also mention that some tribes in Germany would start their day with a bath in the lake or river. So here we have bathing and soap, in Europe, 2,000 years ago. And if we focus just on bathing, we can go back even further. The Minoans in Greece had bathtubs, pressurised showers, cold and possibly hot running water and washing basins 3,000 – and perhaps even 4,000 – years ago. In Scotland, Bronze Age baths and steam rooms (or saunas) have been found, and evidence of Bronze Age steam bathing has also been found in the Netherlands.

Can we perhaps make a case for the Moors *re*-introducing these things? No, not really. The old and generally outdated idea of the 'dark ages' that followed the Romans leaving western Europe, in which people completely forgot how to do basic things within a generation or two, is not only untrue, but especially not true for the area the Moors took over.

The Moors never ruled Europe, they ruled a relatively small part of Europe – an important, rich, powerful region, but not a big one. At their peak, the Islamic Caliphates of Al-Andalus ruled 5 per cent of the continent, mostly in Spain and Portugal. But before the Moors arrived this region had been ruled by Greeks, Romans and Visigoths – all civilisations who cared about bathing, a lot. There were literally bath houses waiting for the Moors as they marched into the towns and cities of the Iberian peninsula. Here, the Visigoths had continued where the Romans left off. They maintained the bath houses, fountains, conduits and aqueducts the Romans had built, and reconstructed and even built new ones, such as the Alcázar conduit of Córdoba and the aqueduct of Reccopolis.

But what about the general idea that medieval people were filthy and didn't care about hygiene? That's not really true either – or at least, things weren't as bad as is commonly believed. Europeans continued to bathe and wash after the Romans left. Why would people suddenly stop caring about being clean and sweet-smelling? If you stink you'll never get kissed, and if you don't wash your hands you'll get sand in your food or grease on your clothes. Medieval people had noses and hated doing laundry, but many people are still surprised by how similar our ancestors were to us. And even if a medieval person was a bit stinky, that smell would have been barely noticeable because of the most overpowering odour of all: the smell of smoke coming from the open fires everywhere.

The big, fancy, Roman-style bath houses were no longer needed because towns and cities decreased in size and population, but medieval European societies were also less dependent on slavery. Without slaves, running a massive spa became a lot more expensive and harder. But bath houses didn't vanish; they evolved. Archaeology and records show us that medieval people loved their bath houses – they were social meeting places you could find in every town. They were popular and were considered essential.

In the thirteenth century, Taddeo Alderotti wrote 'On the Preservation of Health'. Here's an extract:

> *When you get up in the morning, stretch your limbs, so that the natural heat is stimulated. Then comb your hair because this removes dirt and comforts the brain. Wash your face with cold water to give your skin a good colour and to stimulate the natural heat. Clear your nose and your chest by coughing, and clean your teeth and gums with the bark of some scented tree.*

So medieval people used soap, loved visiting bath houses and regularly jumped in lakes and canals to get clean. They washed daily and bathed at least weekly, even the poor. Access to clean water was less of an issue than you may think, as many houses had their own well, and although indoor plumbing was relatively uncommon in medieval Europe compared to Roman times, it also wasn't completely unheard of. Several towns, cities, monasteries and abbeys had fountains, sewers and pipes pumping clean water in from outside springs. In Britain, the Worshipful Company of Plumbers was founded in the fourteenth century and much of their work involved installing, repairing and maintaining conduit pipes.

When Henry VI processed through Cheapside in 1432 on his return from France, the conduit pipes were used to provide free wine to the masses. People could fill their jugs from public fountains across London. That is one bit of medieval history modern society won't be able to replicate, unfortunately.

Towards the late medieval era, there was a bit of a decline in the habit in some parts of the world, but that was mostly because of the plagues and venereal disease outbreaks that made bath houses dangerous to visit. The famous Dutch philosopher Erasmus wrote in 1526: 'Twenty-five years ago, nothing was more fashionable in Brabant than the public baths. Today there are none . . . the new plague has taught us to avoid them.'

Medieval people knew several relatively easy soap recipes with ingredients and techniques that were available even to commoners. After all, at its most basic, soap is nothing but ash and water, sometimes with tallow for binding it. It's even in the Bible:

> Then a man who is clean shall gather up the ashes of the heifer, and store them outside the camp in a clean place; and they shall be kept for the congregation of the children of Israel for the water of purification; it is for purifying from sin.

In Italy and France, soap was not just being produced and traded, it was done on such a scale that guilds had to be set up, also before the Moors arrived. Naples had a soap makers' guild from the sixth century, and France had similar guilds a century later.

There's no need to diminish the contribution of Islamic knowledge to European progress, or to suggest the Moorish caliphates didn't bring anything valuable to Europe; they did. For example, compared to European soap, the soap used in the Middle East and northern Africa was made with olive oil, which was nicer and also smelled better. They also built many new bath houses. So you can say that they improved some of the ways in which people cleaned themselves in Europe. But they didn't introduce Europe to soap, nor did they teach Europeans how to bathe; everybody already did, and had done so for a very long time.

63

The first time women wore shorts they caused a car crash

What you may have been told

As two women wear shorts in public for the first time back in 1937, men stand still and stare, and drivers are so distracted that accidents are caused.

The debunking

This photo does the rounds on the internet regularly and it's easy to see why. The scene is reminiscent of old naughty postcards and cartoons. It appeals to us, either because it makes us smile or because we're offended by it. We start to wonder what it must have been like for those women who just wanted to wear shorts like the men, but who got stared at and saw drivers crash into lamp-posts! Guess who would be blamed for distracting the driver . . .

The women, both in wonderful white sporty outfits, are holding hands, which may lead some modern viewers to think there might be another hidden story in the photograph. The photo caused some online debates about the motives of all involved, who was to blame for the accident and so on.

But the picture is almost too good to be true . . . and that's because it's fake history.

A clue that things aren't as they seem is that the car has no damage to it whatsoever, and nobody is paying attention to the crash that just happened. Of course, there are some 'dames' who have 'gams' (1930s lingo for legs) that are so impressive everybody is distracted, but surely a car crashing into a lamppost would take the attention away from the women, not to mention that the women themselves might notice it too. But maybe it was a very slow bump instead of a crash; maybe it happened long enough before the photo was taken for the men to focus on the ladies again. Which doesn't feel very convincing.

One part of the claim we can instantly dismiss is that this is the first time women wore shorts in public. It may have been the first time *these* two women wore shorts, but women had done this before. In the 1930s, women wearing shorts became more and more acceptable – not in public like in the photo, but they weren't something totally shocking and unheard of. Women were wearing them while doing all sorts of outdoor sporting activities, but they could also be seen in the moving pictures. Chorus girls wore them, as did acrobats, and so on. Wearing them in the street would still be frowned upon and deemed too distracting for men, but, well, that still happens today.

I had to dig deeper. The pictures came from the Toronto Archive and were part of a set that clearly shows the whole scene was staged. The five photos show how a photographer and the two women walked around the city staging reactions and taking pictures. When you see all of them together it becomes obvious that there's very little that's spontaneous about them, and the car also gives the game away, as it features in several photos. There's a photo of the car crashed into a lamppost and the driver staring at the women but with nobody else there, and then we have a photo showing the exact same situation but suddenly with a crowd of onlookers. It looks like the photographer decided that the scene needed more people and got some bystanders to get into the frame.

The photo was made for the Alexandra Studio and it was a commissioned photograph. It wasn't taken by someone who just happened to be passing by. So it's likely that a magazine or newspaper called the studio and asked them to take pictures to illustrate an article.

Unfortunately, I'm yet to find out why the photos were taken and how they were used.

64

A man tested American football helmets by bashing his head into a wall

What you may have been told

These days, everything we use is tested by sophisticated machines in expensive laboratories, but how did people do that a century ago? Well, a photo shows us how a leather football helmet was tested in the United States back in 1912. No robots, no crash-test dummies, no white coats – just some chap jumping into a wall, head first, long before health and safety officers ruined all the fun.

The debunking

Seeing previous generations be really dumb makes us feel good about ourselves, and seeing them daring to take risks that we are now no longer allowed to take also makes us feel good, especially when we're in the mood for being grumpy and annoyed with all the rules of our modern world.

Yeah, test a helmet by crashing into a wall, why not? What a lad! They don't make 'em like that anymore!

But the story is not as it seems. The photo was taken in 1912 and a helmet is being tested, but that's the only bit that's true about the original claim. The helmet is not a football helmet but a flight helmet, and the photo was not taken in the United States but in Britain, where they play football properly, with their feet. The real story is a lot more interesting than someone testing a helmet for sports.

The chap in the photo is W.T. Warren, who invented the safety helmet, which was a novel idea at the time. Besides a lot of horsehair, it also had steel springs inside it that protected the wearer's head. The photo was taken at the then brand-new Hendon Aerodrome in London, a place known for many experiments like airmail, parachute jumping, night flights and so on. It also played a big part during both the world wars but is no longer in use and is now a museum.

In 1912, a reporter for the magazine *Flight*, the 'first Aero weekly in the world', apparently, and official organ of the Royal Aero Club of the United Kingdom, visited Hendon and Warren got to demonstrate his safety helmet.

First the reporter whacked him over the head with a piece of wood, and then Warren launched himself into a hangar wall, head first. At least, that's what's written in the magazine.

Although the reporter claims to have snapped that very scene, I think the image is a trick photo, Photoshop 1912 style. I can't absolutely prove it, but I think they may have taken a photo of Mr Warren banging his head into a wall while standing on the ground and then used a bit of cutting and pasting to make the photo more sensational, by suggesting our brave hero was airborne.

I've asked a few photo experts and they agree, the photo looks doctored.

Because of the shutter speed of most cameras back then it was very difficult to capture fast-moving scenes. Someone jumping through the air would most likely end up as a blur in the photograph, and there's also a difference in colour between the man and the background. No flash was used and the chap is grinning while banging his head – all subtle clues that things are not as they appear.

No matter what the story behind the photo is, it worked, as Mr Warren's safety helmets got a lot of attention. He secured a patent and started selling them, and eventually his 'Warren Patented Safety Helmet' was even used by Royal Flying Corps (the predecessor of the RAF) pilots during the First World War. Interestingly enough, some of the American airmen had to make do and . . . wore American football helmets.

Mr Warren sold the rights of the patent to another company just before the war. I hope he made a good deal and that his life wasn't ruined when he realised he perhaps missed out on the helmet being a huge commercial success. But I'm yet to find out what happened to Mr Warren after that. I'm sure he was at least proud to have made a contribution and possibly saved many lives.

65

Paris Hilton invented the selfie

What you may have been told

Everybody knows that the selfie was invented by Paris Hilton and Britney Spears in 2006. Paris made the claim herself on Twitter; it was seen by millions of people and believed around the world.

The debunking

Of course Paris and Britney didn't invent the selfie! Their fans probably want to believe it and to many it may seem a realistic claim, as in our collective memory the selfie is a relatively new thing. But when we stop to think about what's being claimed, it soon becomes obvious that the selfie is much older than 2006.

Before we dive into the history of the selfie, let's first agree on what a 'selfie' is. I looked at a couple of dictionaries and the general consensus is that it is a photo that you take of yourself that is typically (but not exclusively) captured with a mobile phone or webcam and shared online. But at its core, it is no more than a photographic self-portrait.

I bet you can think of a few that were taken before Paris and Britney had their idea. Perhaps you took some yourself. Even if we decide that you need to be holding the camera yourself when you take the photo, we have pictures over a century old showing that our great-grandparents' generation made self-portraits while holding a camera and pointing it at themselves.

Let's stick to the most basic definition: a photo self-portrait. That means we can include all the photos people ever took of themselves in the mirror, and those go back over a century as well. Humans have been trying to take photos of themselves pretty much since photography was invented.

So we know Paris and Britney were not the first, far from it, but then who was?

When you try to look it up, you almost always end up with Robert Cornelius, who is often credited with making the first photographic self-portrait. It helps that he was a rather dashing-looking gentleman. He looks a bit like a hipster using an Instagram filter, staring into the camera, messy hair, crossed arms. In other words, someone who will get clicks when his picture is shared online.

Cornelius was crazy about chemistry. Besides being a business-man and inventor, he did a lot of tinkering with new technology and, just a month after Louis Jacques Mandé Daguerre announced the invention of his photographic process to the world in January 1839, Cornelius started experimenting with it. In October or November 1839 (there's no proper documentation), Cornelius took that photo of himself, making the first selfie in the United States.

For years, people assumed there were no other contenders for the title of first ever selfie, but in the shadows of history a French photographer was ignored and forgotten.

Besides having a great name, Hippolyte Bayard was, like Cornelius, a gifted man, another tinkerer and inventor. He too got excited by Daguerre's announcement and started experimenting with his own process like crazy. He worked extremely fast and made a lot of progress in a very short time. Within two months, he was showing his first results to his friends.

But when he showed them to politician François Arago, who supported many inventors, he was convinced to keep his invention to himself for a bit longer. Three months later, Daguerre's process was explained in detail to a crowd at the Académie des Sciences and the Académie des Beaux-Arts in Paris by one of his greatest supporters – the very same François Arago who had told Bayard to wait a bit before revealing his work, and who, in advance, had also already arranged a lucrative deal for Daguerre. Sounds iffy, doesn't it?

We'll probably never know what really happened or why, but Bayard was convinced Arago had done this on purpose to help his friend Daguerre. Bayard even held an exhibition of his photos (the first photographic exhibition ever) in June 1839, but he didn't officially present them at an institution and he never got the recognition he thought he deserved, or the state and financial support or success Daguerre did.

But we're getting distracted. Back to the selfie.

Dr James McArdle, Associate Professor in the Image, was researching Bayard's early work and realised that one of the prints shown at the exhibition in June 1839 was a portrait, and in his

Some of Bayard's first self-portraits

well-kept notebook Bayard had also glued his test images. Several are of Bayard, '*autoportraits*', self-portraits, taken with a photographic process. In essence, selfies.

They're not very good; they're too dark, vague, too light – they're just tests. And Bayard didn't have the windswept good looks of Robert Cornelius. His portraits wouldn't get a lot of attention if you shared them online. If anything, people who see them often just shrug – is that all? But the fact remains that although Bayard missed out on becoming known as the inventor of practical photography, we can't deny that the tests he was doing with photography between January and March 1839 are the first ever selfies to survive.

One small addendum: the invention of photography in this case revolves around practical photography. People were taking photos before Daguerre or Bayard made their inventions, but those photos took many hours to make and were thus more experiments than real photography.

66

Wojtek the bear was enlisted into a Polish unit in the Second World War but switched sides and joined the Germans

What you may have been told

During the Second World War, Polish soldiers adopted a bear cub. As it grew, it started to earn its keep by carrying crates of ammo, saluting and becoming their mascot. Eventually, Wojtek was enlisted, becoming a proper soldier, although he enjoyed drinking and smoking a bit too much. But then somehow he ended up switching sides and started helping the Germans! Or, at least, that's what photos shared online suggest . . .

The debunking

The story of Wojtek as it is generally shared is mostly true. He is a very popular bear and in Poland he's a national hero. Thanks to the British connection with Poland and the fact that Wojtek spent his last years in Edinburgh Zoo, he not only captures the imagination of people interested in animals and war, but is also responsible for bringing those two nations closer together. The bear has several statues and plaques dedicated to him in both Scotland and Poland, there's a memorial trust, there are books and documentaries and, as I write this, an animated film is being made about him as part of a Polish–British initiative.

But what about him helping the Germans? I hear you wonder. I'll get to that.

Wojtek was really enlisted, but that's not as unusual as you may think. It's pretty difficult to get command to start sending you special food deliveries just because you couldn't resist dragging a cute pet to the front. But giving the animal a rank and making them an official member of the unit meant it was entitled to food, drink and even cigarettes. You know what those pen pushers are like. And you'll recognise this from the earlier chapter about Bambi, the donkey adopted by the legionnaires.

There is some debate about whether Wojtek really helped carry ammunition, but at least one British veteran claims he saw Wojtek carrying shells during the battle of Monte Cassino and apparently few doubted it back then; high command was even so impressed they let the company change its emblem to a picture of Wojtek carrying a shell. That's good enough for me.

When you share a story online and you want clicks, it helps to have an appealing illustration. But when people start looking for a photo of Wojtek, that's where things begin to go wrong. They often just use a basic Google search and pick a photo they like that claims to show Wojtek, but many of those pictures don't.

One of the photos that most regularly crops up is of a bear sitting in a hole with two German *Fallschirmjäger* (paratroopers) firing a mortar at Monte Cassino.

The eagle with swastika can be seen on one of the men's helmets so it doesn't need a lot of history knowledge to realise something weird is going on here. What is Wojtek doing helping the enemy?! Wojtek, *nie, nie*!

Don't worry, he was a hero bear, not a traitor bear: that is not Wojtek and the photo is not real, it's Photoshopped. There is a whole series of these photos showing a bear alongside German troops during the war. They are pretty well made but none of them shows our Wojtek.

It was relatively easy to find the original photos, which don't have the bear in them, proving they aren't real, but I wanted to know who made these Photoshop creations and why. Finding that out was a lot trickier, but eventually I traced them to a German film school project called *Bär* (2014), by Pascal Floerks.

It tells the story of a man's grandfather during the war, but in all the photos the German veteran is depicted as a bear. There are dozens of photos of 'Opa' during training, on planes, hanging from a parachute, next to burning tanks. And also after the war, at home and in the garden. It is an interesting film, you can find it online on YouTube, just search for '*Bär* (2014)'. But the film is not about Wojtek – our hero bear doesn't even get a mention. So Floerks is not to blame for the misunderstanding. He made the photos for a completely different reason and people simply didn't bother to research the pictures they were sharing online.

Some of the other wartime photos of soldiers with bears sometimes mistaken for Wojtek show 'Misha', a stuffed bear positioned next to the road to Leningrad in a place named Rozhdestveno. Misha became extremely popular among German soldiers to pose with.

People often don't seem to understand that a photo of a bear probably doesn't show Wojtek if the bear is being pals with the enemy! So if you want to share the story of Wojtek and illustrate it with a picture, make sure the uniforms of the men he's with are not German. There are plenty of photos showing the real Wojtek with his Polish brothers-in-arms – use those.

67

This is the guillotine blade that killed Marie Antoinette

What you may have been told

This sinister-looking, sharp-pointed blade attached to a dark lump of what appears to be burned wood with bolts and handles is the one that killed Marie Antoinette. It was on display at Madame Tussauds waxworks museum for many years. Underneath it, a small sign claimed: 'This guillotine blade is the one that beheaded Marie Antoinette in 1793. It was purchased from the executioner's family.'

The debunking

Although most people know very little about Marie Antoinette, they can't help but be fascinated by her, especially by her gruesome death. People haven't been executed by guillotine since 1977 (yes really, that recently) but we can't seem to forget the execution device. It's a pretty macabre scene – the condemned walking up the steps, the lever, the swift drop of the blade, the idea that the head may still show some signs of life . . . it speaks to the dark side of our imaginations – the scene that is, not the head.

I remember visiting Madame Tussauds in London as a kid many years ago and being fascinated by what I saw there. So much so that I bought the way-too-expensive catalogue with colour photos.

Marie Antoinette lost her head on 16 October 1793. Henri Sanson was the executioner who pulled the lever. Henri came from a family of executioners and followed his father into the profession. His son, Henry-Clément Sanson, would later follow him. The Sansons often had curious visitors who wanted to learn more about the dreadful family business, and for a fee they could see a demonstration of the guillotine using straw dolls or, for a little extra, a living sheep. Apparently English tourists were especially interested and lined up to see his home exhibit.

The family needed the money as Henri had a gambling habit, was haunted by creditors, spent some time in a debtors' prison and even pawned two of the guillotines in his possession. He was fired as official state executioner in 1847 and the official guillotine was confiscated by the government, but he still owned one. This he sold to Joseph Tussaud in 1854, after Joseph also paid to have it released from the pawnshop.

So far so good. But where things get iffy is that there are several claims about what happened to the blade.

In his book *Choses Vues* ('Things Seen') the famous writer Victor Hugo (the one who wrote *Les Misérables* and *The Hunchback of Notre-Dame*) claimed to have met the former assistant to the Paris executioner, who told Mr Hugo about the Sanson family, how their house was decorated and how Mr Sanson entertained guests. He also shared an anecdote of an English family who were shown the guillotine but who had a daughter who expected more than just a demonstration of the blade cutting through some trusses of hay. She insisted she was ' put in the oven' , as tying up a victim and placing them under the blade was called. Her parents didn't object, so her legs and arms were tied up and she was strapped to the so-called swinging plank. She even insisted her head was placed in the neck-piece. Much to the assistant's relief, she was finally satisfied and did not demand that the blade be dropped. Guests like these always wanted to see the blade that cut the king and queen's heads off. But according to this former assistant, the blade had been sold for old iron, 'in the same way as all the other guillotine knives when they are worn out'. And Hugo writes: 'If he had cared to trade in them, there would have been as many knives of Louis XVI sold as walking-sticks of Voltaire', another popular souvenir of the time. Countless of them were sold even though there were, of course, only a few genuine ones.

Another theory claims that the entire guillotine somehow ended up on a rock overlooking a penal settlement in French Guiana called Devil's Island. The guillotine there was often one of the first things new prisoners saw upon arrival, a subtle reminder of what awaited them if they broke the rules.

There are a lot of peculiar circumstances surrounding this Tussauds guillotine blade. The fact is that there were thousands of guillotine blades used during the French Revolution and after it, and even if Sanson did once own the genuine blade that killed the royals, it seems he didn't treat the objects in his collection very well, pawning them and letting people try them out. We know Sanson had serious financial problems and the blade used for famous victims would be worth more than a random blade, if, as the anonymous man Victor Hugo spoke to claimed, it had indeed been sold for scrap.

Another thing to keep in mind is that Tussauds was sometimes a little economical with the truth, embellishing some of the stories surrounding its exhibits and Madame herself. For example, in her memoirs, Marie Tussaud, the French waxwork artist and founder of the original Tussauds collection, never mentions being forced to make moulds of the king and queen, but later it was claimed that she somehow managed to model the royal heads before they were buried under quicklime. The quicklime was part of a top-secret operation to make sure there wouldn't be enough left of them to be turned into relics. The Tussaud family has always insisted that Marie was forced to make the death masks, despite the fact that the authorities were at the time desperately trying to erase every trace of the royals and were suspicious of Marie herself, as she had once been a member of the royal household as a tutor.

So much of the story is suspicious that there's no way anyone can claim the blade was used for anyone in particular. Even Madame Tussauds museum now agrees with that. They admit on their website that they 'have no solid evidence of its connection to the "let them eat cake" queen's death'.

Yes, I know, they debunk one myth while repeating another. If you haven't read the chapter on this already, spoiler alert: she never said that.

68

The Minions from Despicable Me were based on photos of Nazi experiments on children

What you may have been told

A group of children wearing strange helmets with small viewing windows line up next to a man in a dark uniform. These are Jewish children being experimented on by Nazis. They called these children '*minions*' – a German word. The children didn't speak German and the guards laughed at how the poor frightened children spoke.

Pixar thought this was a fun story to turn into an animated feature . . .

The debunking

Can you imagine making up Nazis horrors just to get some attention? I mean, it's not like there aren't already more than enough horrific stories and disgusting images of the war crimes committed against men, women and children across all the conflicts humans have endured. There's so much choice, you don't even have to use your imagination. Yet that's what happened. Someone saw a photo, thought the men in the outfits resembled Minions and decided to turn it into something awful.

There's a lot to unpack here. Let's start with the actual photo. A quick reverse-image search debunks the picture in seconds. It's not even a Second World War photo. It was actually taken in 1908 and shows a British submarine crew wearing the so-called 'Hall and Rees submarine escape apparatus', which did what it says on the box. When your sub was sinking you could put on the suit and squeeze through an escape hatch. (The suits were too bulky and took up too much space, so eventually they were phased out.) This explains why the 'minions' are standing on a submarine. Further research tells us that this is the *C7* submarine, which was decommissioned shortly after the First World War. The 'minions' are not Jewish children but British sailors.

Minion is also not a German word. It comes from old French, originally; in German, the word is *Günstling*. Finally, of course Pixar did not base the Minion characters on poor Jewish children who were the victim of horrible experiments. None of the

Minions franchise films was even made by Pixar – they were made by a company called Illumination.

The Minions were designed by Eric Guillon and originally envisioned as robots. And anyway, many Minions actually have two eyes, not one, and thus don't even look like the sailors in the Edwardian photo.

69

The White House was painted white to cover up damage after the British set fire to it

What you may have been told

During the War of 1812, British troops captured Washington, DC, and set fire to the White House, causing a lot of damage. The Americans decided to restore the building right away but it was covered in burn marks that they just couldn't get rid of. So they decided to paint the whole building white. It's been that colour ever since and that's how it got its name.

The debunking

It is an interesting, exciting, even dramatic story that explains something many of us may have wondered about at one time or another. But, of course, it's not true.

The British did attack Washington, DC, in August 1814, two years into the War of 1812, sacking it and setting several buildings on fire, including the White House (after first eating the food and drinking the wine that had been prepared for the president's party). They did a very good job of it, going as far as rubbing gunpowder paste on wooden door and window frames and firing rockets. Robert Ross, the general in charge of the British troops, hoped that it would be such a huge humiliation to the Americans that it would end the war. But the British public disapproved of what was done to Washington, DC, even though it was revenge for what the Americans had done to a few British-held towns and cities.

The damage to the White House was substantial; the interior was almost entirely destroyed and many of the exterior walls had to be torn down and rebuilt due to fire and weather damage. The Americans were humiliated but decided that they had to restore this important building, even though it would take years and cost a fortune.

But it was not painted white to cover up the fire damage. It was not even the first time the building was white. The White House was not only painted white before the War of 1812, it was already known as the White House. The building was constructed in 1798 from sandstone, a rather porous material that needs a lime-based whitewash to protect it from the weather, so it was white before it was even officially finished – it had to be!

Although it's been called the White House probably since it was built, it wasn't the building's official name till 1901. So the name being related to the British setting the building on fire is a myth, but it's still a touchy subject.

When, in 2014, the British Embassy in Washington posted a photo of a cake with a model of the White House, a British and American flag and some sparklers on it with the message, 'Commemorating the 200th anniversary of burning the White House. Only sparklers this time!' not everyone could appreciate the tongue-in-cheek comment, and within hours an apology followed.

By the way, if you ever find yourself in Washington and are allowed to do so, have a look around the building. In some spots you can still see the fire damage!

70

The Tudors used spices to cover up the taste of bad meat

What you may have been told

The Tudors used to drown their meat in spices to disguise its vile smell and taste because in the days before refrigeration it had often gone off or was even rotting.

The debunking

This is a famous one. You've probably heard it during a tour of a Tudor building, or perhaps you were even taught this in school. Although often connected to the Tudors, sometimes the claim resurfaces in relation to other eras, but the general gist is always the same. When you hear this, a few alarm bells should automatically start ringing. Let's destroy this myth bit by bit.

First, why would anyone eat rotting meat? Our ancestors were not stupid – they knew what could happen if you ate food that had gone off. Eating it would be an act of extreme desperation, but of course people regularly were desperate; famines were not unheard of and when you're hungry, you're often willing to do things most of us modern people can't even imagine.

OK, so far so good, but the myth suggests this was a regular occurrence, not something that only happened in extreme cases, as if meat was sold in that condition and then cooked and placed on the dinner table all the time, even at feasts. But we know there were strict laws regarding the selling and preparing of meat, and if you were the servant responsible for people getting food poisoning, you would be in trouble.

It is true that our Tudor ancestors didn't have refrigerators, but they knew how to keep meat. Salting became more affordable after the Middle Ages and people also dried and smoked meat and fish, which was not that difficult as fires were burning in almost every house every day. Sometimes all you had to do was hang the meat above the fireplace. And in some fancy places they even had ice cellars – little basements they filled with ice during the winter and that stayed cold for many months afterwards.

But even if they kept messing that up for some reason and had to deal with meat that had gone rotten all the time, why on earth would they choose spices to camouflage their food? For starters, it does not work.

Try it. No, wait, don't. You could sue me, so officially I'm telling you not to try it. So *imagine* trying it. Get a nice chunk of rancid meat. If you can even hold it while gagging all the time, cover it in spices, cook it and . . . Do you think the spices will be enough for you not to taste the gooey, mouldy, wriggly bits?

Maybe, just maybe, if you use the hottest spices available, you might not taste the meat, or anything, ever again, as your tongue will be numb and probably glow in the dark. But even if you manage to eat the meat, you, your belly and perhaps your backside will soon be regretting this decision. Still, even the fact that it doesn't work is not the main reason the whole story is just plain silly.

Most spices came from abroad. They had to be transported from faraway places, which made them very expensive. The claim therefore suggests that people would use something they couldn't afford, that often literally cost a fortune, to make something comparatively cheap easier to eat after they failed to store it properly.

There are no historical sources that prove that this happened. There are a few very rare recipes that suggest solutions for tainted meat but those never involve spices. The suggestion is to cut the bad parts off and wash the meat.

A good steak, lamb or pork were not types of meat that most people could afford very often, but chicken, rabbit, birds and so on were not rare ingredients. With the money you would have had to spend on a pile of spices to cover up the taste and smell of spoiled meat you could have bought a lot of new fresh meat instead.

Admittedly, medieval and Tudor recipes seem extreme to our modern tastes. Not only did the rich enjoy food that many of us today would find exceptionally strange, they of course also liked the idea of showing their guests that they could afford something really expensive. So yes, they did like to add spices to their food but it was a way of showing off.

We may be tempted to smirk and once again mumble something about how silly people were back then – forgetting we've just seen yet another chef on TV plastering gold leaf on his deconstructed, cucumber foam-covered, charcoal-grilled, oak-smoked potato, so that some celebrity can pay a small fortune for the honour of posing with it on Instagram before scoffing it down in one bite. Perhaps we're not that different from our ancestors after all.

71

Erin O'Keefe was eaten by mountain rats in 1876

What you may have been told

In 1876, on Pikes Peak in the Rocky Mountains in the USA, Sergeant John O'Keefe and his young family were attacked by wild rats that appeared at night from the mountain crevices on the hunt for fresh meat. With stove pipes over his legs to prevent the rats from biting him, he fought back as they entered their cottage through a window. His wife Nora placed wire from their telegraph system on the floor and started electrocuting the rats with a battery, which eventually drove them back. But tragically, it was too late for their two-month-old daughter Erin; the rats had devoured her, only the skull remained.

The O'Keefes buried her on the mountain with a gravestone that said, 'Erected in memory of Erin O'Keefe, daughter of John and Nora O'Keefe. Who was eaten by mountain rats in the year 1876.'

John would tell everybody who visited the peak his story and visitors would pose for photographs. Newspapers wrote about the tale and it became quite famous. Surely nobody could doubt it – there was a grave . . . and a stone!

The debunking

It's quite the tale, isn't it? One of those typical Wild West frontier stories that fit the old-fashioned idea of an exciting, adventurous era of explorers and brave people taking dangerous risks in a new and strange land. It also has so many details that help us imagine the horrifying scene. But none of it is true.

John was with the US Signal Service (later called the Army Signal Corps) and was stationed at the Pikes Peak Signal Station, all on his own, in near isolation, for almost three years. He spent all day and night collecting meteorological information and sending it to his superiors. I'm sure you can imagine that for most of the time this was not a very exciting job. Sometimes visitors would come, and now and then he would go down the mountain for a few drinks with the locals in Colorado Springs, which would be a great distraction for our bored soldier. And what do guests, tourists and drinking buddies like more than anything else? They enjoy listening to amazing stories.

One of the men he told the tale of the rats to was Eliphat Price, a newspaper editor who was very impressed and decided to write about it. The story was published and John received more and more visitors, who of course all wanted to see the grave, hear the story, maybe buy a souvenir photo or perhaps leave a generous donation for the poor, sad father. Soon a gravestone was erected by a large pile of rocks, and nobody seemed to wonder why so many rocks were used for just a baby's skull. But there was no Erin O'Keefe. There wasn't even a Mrs O'Keefe. John made them both and the entire rat story up. The pile of rocks probably covered the remains of the company mule.

There are no wild packs of ferocious human-attacking nocturnal rats in the Rocky Mountains, which by the way does not contain an active volcano and so did not erupt, although John claimed it did. Nor were there any monsters living in Mystic Lake, a claim made by John's predecessor at the signal station. It's almost like people who are really bored and lonely like getting some extra attention by making stuff up.

John was well known for his hoaxes and pranks. He was called the Prevaricator of Pikes Peak and when he resigned from the army his mischievous behaviour and disregard for the truth was mentioned more than once during the toast.

I was not the one who discovered the story was fake. In September 1877, a little over a year after the story was published, a reporter with the *Rocky Mountain News* of Denver debunked the story, which the newspaper itself had also written about when it first came out. He cleverly reminded readers of the fact that rats – whether nocturnal, crevice-dwelling, human-attacking rats or common rats – do not live above the treeline and that it was all a hoax. But as the journalist said, 'People are more ready to believe a good story than a dry truth.'

And he is right about that.

Sergeant O'Keefe continued to tell his tales to all who wanted to hear them, each one crazier than the last. And thanks to the internet and some of those photos of Erin's gravestone surviving to this day, he continues to prank us all in death.

72

Queen Elizabeth II threw food at poor people in Africa

What you may have been told

Shortly after Queen Elizabeth II died in September 2022, grainy old footage of two women throwing something at poor people went viral online. It shows the then young Princess Elizabeth throwing food at poor hungry African children. How awful!

The debunking

When much of the world was in mourning and our television screens and internet were flooded with footage and stories honouring the late monarch, there were, of course, many people who wanted to share a different perspective.

For many, the queen and what she represented was not positive at all; she was connected to oppression, colonialism, nationalism and blind patriotism. Countless stories and pictures were being shared showing how other people – sometimes outside of Britain – felt about the queen and what she, in their eyes, stood for.

There clearly was a need for this alternative perspective, which is perfectly understandable. But I guess someone either couldn't be bothered to find a real negative story or unpleasant footage related to the royal family or British imperialism during her reign (which isn't that difficult), or maybe they misunderstood what they were looking at, but for some reason they found some footage and shared it with a fake claim. The social media posts sharing it were often accompanied with negative comments about the British family, imperialism and so on. It caused many, often fierce, arguments online.

Although the pictures were very unclear it was still easy to see that the claim didn't fit the footage. For starters, the clothing dates either to the late nineteenth century or early twentieth century, and Elizabeth II was born in 1926. The fashion we see in the film is clearly not from the 1920s or later.

It was not difficult to find the source of the original footage, even though it was of low quality and colourised. Just taking a few screenshots and using these on search engines soon led me to the Catalogue Lumière, a wonderful online catalogue of all the films made by the famous film pioneers Auguste and Louis Lumière.

I found the film there. It was shot in French Indochina (today Vietnam but also Laos and Cambodia) in late 1899 and early 1900 by cameraman Gabriel Veyre, who was kind enough to take notes. He wrote down that the women in the footage were Mrs Paul Doumer and her daughter.

Mr Paul Doumer was the governor-general of the colonial territory at the time. The women were not throwing food, but coins known as '*sapèques*', little coins with holes in them that were often kept together with a string. We can see the young woman struggling with them. These coins were worth very little, and the clearly very poor people in the footage would have had to collect many of these coins before they would have been of any use.

According to the Lumière catalogue the film was shot at the 'Pagode des dames', these days known as the Chùa Láng, a temple in Lang Thuong, Dong Da district, Hanoi, but I've not been able to confirm this as the complex is rather large and has been reno-vated many times, and I couldn't recognise the exact same spot while looking at modern-day photos taken there.

I checked with a few Vietnamese people to see if the throw-ing of coins might have been a custom or tradition; if perhaps it was something related to that specific temple, but they couldn't think of anything. Throwing coins in ponds? Sure, that happened, just like leaving them at an altar. People still do that today, just as they give loose change to homeless people. There are also some customs involving giving someone lucky money, but according to the Vietnamese people I asked about this, throwing alms on the ground in front of poor people would probably have been just as degrading and tasteless then as it is today.

Although it's likely that a group of people was begging at the temple, it's still odd that the women decided to get a large number of coins just to throw at them. It's especially distasteful when we consider that at the time when the footage was shot the French rulers were imposing heavy taxes on many necessities, and the husband and father of the women in the footage, Mr Doumer, was directly responsible for some of these taxes that were making life more difficult for many local people. Some of the people having coins thrown at them may have been made poorer because of this man.

Of course, we're not sure if the women just didn't care and were behaving without class, or if perhaps they were talked into it by the cameraman filming them. I'm not trying to find an excuse for their behaviour but as someone who has worked in film and television I also know that what we see never tells the whole story.

The Doumer family later returned to France where Mr Doumer became president of France and was assassinated during a book fair in 1932.

Once more the true story behind the footage is more interesting than the one that was made up. But of course, no matter how many times people responded with the truth, it was too late: millions had seen and believed the lie. Not much later the Russian state television show *60 минут* (60 minutes) shared the footage with the accompanying fake claim and used it as an excuse to attack Queen Elizabeth, the West and 'Anglo-Saxons' in one of their many horrendous propaganda broadcasts during the Ukraine War.

73

In the 1930s, Marlene Dietrich was detained by the police for wearing trousers

What you may have been told

When Marlene visited Paris in 1933, police arrested her on the train platform because she was wearing trousers, something that was forbidden in France! But it didn't bother the actress; as the police escorted her away she looked as cool as she always did.

The debunking

The photos made of Marlene Dietrich's 'arrest' that day in 1930s France are fantastic. There she is, in a man's suit, with a tie, wearing sunglasses, with a man on either side, walking towards the camera. And, of course, this story of defiance strikes a chord with people for so many reasons. Besides Marlene looking brilliant, she is also being a rebel and fighting the good fight for the freedom to dress as you want, for feminism, for gay rights and so on. People interpret the photo in many ways.

Nothing takes away from that, or the coolness of 'La Dietrich', but unfortunately, the truth behind the photo isn't quite as exciting as suggested. When it was first shared, I wanted to know more. I didn't automatically think the story was suspicious, but as a huge fan of Marlene, I was curious about what happened on that day. I soon found out that she wasn't really detained, and then I found a very well-researched article by Gilles Tran. With his permission I am going to share what he discovered.

Marlene was not arrested or detained by the French police. In May 1933, Dietrich was allowed by Paramount to take a European holiday. She boarded the SS *Europa* in New York with her daughter Maria and 'luggage containing 25 suits of male clothes, dozens of men's shirts, neck ties and socks'. She arrived at Cherbourg on 19 May 1933, where she was welcomed by her husband Rudolf Sieber (who is one of the men beside her in the picture). They took the train to Paris to find a mob of reporters waiting for her at Saint-Lazare station. Marlene was tired, so she got in a car and left immediately without stopping for photos, which annoyed some reporters.

The French press did comment extensively on her 'masculine' outfit: trousers, tie, chocolate-coloured polo coat, white shirt, sunglasses and beret. Her daughter was also dressed like her (minus the tie). Some comments were supportive but many mocked her gender-bending appearance and cartoons lampooned it (such as one showing a man ogling an 'effeminate' man and saying, 'Hey, that could be Marlene Dietrich'). Still, she was an immense star and the French press fawned over her, trousers notwithstanding.

In any case, there is no mention of the police arresting Marlene Dietrich, which would have made the front pages all around the world if it had happened. The closest Dietrich got to the French police was when she was invited by Mrs Chiappe, the wife of the chief of police in Paris, to a fundraiser for retired police officers. Dietrich attended the event, 'masculine attire forsaken, [. . .] dressed in modish green with lynx furs, looking very lovely' (*Chicago Tribune* and *Daily News*, 13 June).

Still, Donald Spoto's biography mentions that the French police 'seriously considered a warrant' for impersonating a man, and Steven Bach's biography claims that Dietrich and Sieber 'read official warnings from the indignant Prefecture de Police'. The first claim is unsourced but the second is credited to an American newspaper. And indeed, US newspapers reported that Jean Chiappe, the chief of police, had threatened Dietrich with arrest if she walked around in men's clothes (*Waterbury Democrat*, 22 May). However, no such thing was reported in French newspapers, even though the media followed Chiappe's activities closely. It is unlikely that Chiappe would publicly threaten an international movie star, only to then get her to attend a charity event organised by his wife two weeks later. It is more likely that a US journalist, annoyed at being snubbed by the star when she arrived in Paris, did some creative 'reporting' by listening to rumours. Parisian newspapers did mention a 'law against trousers' and a theoretical action of the police against Dietrich, but only as a joke.

So the idea that women were forbidden to wear trousers was indeed circulating and some did consider Dietrich, famous trousers aficionada, a potential target. But, as noted by historian

Christine Bard in her *Histoire Politique du Pantalon*, the bit about Chiappe was merely a rumour.

There was a law against wearing trousers in France, sort of. On 7 November 1800, the Prefecture de Police in Paris enacted an ordinance (not a law since it was not voted through by the parliament) that stated, 'Any woman wishing to dress as a man must go to the Prefecture of Police to obtain authorisation, which can only be given on the basis of a certificate from a health officer.'

At a fundamental level, the ordinance was against cross-dressing, an old social no-no except in certain circumstances. By the early 1900s, the evolution of women's clothing had rendered the ordinance outdated and useless. However, even though it was no longer a practical concern, the 'law' remained for decades in the public consciousness.

This was notably demonstrated during the civil suit against sportswoman Violette Morris, brought by the Fédération Féminine Sportive (FFS). Morris, who always wore male clothes and who would be considered transgender today, was one of the most remarkable athletes of her time (javelin, shot put, bike racing, car racing, football, boxing and swimming) but she was known to be aggressive towards referees and fellow athletes. When the FFS tried to kick her out, preventing her from participating in the Olympics, one of the arguments used was her cross-dressing. During the trial that took place in 1930, the FSS lawyer, Yvonne Netter (herself a feminist activist), reminded the court that 'the ordinance existed' and that Morris could be arrested by the police since she did not have that famous authorisation. Henri Lot, Morris's defender, argued back that the ordinance was invalid and proved it by showing a letter from Prefect Chiappe (yes, him!) that confirmed that women in trousers were no longer the object of police attention. Morris lost her suit anyway. It was probably on people's minds when the rumour about Chiappe threatening Marlene Dietrich with arrest circulated in May 1933.

Since then, the question of the repeal of the ordinance of 1800 has resurfaced on a regular basis in French politics, usually as an easy way to score points. Who can be opposed to striking down a 'law' preventing women from wearing trousers?

The last iteration took place in 2013, when the Ministry of Women's Rights answered that the ordinance was incompatible with the principles of equality between women and men guaranteed by the Constitution (and other texts) and had thus no legal status, being just a 'piece of archive'. But Christine Bard, after consulting a legal scholar, notes that this is only an opinion, and that the ministry does not have jurisdiction over the prefecture (which has refused so far to consider the issue). So, technically, the ordinance is still valid. Practically, it has been dead for more than a century.

74

Two bullets collided at the battle of Gallipoli in 1915 – a billion-to-one chance

What you may have been told

Two bullets collided mid-air during fighting in the Gallipoli campaign of the First World War, against incredible odds. Did two soldiers, each other's enemies, perhaps survive that day because their bullets didn't reach their destination? Often the picture is accompanied with a challenge to the viewer to name something even more unlikely to happen.

The debunking

The picture and the challenge are social media gold dust. Not only do you have a fascinating historical claim and an amazing photo, but it also tempts the viewer into posting a response.

What is more unlikely than a one-in-a-billion bullet clash?

Of course, it's never really about Gallipoli, the First World War campaign in what today is Turkey, where, during almost a year of fighting, over 440,000 soldiers were wounded and over 100,000 died. The picture has become what the kids call a 'meme'. But is it even remotely based on fact?

The bullets in the photo were clearly once hanging in a museum somewhere, so surely someone had to remember seeing them. Nevertheless, it took quite a bit of detective work to track the photo down. No matter how often I asked on social media, their location remained a mystery for years, literally.

The area of Gallipoli is still covered with objects related to the battles, which has resulted in several museums and collections being set up in the region, but which one had what we were looking for? Eventually, after asking for help on Twitter, one name came up a few times: the 1915 Seddülbahir Ahmet Uslu Müzesi in Çanakkale.

Communicating with the museum was a bit tricky but luckily, thanks to one of my Twitter followers, I was reminded of the fact that Google Maps often has photos of certain places taken by visitors, so I could have a look inside the museum without having to travel there. I looked through countless tourist snapshots and finally found the bullets. This confirmed that at least the connection with the Gallipoli campaign was true.

But did they really collide in mid-air?

I'm not a ballistics expert so I had to check with a few old friends who know more about this sort of thing than I do, and the general consensus was that this part of the story is not true. When a bullet was fired from the rifles used at that time, the barrel left 'rifling' marks on the projectile. The inside of a barrel is never perfectly smooth and often it's even spiralled to give the bullet more stability during its flight. You've probably heard this mentioned during a crime drama or film, when forensic science is used on such marks to trace the bullet to a specific weapon. And that is where this story falls apart: one of the bullets doesn't have rifling marks. This means that when the bullets met, one of them was stationary, probably stored in a cartridge box or maybe in a soldier's bandolier (a belt with pockets for ammunition).

This happens a lot more than two bullets colliding in mid-air. I wouldn't say it's a very regular occurrence, but it's common enough that quite a lot of museums have several such bullets on display. Unfortunately, some of those museums either forget to mention that the bullets probably didn't meet in mid-air or even suggest that they did, despite knowing that they couldn't have.

After all, why let the truth get in the way of a good story, right? Well, that's what I'm here for. To get in the way of a good story, and hopefully reveal some better ones along the way.

Do bullets ever collide mid-air? Yes, but that really is quite rare.

I'm terrible at maths, but as rare as even that is, it's probably not one in a billion, especially considering the number of bullets fired at Gallipoli. However, if modern bullets hit each other after they've been fired, generally very little remains of them – they pretty much explode into tiny bits. So the examples that do exist of these collisions date back to the nineteenth century, when bullets were made of a softer material and travelled at slower speeds.

Just to add to the confusion, there is some talk of soldiers, perhaps engineers, with a bit of time on their hands and access to plenty of ammunition, tools and workshops, faking collided bullets like these. After all, they make great souvenirs and collector's items – like bullets that struck a bible, coin, cigarette case and so on.

But that's not what we are seeing in this picture. What we're looking at is a bullet fired at stationary ammunition. Which is not as rare as the claim suggested.

75

These mysterious photos show an abandoned medieval village

What you may have been told

This wonderful photo shows an old well in a little square surrounded by medieval houses. Isn't it amazing, isn't it romantic? Some claim it is in Scotland; wouldn't you like to visit it some day? It looks like the people have only just left, or maybe it's been deserted since the days of the Black Death. This is a real medieval village that was abandoned, but nobody knows where it is . . .

The debunking

This gorgeous photo sparks your curiosity and makes your imagination run wild. Where exactly is it, are you able to visit it, why was it abandoned? And actually, how has that very old bucket survived hanging in water like that for all this time . . . ?

As romantic and exciting as the idea of an centuries-old deserted village is, and although there really are abandoned villages in Scotland, that is not what we are seeing in this photo.

The scene almost looks like something out of a fairy tale and that's because it is – a modern-day version of a fairy tale: a film. It is relatively easy to find out where the photo was really taken. Several fact checkers have already discovered that it was taken at Studio Babelsberg just outside Berlin in Germany, which is the oldest large-scale film studio in the world. The property covers a total area of about 460,000 square metres (5,000,000 square feet) and thanks to its size, film sets can be left standing instead of being demolished as soon as the filming is finished.

Although the studio has a very popular large film theme park attached to it, with a 'medieval' area, the place where the photo was taken is not accessible to the public. So the photo had to have been taken by someone working on a film. On the Babelsberg website, I found out that the film set was last used for the shooting of *Hansel and Gretel Witch Hunters*, filmed in the first half of 2011. Could the photo be from that shoot? I didn't know.

The photo started getting attention when it was shared online on the Imgur image-hosting website with the title 'Skyrim in real life', after the popular video game. Even though one of the commenters had explained that it was a film set, the picture soon started living a life of its own. When someone shared it online as an abandoned village in Scotland, it triggered people's imagination and it went viral.

I hadn't considered writing an article about the photo because so many fact checkers had already debunked it, but it did annoy me that the real origin of the photo had remained a mystery. So I decided to take one last look at this case and had a breakthrough.

I stumbled upon an account on the photo-hosting website Flickr with the mystery photo, along with several other pictures that made me wonder if the person who uploaded them was perhaps the original photographer. The photo was uploaded in 2013, earlier than any other copy of the photo I found online. From this Flickr account, I could tell that user 3PASSA was into urban exploring (or urbex, if you're hip and cool), which involves going around old, abandoned places – sometimes hospitals, army barracks and factories, with broken windows, forgotten artefacts and spooky rooms – and taking pictures. The results are often gorgeous and always fascinating.

Many of the photos uploaded by that account were taken in and around Berlin, another clue. The account also shared photos of props and models the photographer had taken as part of their job. I clearly was on the right track: someone living in Berlin, working in the film and TV industry, who had uploaded a photo of the Studio Babelsberg film set . . . yes, I was close!

I did a bit more detective work. Via his Flickr profile, I learned his name was Alex. I've been in the same line of work for quite a few years. Besides being a film and TV researcher, I've also dressed a few historical sets, made some props and was even involved with special effects. So I pulled a few strings, bothered some of the people in the business I used to work with and looked everywhere.

Once more, luck was on my side. I found a certain Alex Friedrich on LinkedIn and when I checked his website it was clear that I'd found the right man. I contacted Alex and he confirmed that he had taken THE photo and that he knew the photo was being shared with the fake story attached to it. He also told me that the village was originally built not for *Hansel and Gretel Witch Hunters* but for *Anonymous* (2011), a film about Shakespeare. Originally, it even included a replica of the famous Globe theatre, but once filming was done that was demolished, while the rest of the buildings were turned into the town we know from the later film.

Alex worked on *Hansel and Gretel* as a props maker and took a few pictures after the filming was done. He also told me that both sets were built during the winter, sometimes with temperatures of −10° C! Which may sound insane, but most films are recorded in spring and summer and building a set takes a while, so sometimes there's no other time to do it.

There *are* real abandoned villages in Scotland, although of course none of those looks like the one in the photo. For instance, there is the archipelago of St Kilda, which was inhabited for almost 2,000 years but abandoned in the 1930s, and the village of Lawers in Perthshire, which recently made the news when it was put up for sale (including old ruins and a ghost, although I doubt the estate agent dared to guarantee that the place was definitely haunted).

I felt like a detective who had cracked another case – albeit a relatively trivial one. But it is just so rewarding to solve a mystery, no matter how important it is.

76

Hugh Hefner's grandpa invented the Playboy Bunnies

What you may have been told

It is quite a peculiar Victorian photo: a gentleman is standing on the porch of a house with four lovely ladies, who all have bunny ears on their heads. A sign above the door states 'The Jack Rabbit Club'. The man is Hugh Hefner's grandfather and the women are the very first Playboy Bunnies!

Did you know they've been around this long? No, me neither. I thought they were a 1960s thing, but photos don't lie . . . do they?

The debunking

Of course photos lie, a lot. I think we've established that!

It is a fun photo and of course people want to believe it really shows the early history of the Playboy Bunnies, because when you see a woman with bunny ears, that's what you think about. At least, if you're of a certain generation.

I started by looking for 'The Jack Rabbit Club' in archives and old newspapers and did find one, but it was a veterans' sports club, founded in 1891. Although a club whose stated purpose is to 'cultivate sports of the gun and rod' sounds like a good cover-up for a place where chaps get to hang out with pretty lasses without their wives finding out, nothing of what I discovered about the club suggests it was even remotely more exciting than what it claimed it was.

One of the first steps I take when investigating a photo is finding the biggest copy of it with the best resolution. This is relatively easy with a good search engine. I then realised that the picture that was being shared online was missing a bit. Someone had cut the bottom off the photo but it was still attached to the version I found and there was text on it: '© Steven Cook 2011'.

Well, that of course unlocked the case!

The photo itself is real but has been altered by British-born artist, photographer and graphic designer Steven Cook for his *Alternity* series. For this collection, he created strange and wonderful scenes by mixing his own photography and old photos, with unusual and sometimes magical results. After finding the source of the picture, I got in touch with Mr Cook, who was kind enough to answer all my questions.

Unfortunately, the original, unedited photo is currently lost in his archives so I couldn't add it here as the ultimate proof. Mr Cook confirmed that he added the sign above the door to the picture, and obviously the bunny ears are also not original. So besides not crediting the artist and owner of the picture, people are sharing it online without mentioning (or even realising) that it is not a genuine photo, and are thus spreading fake history.

77

This is the world's first Miss World

What you may have been told

A very old photo shows a beautiful lady, but not just any lady — she is the first Miss World ever! Did you know that kind of thing has been going on for over a century?

The debunking

The Miss World contests have played a part in most of our lives – we've either seen them, read about them or tried to avoid them. Seeing the very first winner and realising that the contest has been going on for that long is interesting to most people and that makes it a popular social media topic. But the photo does not show the first Miss World.

A relatively basic reverse-image search quickly told me that the lady in the picture is Cléo de Mérode, a woman famous for dancing and performing, for being glamorous and for her beauty. The illegitimate daughter of a baroness and a judge, her talent for performing was soon obvious and she first performed at the Paris Opéra aged 11. But she became even more famous because of her appearance – the clothes she appeared in and how she wore her hair were the talk of Paris, and she was copied everywhere. Famous artists painted and made sculptures of her, and photos of her became incredibly popular, both in France and abroad.

Soon her appearance was known across the world. Of course, there were countless rumours spread about her as well, like the claim that she had an affair with King Leopold II of Belgium – yes, the monster of the Congo Free State. The press even made up the name 'Cléopold'. Sounds familiar, doesn't it? They still do that today, combining names of celebrities. That whole story was nonsense, though, more fake history.

We can say that she was perhaps the first modern global image-based celebrity, more famous for her image and behaviour than for her talent. In a way, she was perhaps the first unofficial Miss World, famous for her looks, considered the prettiest woman of her time. She may have won the first Miss World contest if it had existed at the time, but it didn't. She wasn't given the title. She was not the first Miss World.

The Festival of Britain Bikini Girl beauty contest was organised in London in 1951, but with a title like that it's no wonder the media went with Miss World, which the rather smart organiser Eric Morley quickly registered as a trademark. And when he heard of the Americans organising Miss Universe a year later, Eric made his alternative – originally a one-off event – an annual thing; that'll teach 'em.

Anyway, when this event took place, Cléo de Mérode was 76 years old and, unsurprisingly, she did not take part in the pageant. The winner was Kerstin 'Kiki' Håkansson from Sweden. She was 22 and not easily confused with Miss de Mérode at the time.

78

This is the world's first robot

What you may have been told

An amazing photo shows a robot standing among several Black soldiers, somewhere in America in the 1890s. We're not told anything about who the men were or what the robot is doing there, but it looks like he is ready for battle. The only thing the text accompanying the picture tells us is that this is the world's first robot...

The debunking

It may be difficult for you and me to understand that people are falling for this, but they are.

It is a great picture, a first-class Photoshop job, but most of us will automatically dismiss it because, well, it just doesn't make sense, no matter how cool the picture looks. It's appealing, it has steampunk and H.G. Wells vibes about it, but alas, it isn't really a Victorian robot.

The robot in this picture is called Boilerplate and he's a fictional character invented by artist Paul Guinan, not in the 1890s but over a century later. Mr Guinan made a model robot and created a whole website about the adventures of Boilerplate, placing him in real historical situations. A wonderful book, *Boilerplate: History's Mechanical Marvel*, was produced with co-author Anina Bennett, and there's even merchandise. Mr Guinan did such a good job that it fooled quite a few people but it was soon debunked. Still, it's quite impressive that people fall for it to this day.

The photo into which Boilerplate was Photoshopped is fascinating, even without the robot. The men in it are so-called 'Buffalo soldiers', originally members of the 10th Cavalry Regiment of the US Army, which consisted of Black soldiers, taking a break while escorting General Wesley Merritt across the country in 1894. Native Americans gave them the Buffalo nickname and it was adopted by several regiments of the then-called 'colored cavalry', formed after the American Civil War. They saw action in several wars, including the Indian wars, the Mexican border war and even the First and Second World Wars.

But the picture has left us with a question – if good old Boilerplate wasn't the first robot, what was?

The answer, of course, depends a lot on how we define 'robot'. If we go for the very basic meaning of the word and start looking for the first device that can replicate human movement and function automatically, one could claim that automata were the first robots. These mechanical wind-up devices, often depicting humans or animals, could follow a pre-determined sequence of operations, though they are perhaps best compared to today's animatronics. There have been stories about automata – statues, furniture and so on – that moved on their own and reacted to humans dating back to ancient times. So it's likely going to be impossible to find out which one was the first. Some were clearly mythical; stories about them were probably made up, or are of dubious origin, which does not make things any easier.

Still, it is worth looking up automaton videos online. It is absolutely amazing what extremely smart people could create centuries ago. The one that German cabinet maker David Roentgen made in 1784, of Queen Marie Antoinette playing eight tunes on a dulcimer, is especially impressive.

79

The pyramids were
built by slaves

What you may have been told

The great pyramids in Egypt were built by slaves; it even says so in the Bible.

The debunking

We all know the image: slaves dragging huge stones up ramps while a master whips them; but the scene is mostly fantasy. Yes, there were slaves in ancient Egypt and somewhere along the production line they were very likely involved in the building of the pyramids – after all, slavery was part of daily life. So I don't think we can say they had absolutely nothing to do with the construction of the pyramids, but there is no evidence that they actually built them.

And no, it is not mentioned in the Bible either. The book of Exodus does mention that Hebrew slaves were forced to work 'in mortar and brick' but it doesn't specify that these were used for pyramids:

And the Egyptians were in dread of the people of Israel. So they ruthlessly made the people of Israel work as slaves and made their lives bitter with hard service, in mortar and brick, and in all kinds of work in the field. In all their work they ruthlessly made them work as slaves.

The myth was probably born because someone misunderstood what Herodotus, the ancient Greek historian known as both the 'Father of History' and 'Father of Lies', wrote in his *Histories* (in 430 BC, long after the fact) about the pyramids:

> *To some, [the king] assigned the task of dragging stones from the quarries in the Arabian mountains to the Nile; and after the stones were ferried across the river in boats, he organised others to receive and drag them to the mountains called Libyan. They worked in gangs of a hundred thousand men, each gang for three months. For ten years the people wore themselves out building the road over which the stones were dragged, work which was in my opinion not much lighter at all than the building of the pyramid.*

Somewhere along the line someone added one and one and ended up with three. And then Hollywood got involved and the image of a shirtless Charlton Heston asking Pharaoh Yul Brenner to let his people go embedded itself in the general consciousness.

It wasn't until relatively recently that historians and archaeologists started to find evidence that clashed with the long-accepted story. Historians started to wonder where the people who worked on the pyramids lived; building them would have required thousands of labourers who all had to live somewhere. Near the pyramids, they found the workers' city. As expected, it was huge, but it didn't look like a place where you'd keep slaves! Along well-made streets there were large dormitory-like houses surrounded with evidence of fish preparation, cattle being butchered and bread being baked on a huge scale. These workers enjoyed a good diet of high-quality food – luxurious even, the kinds of meals that wouldn't be wasted on common slaves that had been whipped and worked to the bone all day. That would just be silly.

In one papyrus letter, an expedition leader complains about how it's going to take too much time to provide his workmen with clothes. So the labourers were given good housing, great food and clothing. This shows that the men were looked after very well but it may also mean they received all this as payment for their work. Slaves don't get paid.

The archaeologists found graffiti on some of the buildings, including the names of some of the workers' crews. One called their group 'the drunkards of Menkaure', who sound like they were a fun bunch. Does that sound like something slaves would do? Give their gang a funny name? Would slaves even be able to become drunkards on their likely meagre rations?

They also found the remains of some of these builders in a special cemetery near the ruins of the city and very close to the tombs of the pharaohs. If you were a rich, powerful person, a demi-god, would you want your slaves to spend eternity near you? I wouldn't. Their ghosts can stay out of sight and float to work every day. Their proximity to the pharaohs was a sign of respect, something not afforded to the average person. The human remains showed signs of arthritis, damage and wear on their spines; the work was evidently tough and demanding. This makes it tempting to assume they were forced to do this work, but there are many reasons people will do hard, punishing work. Some of the skeletons actually showed evidence of medical treatment: damaged hands and legs that were operated on. Someone had cared for them for days, perhaps weeks or even longer, while they couldn't work. Which, again, is something people probably would not have bothered with if these workers had been ordinary slaves. Some of the labourers may have been working in order to pay their taxes, which is a little less voluntary, but still not slavery.

But why would they have done this dangerous and very demanding hard work if they weren't forced to? Besides being paid, spoiled and perhaps paying their taxes by doing this work, they may have also considered it an honour to work on such important buildings, and believed they would be rewarded in the afterlife. It was, of course, also a steady job – building a pyramid took decades! Besides, people have been risking their health for work throughout history. Those who worked on the European medieval cathedrals risked their lives, but they were not slaves. Victorian mineworkers destroyed their lungs to make a living, but they were not slaves. And today many of us ruin our backs by sitting in front of a computer screen from nine to five and we're not slaves either – well, not technically, anyway. We may not always have much of a choice, but we still get paid and aren't someone's property.

So, in conclusion, there is a lot of evidence that shows the pyramids were built by well-looked-after labourers, and no evidence at all that they were built by slaves. Oh, and the pyramids were also not built by aliens, just so you know.

80

This is a photo of Bill the Butcher, the infamous nineteenth-century street-gang leader

What you may have been told

Have you seen *Gangs of New York*, the 2002 film directed by Martin Scorsese starring Leonardo DiCaprio, Cameron Diaz, and Daniel Day-Lewis as William 'Bill the Butcher' Cutting? That character was based on a genuine nineteenth-century gang leader called William Poole and this is a photo of him, looking even scarier than he was portrayed in the film. Just look at him, standing there – a dirty apron with a large knife attached to it, holding a saw and a cleaver. Under his fancy top hat, he stares out at you, with one arched eyebrow . . . yeah, he sure was a scary chap.

The debunking

The film *Gangs of New York* made quite an impression on many people and is still relatively well known. One of the reasons the film is still popular is because of Day-Lewis's portrayal of Bill the Butcher, a dangerous, violent psychopath who somehow manages to still be appealing (sometimes, a bit), with his tongue as sharp as his knives, his wit as powerful as his fists. He has achieved a cult status that may have transcended the film itself, as his lines are still shared around by people who've never seen the film. He's been turned into a popular gif on social media. People even used his image and words to get people to support Donald Trump, not realising that Bill was a bad guy in the film, I assume.

Anyway, the film character was charismatic and popular and roughly based on a real historical character, so it makes perfect sense that people started looking into the story of the real William Poole.

He was a butcher, trained by his father, but also a volunteer firefighter, which was a very competitive side-job back then as there were many fires and several fire companies who, sometimes literally, fought over who would extinguish the fire. William founded and led the Bowery Boys gang – tough guys who would often try to stop other firefighters from doing their job till the ones William worked with arrived on the scene.

Bill was someone you wouldn't want as your opponent. He stood six-foot tall and weighed over 200 pounds, was good at boxing but also a very dirty fighter who broke all the rules. If you got into a scrap with him, you'd be lucky if he didn't bite your nose off, gouge your eyes out or kill you. He also despised everyone who didn't share his race or religion, who were new immigrants to the United States, who disagreed with his views or just looked the wrong way at him. He made many enemies and eventually this was his undoing: in 1855 he was shot and it took him several very long and painful days to die.

But the man in the photo is not him.

He looks fascinating but unfortunately all I can tell you about him is that he was a butcher who had his photo taken *c.* 1875, 20 years after Poole died. I'm also not sure if he fits the description of the rather large and heavy Bill. This photo is a professional portrait of a man wanting to show the tools of his trade; it's not his fault that those objects look scary to us. Mind you, that jaunty top hat does add something unsettling, at least to our modern eyes.

The first step most people take when they want to know more about something they've just seen in a film is of course rushing to Wikipedia. Don't get me wrong, I love Wikipedia; it's an amazing site of immeasurable value. As a researcher, it's always my first step as well, but I make sure that it is never my last.

As wonderful and rich as each article on that website is, there's always a chance a mistake has slipped in. While this is not as common as people often claim, especially if the page in question tells them something they don't want to hear, it is still something to keep in mind. And I fear this is one of those cases where we can probably blame Wikipedia for a bit of fake history, as the page on William Poole added this wrong photo in August 2016. The photo was removed within a couple of months but the damage was already done. Before the error was fixed the photo was also shared on Reddit and it's been going around ever since.

I can't find an earlier use of the photo with the claim that it depicts Bill the Butcher so I'm blaming Wikipedia but, to be fair, the editor who uploaded the photo may of course have seen it used as such elsewhere.

I can't help but wonder if there's a ghost of a butcher somewhere out there who's either really angry or honoured to be mistaken for William Poole.

81

The world's first computer virus was a universal message of peace

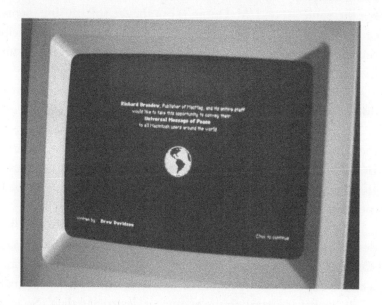

What you may have been told

Yes, it's another 'world's first' claim. There are entire social media accounts based on this subject and they are almost always wrong. But *surely* this time it's real. Look, they've even got a picture! Folks, step right up, take a peek. This text about a Universal Message of Peace is the very first computer virus ever, created all the way back in 1988! It must be true, it's on an old computer monitor – remember those heavy plastic beige monsters?

The debunking

The history of things like computer viruses is now actual old-timey stuff that young people don't know about, while to some of us it feels like it only happened yesterday.

We've all dealt with computer viruses. They don't seem to be as big a deal as they used to be a couple of decades ago (remember the panic around 'MyDoom'?) but they're still causing plenty of trouble and, of course, may one day end civilisation and help the robots take over the world, but I'm not here to write about the future.

Anyway, let's start the debunking before my computer starts doing weird things.

The photo shared does show a virus. So far, so good. It shows the so-called 'MacMag' virus in action. It was created by Richard Brandow and Drew Davidson in 1988 and was relatively harmless. It only infected Macintosh computers and all it did was show a message of peace. Which is nice, but was it the first?

As always, researching such claims begins with looking up the definition of what we're talking about, so according to the *Oxford English Dictionary* (2010), a computer virus is: 'a piece of code which is capable of copying itself and typically has a detrimental effect, such as corrupting the system or destroying data'. So just to be sure, it does not need to be spread via the internet.

The MacMag virus was predated by several other computer viruses. Here's a short list of the ones I could find. There may have been more and even earlier ones, so if you know any, get in touch.

'Creeper worm' 1971
'Wabbit' 1974
'Animal' 1975
'Elk cloner' 1982

'Brain' 1986
'Vienna' 1987
'SCA virus' 1987
'Lehigh' 1987

So it seems that, for now, the 1971 'Creeper worm' was the first virus. There was an earlier attack on the Burroughs 5500 at the University of Washington Computer Center in 1969, but I don't think it technically qualifies as a virus as it was more of a hack.

I stopped adding viruses to the list after 1987 because that's when things started getting out of hand. But the 'Morris' worm from 1988 deserves a special mention as it was the first that spread via the internet.

82

Europeans built a bridge in Ethiopia but locals couldn't repair it and crossed the river with ropes

What you may have been told

A picture shows men using a rope to climb across a river via the ruins of a very old-looking bridge. The caption tells us that the bridge is in Ethiopia, and was built by Europeans centuries ago but that the Africans never rebuilt it. Which just proves that Europeans are better, built lots of great things in Africa, and that

Africans just are not advanced enough to properly repair things when they break them.

The debunking

First of all, sorry about that intro. It's pretty vile, but the intent here is quite obvious – the caption suggests that Europeans built great bridges but that Africans are clearly unable to maintain or restore them. This is one of those examples of fake history that instead of being a relatively harmless bit of nonsense is being weaponised to spread an awful ideology.

The claim perfectly fits a bias many people have, conscious or unconscious. Many of us outside Africa have grown up knowing nothing about Ethiopia but what we occasionally saw in the news – wars, genocide, political chaos, famines and poverty. The way this caption works is smart, which makes it even more dangerous. 'Look, there's the photo, we see the bridge, it's old, it looks European, kind of Roman perhaps, and it's been clearly broken for a long time and there are people climbing to the other side.' And because many of us know so little about Ethiopia, it is convincing. But it's nonsense, of course.

So, let's start with the basics.

The bridge is real. It's called the Sebara Dildiy, which means broken bridge, so unsurprisingly it is really broken. It also is really in Ethiopia. It is one of several 'Portuguese' bridges across the Blue Nile. They all look similar and they all have a style that looks a bit Roman. It is not clear who built them but there appears to be a clear European influence. Some people think that the technology to build this specific style of bridge may have come from Portuguese soldiers who were in the region during the seventeenth century, and they may even have built them.

Professor Richard Pankhurst, a well-known Ethiopianist (yes, I also didn't know that was a word) and son of the famous suffragette Sylvia Pankhurst, moved to Ethiopia with his mother in 1956 and stayed for 20 years. He taught at the university there and was the founding director of the Institute of Ethiopian Studies. According to him, the first of the 'Portuguese bridges' was built by Indian stonemasons during the reign of Emperor Susenyos I, who reigned from 1607 to 1632, and later bridges were built in the same manner during the rule of his son, Emperor Fasilides. Several contemporary accounts by Jesuits confirm this. I find Pankhurst convincing as a historian – after all, he lived in the region and did not just study physical, mostly European, sources, but also had access to local oral history. I think this claim is more convincing than the one about Portuguese soldiers building them.

Emperor Fasilides was also responsible for the building of Fasil Ghebbi, an amazing castle in Gondar. When looking at it, you may think it looks European, but it was actually influenced by Arab, Nubian and Hindu architecture. Ethiopia adopted Christianity very early on (second century AD), traded with both the Roman Empire and India, and had other cultural connections, so the region was not as isolated from the rest of the world as some may have thought.

So although Ethiopians already knew how to build bridges, it is not completely clear who brought the technology and knowledge for building these specific bridges to the region, or who physically built them. I'm leaning towards the claim that it was Indians who brought the knowledge and who, together with the locals, built them by order of the emperor of Ethiopia. Which makes sense, as it seems the Portuguese may have been expelled from the region before some of the bridges were built.

Unfortunately the Blue Nile is a temperamental river that regularly floods and the bridges were often damaged and had to be repaired many times – by the Ethiopians, who of course knew what they were doing. So the Sebara Dildiy was broken and repaired frequently, thereby earning its name. But the damage we see on the photo was done on purpose and for a good cause.

In 1935, Ethiopia was invaded by Fascist Italy. To hinder the progress of Mussolini's troops, local people decided to destroy the bridge. A large group demolished part of it using farming tools, but sadly its collapse killed 40 of these brave heroes. That was the last time the bridge was seriously damaged.

So it's not like it's been damaged and neglected for centuries, like the claim suggests. After this last destruction it was repaired a few times, but temporarily, with simple wooden crossings, wires and so on. Repairing it properly would cost a lot of money and Ethiopia had more important things to spend money on after the war.

Another bridge destroyed during the war that was more important, the Abbay bridge, had to be rebuilt. A massive, state-of-the-art modern concrete bridge was opened in 1948 and others were to follow. So it wasn't like Ethiopians didn't know how to maintain bridges, they just chose not to repair some of them and instead focused on building better, newer bridges elsewhere.

It's just not cricket to post a picture of an old ruined bridge and suggest it's that way because of neglect and the inability of local people. Imagine if we did that with European landmarks. There are quite a few aqueducts, theatres and bridges in that part of the world that haven't been repaired for centuries! Can someone please help those poor natives fix Hadrian's Wall already?! It's been neglected for almost 2,000 years!

83

In Victorian times, Dr Batty's Asthma Cigarettes were advertised as good for your health

What you may have been told

A wonderful old Victorian enamel sign wants to sell us Dr Batty's Asthma Cigarettes, for the temporary relief of paroxysms of asthma. It claims to effectively treat asthma, hay fever, foul breath, all diseases of the throat, head colds, 'canker sours' and bronchial irritations. But it is not recommended for children under six years old. It's just the typical kind of wacky Victorian advertising we've come to expect from that era. Oh, silly ancestors! They really didn't know anything about health, did they?

The debunking

Weird historical adverts are always popular. There are loads to choose from and they're often racist, sexist, make no sense to us whatsoever or remind us of the crazy times when nobody seemed to care about health and safety. Which either amuses, annoys or makes us long for a past that never really was.

But when I first saw this advertisement, I immediately knew something wasn't quite right. I've studied countless Victorian images, adverts and enamel signs over the years and this one set off a few alarm bells.

Purely on visual terms, it isn't a real Victorian enamel sign but a picture trying to look like one. It is not embossed, painted or even printed on to the enamel. This is not a photo of a physical object.

One of the first things you can do when you're suspicious of something that uses text is to look up the font used. There are websites and apps that can help you figure out the name of the font and with that information you can easily figure out who made it and, more importantly in this case, when it was created. The results all suggested fonts that were not around in the Victorian era.

There actually were asthma cigarettes back then. This may sound weird to us but administering medication through smoking (inhalation therapy) is not that unusual and, of course, marijuana cigarettes are still used for the benefits they offer people suffering from certain conditions to this day. A genuine 1881 advert I found in a London newspaper tried to sell readers 'Cigares de

Joy' – because, you know, it sounds more fancy in French. They did not just promise immediate relief in cases of asthma, wheezing and winter cough – they promised a permanent cure. And unlike Dr Batty's cigarettes, they could be safely smoked by ladies and children. Phew!

As I was researching this ad I started focusing on Dr Batty's picture. Why did his face seem familiar to me? Suddenly I knew I had seen him before, very recently – in my house! No, not the actual man or his ghost, unfortunately, but the image of his face. As a historian, time traveller and general collector of old stuff, I've gathered quite a large collection of all sorts of peculiar artefacts. On my kitchen shelf I found the good doctor staring at me from the label of an old bottle of Sloan's Liniment, a painkiller. How did I not recognise him right away? And what are the odds of me actually owning evidence in a case I was investigating?

Anyway, the packaging on my old bottle identified the man as Dr Earl Sawyer Sloan (1848–1923), not Dr Batty. Dr Sloan was a famous American entrepreneur and philanthropist who didn't receive a lot of education but devoured books and spent so much time looking after and healing animals, especially horses, that he became a well-respected self-taught veterinarian. His father had used a sort of ointment on horses that would make their stiffened muscles relax and it became very popular. Sloan sold a lot of it but when one day a customer used it on their own back instead of their horse's they discovered it worked fantastically on humans as well. Sloan started calling himself a doctor, although he wasn't really one, put his face on the product, and soon became famous and rich.

It is highly unlikely that a contemporary brand would be stupid enough to steal this very famous face for its asthma cigarettes under another name. Not only would countless people have realised that this face was not that of Dr Batty and that the brand was thus dodgy, but Dr Sloan's lawyers may also have pounced on it.

While continuing my search, I eventually stumbled upon a website discussing this image that contained a confession by someone claiming to have made it:

I should be able to shed some light on this. The two fonts used are 'Manzanita' and 'Aristrocrat'. I work at a sign company and I designed this one as a fledgling graphic designer about 8 years ago. We still sell this one quite often. I found most of the wording from old ads for actual asthma cigarettes. I made up the line 'Not recommended for children under 6.' Seemed appropriate for the time . . . I think it is really funny how this has been presented as an authentic vintage advertisement on more than one site. Looks pretty fake to me!

Aaron Howe, 2011

I contacted Mr Howe and he replied, confirming his earlier comment on the ad that I had found. He was the designer. Case closed!

By the way, you can still get Sloan's Liniment today; asthma cigarettes, not so much.

84

This massive device was the world's first camera

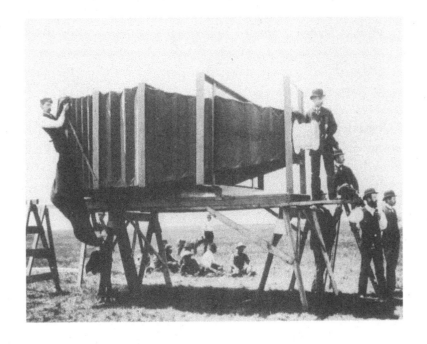

What you may have been told

Just look at this amazing photo! That massive camera needed a team to operate it and was the world's first ever camera. It says so on the picture, so it must be true.

The debunking

Another one of those 'world's first' claims. Don't they ever get one right?

It's a great photo, though, and if you don't know much about photography it sort of makes sense that the first camera was huge. After all, we old-timers remember how cameras used to be bigger when we were young and now they fit in a portable electronic telephoning device.

But it is a famous photo and the truth behind it is not that hard to figure out, so I think whoever wrote that caption knows it's not true. It's not the world's first camera, so what are we looking at? What is this giant camera?

This is the Mammoth camera, invented by George R. Lawrence (1868–1938), who is in the photo; he is the one standing by the lens on the right. Mr Lawrence was a bit of an inventor. Besides running a portrait studio he also kept tinkering and improving photography technology. He liked experimenting and took pictures by hanging his camera under kites and balloons, and later by taking photos from planes.

In 1899 or 1900 he was asked to take a detailed and very impressive photo of the Alton Limited Train, owned by the Chicago and Alton Railway. The train offered a type of luxury travel that we can barely even imagine today. But there was one problem: the train was long, it had eight cars and using a regular camera from a distance wouldn't do it much justice, as you'd have to stand very far away for the train to even fit in the frame.

Mr Lawrence explained to the train manufacturer that the way to photograph it would be to take lots of separate photos and then stick them together. But the company was not impressed. Its train was faultless, a perfect design, so sticking photos together wouldn't do the train justice. It wanted the train in one, massive photo.

So our hero took two months to build a special, giant camera just for this one photo. It weighed 900 pounds (408kg), 1,400 pounds (635kg) with the plateholder loaded. It contained the largest photographic lenses ever made (up to that moment), took a 243cm x 137cm (8 x 4.5 feet) photo plate, and had to be transported by train and set up by a team of men. It was rumoured to have cost over $5,000, which would be over $160,000 today.

After two and a half minutes of exposure the photo was taken and the result was amazing – a photo 244cm wide (96 inches) that showed off the train in perfect detail. It made a huge impression on anyone who saw it and a print was even shipped to the Exposition Universelle in Paris, but nobody believed it was real. The French consul-general was sent to inspect the camera and affidavits had to be signed to convince the organisers it was an actual giant photo.

There's no way for us to comprehend the quality of this photograph or the impact it made on the people seeing it in 1900 because, as far as I know, no full-sized or even half-decent quality version of the photo exists. It was a very impressive achievement, so it's a bit sad that the photo of Mr Lawrence's camera gets more attention than the photo he took that day.

A wonderful pamphlet was published shortly after the photo was taken detailing the making of it, with impressive photos of the camera being put together, transported and so on. You can download a PDF copy of the leaflet on the Indiana Historical Society website.

Just a few years later, Mr Lawrence got quite a lot of fame with his amazing photo of San Francisco just days after the horrific earthquake of 1906, taken by hanging a 49-pound (22kg) camera from several kites. The result was a highly detailed, massive photo, like nobody had seen before. Copies sold like hot cakes and this one photo made Mr Lawrence a lot of money. Please look for a high-resolution version of this photo online; the detail is stunning.

We now know that 'the Mammoth' was not the world's first camera. So, what was?

As always, that depends a bit on your definition of a camera. One could argue that they've been around since people started experimenting with the camera obscura: a dark room or box with a lens through which rays of light travel, projecting an image of the outside on to the opposite wall – a technique discovered over 2,000 years ago.

But photographic cameras that could be used to make actual photographs have been around since the early 1800s. Lots of people experimented with photography but many of those early cameras were nothing more than that same camera obscura idea with a sensitive plate installed to catch the image – and unfortunately it always faded away again very quickly. It wasn't until someone managed to fix the photo and stop it from vanishing that, I think, we can start calling them proper photographic cameras.

And that was in 1822 when Joseph Nicéphore Niépce made the first photographic image of an engraving of Pope Pius VII, which was sadly lost. But many people know the photo he took in 1827, which survives to this day, and, as it doesn't just record an old engraving but an actual view out of a window, it is generally considered to be the first (surviving) photograph. This means that the camera Niépce used in those early days and that is now on display at the Musée Nicéphore Niépce could be the world's first camera – IF it is the one he used to make the world's first (surviving) photo with and IF we decide that a camera is only a camera if it can be used to make a permanent photograph.

If we decide that anything ever called a camera can technically be the 'world's first camera' then things get even more complicated, as it comes from the ancient Greek καμάρα, which roughly means 'anything with an arched cover, a covered carriage or boat, a vaulted chamber, a vault'.

Good luck finding the first iteration of that type of camera!

85

This is the first cat photo ever taken

What you may have been told

The internet loves cats. That should not come as a surprise to you, if you've ever been anywhere near the internet, as they really are all over it. And just look at this wonderful creature: this is the oldest photo of a cat ever made!

The debunking

When the photo is shared the claim is generally something like, 'The first ever photo of a cat, 1880'. That date was the first thing that caught my eye, as we know that photography has been around since the 1820s. Although animals are of course notoriously bad at sitting still, and cats are notoriously stubborn, so I could understand there not being a lot of photos of them in the early years when a photo still took a couple of minutes, 60 years of nobody photographing little Fluffy still seemed highly unlikely.

I tried to trace the photo to its origin but have to admit I couldn't. It was uploaded to photo-hosting site Flickr in 2009. Perhaps it was just a random old photo someone found, possibly a postcard, but we may never know as the account is no longer active and the post has vanished. I've studied a lot of historical photos (it's my job, after all) but I wouldn't want to make a claim about the age of the photo. I don't think it is from the 1880s, but can't really say anything certain about when it was made. Still, even if it really was taken in the 1880s, we know there were people making cat photos before that time.

In the 1870s, Harry Pointer from Brighton, England, was not just making cat photos, he made so many and they were so wonderful that this work was making him famous. Harry was a former corporal in the 1st Regiment of the Life Guards, protecting Queen Victoria at Buckingham Palace. He lived with his wife and children in Brighton and for a while made a living as an instructor in military drill at a public school, which was considered a sort of physical exercise at the time – learning a bit of strict discipline while you get healthy!

Harry's wife, Rosa Myra Drummond, was an accomplished artist in her own right, making wonderful paintings and drawings, mostly portraits. Maybe it was her work that inspired Harry to switch careers and become a photographer, a job she probably helped him with. At the time, '*carte de visite*' portrait photos were a huge craze. Everybody wanted a little business card-sized portrait to trade with friends, to collect or to try to impress someone you fancied. Perhaps a bit like Facebook.

Harry was a good photographer but his photos didn't stand out. But that all changed when he started taking pictures of cats in the late 1860s. Sometimes the cats were just doing cat stuff, like sleeping, eating, sitting, planning world domination – the usual. But he also decided to have a bit of fun and started to create little scenes with the cats and then added amusing captions. Yes, I guess we can say he invented what the internet now knows as 'LOLcatz'.

According to the media at the time, Harry had a special way with cats. So he went from screaming orders at schoolchildren to somehow convincing cats to sit and look just the way he wanted and then not move for a bit. I can't help but imagine this big, stern, shouty man whispering sweet little nothings at kittens so they pose for his adorable little photos. Within a couple of years, he had made over one hundred of these photos and they became very popular. Our Victorian ancestors felt the same way about adorable and funny cat pictures as we do.

Harry got a lot more work and even showed his photos at prestigious exhibitions, so he wasn't just taking funny pictures of pets. He kept working till his wife died and he was so overcome by grief that it may have been the cause of his own death a few months later.

Harry was famous for his cat photos by the early 1870s, but these weren't the first. So what was the first cat photo?

I wish we knew.

When Harry started his career as a photographer in the 1860s, people had been taking daguerreotype photos of lots of subjects. You name it, some photography pioneer tried to capture it on plate. So if we want to try to find the first cat photo that survived, we'll need to look at those early experiments.

There are lots of photos of cats that were made going back as far as the 1840s and 1850s, but unfortunately not every photographer realised that one day in the far future, people would want to know exactly when they took which photo, where, and what the cat's name was.

So we do have some very old cat photos but we don't really know when exactly they were taken. Most early cat daguerreotypes are from the 1850s, so for now, a good contender is one dated between 1843 and 1850 (image EGH064 on www.daguerreobase.org) that shows a group of people having a fancy dinner. In a corner you see a cat, clearly waiting for the perfect moment to steal food.

86

This is the first dog photo ever taken

What you may have been told

So that first cat photo you saw online wasn't the first cat photo ever made. That's sad. But not to worry, surely we know when the first ever dog photo was taken? If I put 'first dog photo ever made' into Google then it comes right up! It's a glorious poodle, with a bow around her neck, in a gold frame. It looks like a daguerreotype, the first photo technology available to the public, surely this must be right . . . ?

The debunking

I agree, the photo is wonderful. What a fabulous poodle! Yes, she is a good girl, of course she is. But is it the oldest photo of a dog ever taken? Probably not.

Just like with the cat photos, we have the same problem: photographers of old who don't realise they're making history and thus didn't keep detailed notes for us future historians. (While we're on the topic, come on, reader, run upstairs, grab that old box with photos from the attic and write as much information about the picture on the back of each one. Please, I'm begging you. One day someone is going to be so happy you did.)

Anyway, the photo that often pops up with the claim that it's the oldest dog photo was first shared online in 2009 when Sotheby's was auctioning off a collection of old photographs. Lot 73 was described as: 'Anonymous American Photographer. POODLE, WITH BOW, ON TABLE. Sixth-plate daguerreotype, modern seal, cased, 1850s. Estimate 5,000–7,000 USD.'

It eventually sold for $8,125.

But alas, we don't know who took the photo or when and where. All we have is an educated guess that puts it in the 1850s. The experts at Sotheby's know what they are talking about and so will have done a good job of dating the photo, but they would agree with me that this is as close as we're going to get to putting a year on it – it could be older, it could be more recent. At the time, this was reported as being *one of* the earliest dog photos ever, which is true. But then, somewhere along the line, someone lazy, in a hurry, unbothered, forgot these crucial words and it became 'the earliest dog photo ever'.

There are two photos that I think are contenders for the earliest dog photo and they both predate the 1850s. So if the Sotheby's experts are right, which they probably are, both of the following photos are older.

The first contender, oddly enough, looks a lot more recent

than any of the others. My first thought was that there had been a mistake and this photo was from the 1920s but that's because the paper frame of the photo has a little doghouse drawn on it in a very modern-looking way.

The photo was made by Louis-Auguste Bisson, one of the countless daguerreotype pioneers who were experimenting with the new technique at the time. Louis-Auguste was a fascinating man who took some amazing photos, including on Mont Blanc (climbing up there with almost an army of porters just to carry his equipment), and he made one of only three known photographs of the composer Frédéric Chopin.

He took the photo of the dog and made the pretty frame for his childhood neighbour Rosa Bonheur, who became his sister when her mother died and Louis-Auguste's family adopted her. Once more we have to rely on the research done by historians and museum experts from the Metropolitan Museum of Art in New York, but this photo has been dated to 1841–9.

But there's one final contender, even though it is really difficult to find any information about this photo.

While researching this subject, I stumbled upon a great website run by Claude Marillier. It is full of fascinating articles about photography written by Claude's late father, Pierre G. Harmant, and her husband, Paul Marillier. Pierre had been fascinated by history and photography and wrote lots of wonderful articles on the subject. It was a joy to read through the articles and on one page there is a collection of photos taken by Daguerre himself – yes, the 'father of photography'. All of his pictures are among the earliest ever taken; most are from the 1840s. When he started using smaller format plates he began to take photos of every-thing: family, friends and . . . his dog Médor?

This is from a letter written in 1837:

I thank you, my dear Isidore, for sending us gingerbread, which you make for our little Médor, I am convinced that he will be very sensitive to this kind memory from you and that at the next occasion he will devour you with caresses.

The photo placed by this letter on that website shows a lovely white dog holding a stick.

I've tried to trace the photo to a source but can't, so all we know is this photo was used to illustrate a letter on a website. It proves nothing, but goodness it's tempting to think there's a connection. I've contacted experts and looked through countless books, but unfortunately I only have what's on the website to go on. But if it's Daguerre's, I reckon it was made between 1843 and 1844, not much later. So I think it might be the world's oldest dog photo . . . if only it could be proven.

Either way, Médor was a good boy! Yes, he was.

87

The Victorians covered furniture legs because they were too arousing

What you may have been told

The Victorians were so prudish and sexually oppressed that they covered up furniture and piano legs to avoid causing arousal.

The debunking

Let's get one thing firmly established: the Victorians were a randy bunch. Yes, it may not be obvious from the image they projected to society, and it may clash with the view we have today of that era, but they were into sex, big time. They had crazy wild parties, wrote passionately about their steamy adventures in diaries and correspondence, and used any excuse to wear wild and often scandalous outfits. Sellers of erotica did big business, and guess what Victorians very quickly started using the relatively new invention of photography for . . .

Queen Victoria herself had an impressive collection of nude paintings. In short, and this may suprise you, Victorians, like us, were human.

They did NOT cover up the legs of furniture. Although I am sure someone, somewhere, sometime, was aroused by a well-shaped part of a piano or comfortable chaise lounge, furniture legs were not things that your average Victorian was so worried about that they obscured them from view.

The story started with Captain Frederick Marryat CB FRS, an Englishman who in 1839 published *Diary in America*, a book that was rather critical of American society and even mocked it. He went so far that Americans burned his books. Marryat wrote about a young American lady who was shocked by his use of the word 'leg' in front of a lady, which was just not done in polite society. She explained that the word 'limb' should be used instead. There is some truth to this claim; some did prefer to use the word limb to leg.

A few weeks later the captain wrote about having witnessed the following furniture-dressing scene:

However, that the ladies who visited their daughters might feel in its full force the extreme delicacy of the mistress of the establishment, and her care to preserve in their utmost purity the ideas of the young ladies under her charge, she had dressed all these four limbs in modest little trousers, with frills at the bottom of them!

So for once we know exactly how a myth was born. It's not certain if Marryat was poking fun at prudish Americans and made it up as a bit of satire, or if some Americans were pulling his limb and told the silly Englishman this as a joke, but there's no evidence at all for this being an actual habit, even in America. I'm yet to find a nineteenth-century photo of furniture with leg coverings; if you find any, please let me know.

British readers, of course, loved the story and couldn't resist poking fun at those strange Americans. It even became a running gag and a song about it was performed on stage. But then the French heard about it and started using the story to make fun of the English! That's just not cricket. And to make things even worse, the following generations, who, as is tradition, enjoyed mocking the silly habits of their parents and grandparents and who, naturally, think they're smarter and better than their ancestors, started mentioning the claim to mock the Victorians while forgetting that it was all just a silly joke!

88

During the Middle Ages, there were torches everywhere

What you may have been told

How did people light up their surroundings during the Middle Ages? With torches, of course!

We see them in every film and TV show, dramatically illuminating castles, inns, churches, generally stuck into handy holders, but they were also very practical to walk around with.

The debunking

They look fantastic and they fit the vision we have of that era so well. Dark castle corridors, the flickering light of the torch on the wall. Oh no, a baddy! So our brave knight grabs the torch and uses it to fight with. We've seen the scenes countless times and it makes sense – surely they must have been used a lot; medieval people didn't have electricity.

The main problem with torches is that they don't burn for very long. Fire needs fuel and if you look at the average torch, especially the ones on TV and in films, they're generally just some rags tied around a stick. But even a good-quality torch with the right fuel will rarely burn much longer than half an hour. Which makes them fine to use when you just need to walk a short distance at night but pretty useless to light hallways, rooms or even streets.

Just imagine the scene: the king is giving a speech to his men about the upcoming battle, suddenly the room starts getting dark and some servant with a basket full of torches enters the room and starts replacing them all, while mumbling apologies and annoying everybody.

He finally leaves, people can see again, the speech continues, the men cheer, time to look at the map and prepare for battle and . . . oh no, it's getting dark again and there's the irritating servant again . . . Every single torch would have to be replaced once or twice an hour, all evening, all night. It's no problem if you're making a film and have a crew of special effects assistants. I know because I used to be one. I was the one who rushed around grabbing burning torches from actors, extinguishing them and then lighting new ones for the next scene. It was quite scary to be honest because the extras all wore fancy hats and had their hair done with a ton of hairspray. One stupid move and the actor would have turned into a torch themselves. And that's of course another problem with torches: you've got an open fire at head height and sometimes also scarily close to wooden ceilings and beams. It's just asking for trouble, especially when people are walking around with spears, helmets, cloaks and pointy hats.

In medieval times, people did use torches but they often looked quite different from what we see on the screen – they were longer, thicker sticks on poles, which makes sense as that meant they could contain more fuel and burn for longer. People also used braziers, metal holders for coal or other fuel that were used for light but also as little portable heat sources.

One popular, longer-lasting, less dangerous and smelly alternative was, of course, the candle, but what we often don't realise is that for most of the Middle Ages these were quite expensive. Which means that although a room or hall lit with a ton of candles looks great, it would also have cost a fortune. This would be possible in a castle, a rich family's home or a church during a special event, service or feast, but not something you'd see that often. Beekeeping became big business around this time because beeswax for candles was in demand, but a simple beeswax candle could still cost as much as a day's wage.

People also made candles out of tallow, a rendered form of animal fat. Tallow candles were a lot cheaper but not as good – they were smoky and didn't smell very nice. But they did at least provide light!

The demand for candles kept increasing so wax had to be imported from countries that still had plenty of woods and land for bees to do their thing, which is how the Hanseatic League, a federation created to protect the interests of merchants and towns in several European cities, made part of its fortune.

It wouldn't be till the German Karl von Reichenbach in 1830 invented a method to turn petroleum into paraffin wax that good candles became affordable to most people.

So what would most people have used then? I find it interesting that this question doesn't seem to be an issue when we're talking about the Romans. Ask people what Romans used for light and many will tell you they used oil lamps. But that's what medieval people used as well! People often think that when the Roman Empire era ended there was some sort of apocalypse in Europe and people spontaneously forgot everything and went back to the Stone Age. But that really wasn't the case. Besides beeswax and tallow candles, common people and also the rich used oil lamps in all shapes and sizes, burning animal fat and various types of oil – including olive, sesame and grape seed, along with other kinds. They could be simple or fancy, with just one wick or several, hanging from the ceiling or placed on a table. They burn a lot longer than torches and are safer and cheaper. Still, try not to bump into them.

Oil lamps would be the most historically accurate lighting for film and TV series set in medieval times. And because they were often hanging from the ceiling or even enclosed in lanterns and lamps, you wouldn't even see the flame, so the set dresser should be able to cheat and just put a little LED light in them. This is one of those cases where the realistic solution is easier and cheaper than the nonsense one.

There was one more alternative way of lighting a room that you don't see represented very often on TV, so if you happen to spot one you know you're watching a well-researched production. This is the rushlight, which is the dried pith of the rush plant soaked in fat or tallow and placed in a holder. It's essentially just a little stick that slowly burns like a match – not very brightly, but the cheapest alternative besides the fireplace.

Then again, for many the day ended when the sun set anyway. It's really hard for us to imagine life with no electricity but for most of our ancestors, for most of history, the evenings were dark, very dark.

89

Beethoven was Black

What you may have been told

Did you know that Beethoven was Black? During his life, people called him swarthy. His family came from Flanders, which was once ruled by the Spanish, who were once ruled by the Moors, and his mother had an affair with a Moor so he was mixed race! But they whitewashed all the paintings of him to hide that he was Black, because of course racist white people didn't like it that such a famous composer was Black.

The debunking

I can understand why someone would want to believe this story. Beethoven was an amazing composer whose impact on music is undeniable, so any little-known 'fact' about him will be of interest, but you also get to upset a lot of people who for some reason can't stand the idea that Beethoven was not white. More importantly, it allows Black people an association with a genre and genius that they were and are so often denied in some parts of the world.

This may sound like something that is relatively recent, but it's a very old claim that just keeps coming back. People have been suggesting that Beethoven had African heritage since the early twentieth century.

Beethoven's family tree has been extensively researched, so we know who his parents and grandparents were, and we know what they looked like as they had their portraits painted. The

Beethovens can be traced back to before 1500 and pretty much all of them were Flemish; there's no trace of Spanish or African ancestors. Could one of Beethoven's ancestors have had a baby with a dark-skinned Spanish person descended from a Moor? Yes, it's possible, but unproven.

The 'Moor' bit is a strange part of this story. The low countries of Europe were indeed occupied by the Spanish in the sixteenth, seventeenth and early eighteenth centuries, long after the Moors had occupied Spain. The Moors, who hailed from the area we now call Morocco, had lost control over most of Spain by the thirteenth century and were, as far as we know, typically fairly light skinned. All of this was long before Beethoven was born in 1770.

Beethoven had dark hair and dark eyes, according to his portraits, and was described as being 'swarthy' by some of his contemporaries, which does mean 'dark' and could be used for someone with a very dark skin, but also for someone with just a slightly darker skin, a tan or even someone who just had dark hair. Blond, blue-eyed Germans may have considered someone who was white but had black hair and dark eyes 'swarthy'.

Beethoven's nickname was 'the Spaniard' and his childhood friend Gottfried Fischer described the boy Ludwig as having a 'dark-brown complexion', which can of course be interpreted as him being Black, and it may be the origin of the myth. But it could also describe someone whose skin and hair were darker than that of most people, as seen through the eyes of eighteenth-century Germans.

If Beethoven had been very dark skinned, people would have probably used other words to describe him. A girl who knew him when he was young, Fraülein von Kissow, described him as having an ugly red face full of pockmarks. Ouch, brutal.

Beethoven was a very famous man for most of his life and many portraits were made, including some he sat for, in person. We also have accounts from people who met Beethoven in person and then compared him to the portraits they had seen of him, which were at the time being sold in music stores. You'd imagine that if Beethoven looked nothing like his portraits, for instance by being brown or black skinned, someone would have mentioned it. I bet that people would even have noticed if he used make-up to hide his dark skin, as some people claim.

There are some prints and etches that make him look a bit darker. In part this has to do with the printing technique of the time; if you want to add depth or contrast but without colour, you do this by making some parts darker and others lighter. Beethoven looks different in different prints but many of these were mass produced, made by artists who never even met Beethoven, and sometimes they were coloured in with a bit of a tan. Louis Spohr, a violinist who had known Beethoven personally, was once asked by a Beethoven fan which of the many very different-looking portraits the girl had of him in her room was the most realistic. This tells us that Beethoven had fans who decorated their rooms with pictures of their idol, just like teenagers now who are obsessed with pop music, but it also confirms that it's dangerous to assume a portrait of anyone alive back then is necessarily accurate and realistic.

Although people gave him nicknames based on his dark hair and dark complexion, nobody who ever met him actually described him as being a Black man. That includes George Bridgetower, a composer who was Beethoven's friend (and later enemy) and had a Black father. If Beethoven came from a similar background, George would have mentioned it!

So there's no evidence that Beethoven was Black or mixed race. If he had been, people would have mentioned it, a lot. He could, of course, have had a Black ancestor we don't know about – anyone could – but again there's no evidence for that, just rumours and 'what if's.

Looking back at the world he lived in, most of us would assume that Beethoven would not have had the opportunities he had if he had been Black. This is true in some ways but we also know that

it didn't stop other Black men from becoming famous composers in the same time and place. Their skin colour and ethnicity
were often mentioned, not kept secret, and their portraits were
not white-washed: they were celebrated. This may be difficult
for people to believe, especially those who look at history from
an American perspective, who may assume that the situation in
Europe was the same as or worse than the situation in their own
country at the time. There was certainly racism, but there were
also famous Black artists. Both these things are true.

Claims that Beethoven was Black are easily debunked and
not taken seriously, but the real shame is in the fact that there's
time wasted on this discussion while it could be spent talking
about actual Black composers who were talented and famous in
their own right, who are being ignored. So instead of pointlessly
arguing about Beethoven being Black, let's talk about genuine
Black composers, including contemporaries and even friends of
Beethoven.

- George Augustus Polgreen Bridgetower (1778–1860) was
  born in Poland to a Swabian mother and a (probably)
  West Indian father who, according to George's baptismal
  record, was an African prince. He moved to London
  and was wooing the public on stage at the Drury Lane
  Theatre as a solo violinist when he was just ten years old.
  He toured Europe, performed for royals and presidents,
  and also with Beethoven, who was very impressed by
  George's talent.
- Joseph Bologne, Chevalier de Saint-George (1745–
  99), was born in the Lesser Antilles. His father was
  a planter and his mother an enslaved 16-year-old of
  Senegalese origin. Although Joseph was illegitimate,
  his father still acknowledged him, gave him the family
  name and took him to France for an education.
  Joseph became an officer of the king's bodyguard, was

admired for his fencing, horsemanship and dancing, and was quite popular with the ladies (which, if you see his portrait, makes a lot of sense). He was very talented with the violin and started composing music and operas, and became a star in France and England, both as a fencer and composer.

- Charles Ignatius Sancho (*c.* 1729– 80) was born on a slave ship, taken to England and given to two sisters to be their servant when he was only two years old. But he couldn't bear working for them and ran away to a duke who had often visited the sisters and was impressed by the boy. At the duke's house he was taught to read and immersed himself in music and poetry. When the duke and his wife died, they left Charles a substantial amount of money. He got married, had seven children, opened his own shop, wrote stories and plays, and composed music. He was the first person of African descent to vote in a general election in Britain and the first to receive an obituary in the British media.

All these men were talented and well-known composers, and they deserve more attention, more than an unprovable thesis about Beethoven maybe having a granny who could have had a baby with some chap who might have been Spanish and whose grandparents maybe were a bit Moorish. So do them and yourself a favour, forget about Black Beethoven and look up the gorgeous music these men made and start sharing their story instead.

An addendum: as I was finishing my book, an international group of researchers published a paper on the results of genomic analysis of Beethoven's hair. Enough locks had been gathered to determine which ones actually belonged to the composer and the scientific tests revealed a lot about him. Although their main goal was to learn more about his health (he had a genetic predisposition for liver disease and had a hepatitis B infection shortly before he died) the researchers also discovered that some people who have been claiming to be related to him were not (ouch), that a famous lock of his hair that a bestseller was written about was also not his (ouch again) and that his grandfather was not his grandfather! So at least that part of the rumour was true; his grandmother apparently did have an affair, but . . . Beethoven's real grandfather was not African. His ancestry is over 99 per cent European and the geographic clustering of his family tree is slap bang in the middle of Europe. There is no evidence whatsoever of any non-European genetic material in Beethoven's recent ancestry.

90

These women in China in 1922 are being punished for the crime of witchcraft

What you may have been told

A photo from 1922 shows three women with their heads stuck in a wooden board; it's their punishment for being witches! Even as recently as the early twentieth century, innocent women were suffering because they had been accused of witchcraft.

The debunking

The object the women are locked into is called a cangue. It really existed and was a common punishment for all sorts of crimes. Besides, of course, being humiliating, it was also very uncomfortable and painful. It's very much like a portable version of the 'pillory' we know from films and television, which is also impossible to avoid at countless museums, castles and fairs. But instead of sitting or standing with your hands, head and/or feet stuck in some holes, the cangue was worn around the neck. Sometimes it was chained to another criminal or a wall so that you couldn't walk very far – like to the nearest locksmith to let you out, for instance. But unlike the pillory or the stocks, being locked into a cangue sometimes involved a truly horrific fate: death by starvation.

While wearing this and being unable to go anywhere, prisoners depended on the kindness of passers-by to feed them, as they couldn't do that themselves. The crime the prisoners had committed was written on a piece of paper attached to the board, so you could read what they had done and decide if you wanted to help them eat or let them starve. If prisoners were in there for a long time and everybody in the village hated them, well, you can imagine how that might end. To make things even worse, the wooden board might be extra heavy, depending on the crime, slowly cutting into flesh the longer it was worn. And the shape meant the people wearing them couldn't really lie down and rest, so sooner or later it would drive them mad, sometimes literally. But often people were made to wear them for a only short time and being seen by everybody was the main punishment. They seem to have been quite common, especially in China.

So, back to the photo. Were these women accused of witchcraft? No. Or at least, there's no evidence of that whatsoever.

The photo was taken in the late 1870s or early 1880s, not in 1922, by William Thomas Saunders, a London-born photographer who travelled all over China and even opened a studio in Shanghai. He became a very successful portrait photographer but also took pictures of important events, the region and common people as they went about their business. The pictures he took became hugely important as he was one of the first and few outsiders who recorded daily life in China at that time.

He published several books and his photos appeared in countless magazines all over the world for decades to come. The photo of these three women appeared in one of his collections with the description: 'Shanghai, female prisoners.' There was no mention of them being witches or any kind of witchcraft being involved. It seems like someone just made it up or misunderstood what they were looking at. We don't know what these women were accused of – or if they were even accused of anything. They may have been completely innocent, just posing for the photographer.

Régine Thiriez from the Institut d'Asie Orientale, who has studied and written about the history of photography in China, has looked at the photo and thinks it was probably staged. She makes a few convincing points – for one, the paper strips documenting the women's crimes are missing, whereas these always had to be pasted on to the board. There is also another photo in the same collection that shows two men wearing a double cangue. It's a bit suspicious to have three women and two men in the same situation, patiently posing for you, in the exact same spot, both wearing cangues that are missing the legally necessary pieces of paper announcing their crime. And although they look a bit miserable, they don't look like they've been wearing it for a long time.

So I too think that it's quite likely that these photos are staged and the women were not accused of anything at all, let alone witchcraft.

91

Thumb down meant death for the gladiators of ancient Rome

What you may have been told

During the time of the Roman Empire, people often went to see gladiators fight in arenas. When a fighter was defeated, the victor would look up to the important fancy people in the expensive seats, politicians and sponsors of the fight, to see what they wanted the loser's fate to be. The most important person would then stick his thumb in the air, like a hitch-hiker, if the gladiator was allowed to live. But if he put his thumb down, the man would be killed. Often the public would try to influence the vote by sticking their thumb up or down as well.

This is the origin of the thumbs up and thumbs down gestures we still use today.

The debunking

I know, this one sounds so good. We have seen it everywhere and it seems so believable. What a wonderful origin story for a gesture we use all the time! Well, it is kind of true – but also not true at all.

Let me explain.

There *was* a thumb gesture and yes it was used to decide if a gladiator who lost the fight should live or die but . . . we're not completely sure what the gesture was. It was called the *pollice verso*, which is Latin for 'with turned thumb'. We know it existed because contemporary Romans were kind enough to write about it.

'They hold shows of their own and win applause by slaying whomsoever the crowd, with a turn of the thumb, bids them slay,' wrote the poet Decimus Junius Juvenalis. And according to Aurelius Prudentius Clemens:

> The modest virgin with a turn of her thumb bids him pierce the breast of his fallen foe so that no remnant of life shall stay lurking deep in his vitals while under a deeper thrust of the sword the fighter lies in the agony of death.

But unfortunately, no one bothered to explain a bit better what this meant. Thumb up, down, sideways, stuck up your nose . . . they never explained it properly.

Despite all their mosaics, sculpture, writing and leaving graffiti all over the place, no Roman thought it might be nice to leave a clear infographic for us people from the future. Thanks a lot, guys.

To make things even more complicated, there were several gestures with different names, also rarely described with any clarity. Aside from the *pollice verso*, there was the *pollice compresso*, the pressed thumb, which some historians think involved hiding your thumb in your fist and meant the fighter was to be spared. It may have symbolised the sheathing of a dagger – the thumb being the weapon, the fist symbolising the scabbard. Sticking the thumb in the air would then mean that the knife had to be drawn and the gladiator killed.

And maybe they even used the thumb to show how the knife had to be used by jabbing the thumb in their chest. And it's obvious what they'd expect if they dragged their thumb across their throat – another gesture that's still known today, although I'm not sure if there's a connection with the Romans there.

Interestingly enough, this is what the Victorians thought as well. Yes, I'm as surprised as you are: for once the Victorians were spreading real history and us modern folk were responsible for messing the whole thumb thing up.

In *Brewer's Dictionary of Phrase and Fable* of 1898 we read:

> *When a gladiator was vanquished it rested with the spectators to decide whether he should be slain or not. If they wished him to live, they shut up their thumbs in their fists* (pollice compresso favor judicabatur); *if to be slain, they turned out their thumbs. Adam, in his Roman Antiquities (p. 287), says, 'If they wished him to be saved, they pressed down their thumbs; if to be slain, they turned up [held out] their thumbs.' (Pliny, xxviii. 2; Juvenal, iii. 36; Horace: 1 Epist., xviii. 66.)*

There's even the following note:

> *It is not correct to say, if they wished the man to live they held their thumbs downwards; if to be slain, they held their thumbs upwards. 'Police compressio' means to hold their thumbs close.*

Mr Brewer's inclusion of this note suggests he felt the need to set the record straight, so it's likely that people were getting the thumb thing wrong even then, making this myth a very old one.

As are attempts to debunk it – perhaps Mr Brewer would be a fellow Fake History Hunter, if he was alive today!

We do have some more evidence of the gesture; there is a medallion that shows two gladiators with a man standing next to him raising his fist in the air, his thumb covered by his fingers. It's really prominent and clear, so the artist obviously thought the hand deserved extra attention. Above it is written '*Stantes missi*', which stands for 'released standing', so it appears to show two gladiators who are allowed to walk away after the fight.

Pretty convincing, right? Yes, but not convincing enough for all historians to agree that this is what the mercy gesture looked like. Historians are annoying that way.

So there were several gestures with different meanings and we can't say for sure which one meant mercy and which one meant death. But what we do know is that the thumb down most likely did not mean the gladiator had to be killed – there's no evidence for it and it seems much more likely to have meant the loser got to live. That's what the majority of Roman experts these days seem to agree on. Well, most of the time, anyway.

In 1872, the painter Jean-Léon Gérôme created a magnificent painting with the title *Pollice Verso*. Mr Gérôme, unlike most artists and quite a few historians at the time, put a lot of work into getting everything right. He visited museums, examined original Roman armour and did a ton of research. So it's no wonder that when he put the thumb-down gesture in the painting everybody accepted it as truth.

On a side note, it was this exact painting that convinced famous director Ridley Scott to direct the blockbuster *Gladiator* with Russell Crowe. That is probably why he put the thumb-down gesture in the film even though he was apparently told it wasn't authentic . . .

Is there any connection between the Roman thumb-up gesture and our modern one that means everything is OK? No, most likely not. In Italy, for instance, it seems that people didn't consider it a positive sign at all until the 1940s.

As another side note, gladiator fights rarely resulted in death. These men and women were expensive possessions: buying them, training them and looking after them was a big investment. Many of them also became quite famous and loved by the public; they pulled in the crowd. So it was not the audience, probably not the referee or even the VIP guests who decided if a fighter got to live or die but the sponsors, as they financed it all. Although, of course, the public probably did try to influence the decision.

92

This horrifying photo shows serial killer Leonarda Cianciulli making soap out of humans

What you may have been told

An old lady stands by a boiling pot. She stares at us through the ages, perhaps even through us. She may appear to be just a harmless woman but this is actually a photo of the serial killer Leonarda Cianciulli, who killed a whole bunch of people and turned them into soap and teacakes to protect her son!

The debunking

I admit that I had never heard of Leonarda Cianciulli till I saw her photo being shared online, which is a bit embarrassing because crime is one of the subjects I specialise in as a researcher. So when I first heard about this Italian murderer I thought I ought to find out more and started doing a bit of research. I pretty quickly realised that the photos I found of the murderer looked nothing like the little old lady with that old cauldron.

Surely people wouldn't use the picture of a poor innocent woman to tell the story of this vile creature? Well, they did. And although the woman had died long ago I still got a bit angry and wanted to rescue her. Yes, she looked a bit suspicious stirring that big pot but I bet she would be very upset to find out that people were claiming she was a serial killer. Wouldn't you be?

It was not difficult to debunk. A bit of reverse-image searching led me to a collection of photos taken in early twentieth-century America, far away from Italy where Cianciulli committed her crimes. There she was, just an innocent granny making soap. So I guess whoever made the mistake at least found a picture of someone making soap.

Unfortunately we don't know anything about her besides her job and that she lived in a place called Santa Claus in Indiana. The photographer, Frank M. Hohenberger, working in a photo shop in the busy city of Indianapolis, became fascinated by some photos a customer once brought in. They showed the wonderfully quiet and old-fashioned way of life in the country-side Frank had been looking for. The man told Frank he had taken the idyllic pictures in a small village called Nashville, also in Indiana.

Not much later, Frank, then 41, quit his job, packed his bags and travelled to that place he had only seen a couple of photos of by chance. He loved the countryside and the old pioneer architecture but at first the locals didn't trust him and some even thought their souls would be captured by his camera.

So at first, Frank only took pictures of the fields and houses. They became popular, which meant he had quite a good income, even though it was the Great Depression. Eventually, the locals got used to him and allowed him to take their photos – not just serious formal portraits but also snapshots of regular folk going about their daily business. Frank loved capturing that the most. When he died in 1963, he left behind an invaluable record, both in photos and writing, of a world that had vanished forever.

But, I hear you ask, what about the real soap-making serial killer?

Are you ready for this? Cianciulli was what some would describe as the typical Italian mama, who would fit very well into one of those stereotypical pasta adverts. Her life had been pretty difficult. She had married against her mother's wishes and believed that this was when she was cursed, literally. Her husband got locked up, their house was destroyed in an earthquake and of the seventeen pregnancies she endured, only four of the children survived childhood. She thought she was followed by misfortune.

Eventually, things started going a bit better. She opened a shop in a town called Correggio that did pretty well and her neighbours liked and respected her, even though they thought she was a bit eccentric. She was extremely protective of her surviving children but at the same time she was still haunted by the idea of being cursed. She was very superstitious and had her palm read and fortune told several times. The predictions were often the same: doom and misfortune.

By 1939, her husband had left her and, as the dark clouds of the coming war gathered above Europe, Leonarda's oldest son Giuseppe joined the army. What with the curse, all the bad luck and what the fortune tellers had told her, she was terrified and she became convinced she had to do something to protect him.

So, obviously, she came to the conclusion that human sacrifice was just the ticket.

One by one, she murdered three of her friends: Faustina Setti, Francesca Soavi and Virginia Cacioppo. All were elderly single ladies who came to Leonarda for help but who instead were killed with an axe by Leonarda, who then collected the blood, cut the bodies into pieces, put them in a pot, added caustic soda and dumped the resulting goo in the sceptic tank. The last victim's fat was turned into soap that Leonarda gave to neighbours. But it gets worse.

She used the blood of her victims to make 'crunchy tea cakes' – her words, not mine – that she served to visitors and local children . . . and she and her son tried them as well. The police soon got on to her and when Leonarda realised they suspected her darling son Giuseppe of being involved with the crimes she admitted it all: *'Non ho ucciso per odio o per avidità, ma solo per amore di madre.'* ('I did not kill out of hatred or greed but only out of mother's love.')

She was sent to a criminal asylum where it is claimed that she wrote her memoirs, including tips on how to turn people into soap, but I can't find a copy. According to a nun who worked there she also made tasty sweets but nobody dared to eat them. She died in 1970.

If you want you can see the pot she used to boil her victims in at the Criminological Museum in Rome. Her life has since been turned into a film and musical.

93

These girls are saying a sad goodbye to sailors during the Second World War

What you may have been told

It is a classic photo: young sailors are leaning out of the portholes of a big ship to say goodbye to their girlfriends on the dock. A last hug, a final promise, one more whisper and a kiss whose memory will have to last for a long time. It is such a poignant scene as it's not just a sad goodbye, it may be a farewell for eternity; these young men are going to war. The photo was taken during the Second World War and we're left to wonder how many of the boys ever made it back home and how many of these couples never got to hold each other again.

The debunking

It is a classic photo and these couples are saying goodbye but that's the only bit that's correct about this story, which has been going around the internet for ages.

When I looked at this photo I instantly saw that it was not a 1940s photo. It is clear that we're looking at something that took place long after the war. The hair, the handbags, the clothes, even the box camera one of them took along that day tell us that the photo was taken in the 1960s. But as you should know by now, that is not enough to satisfy my curiosity and it is sometimes not enough to convince people online. We know the photo is not a Second World War photo but what exactly *are* we looking at?

Details in the picture suggested the photo may have been taken on an Italian ship, and to find out more, I got in touch with the Italian Navy Historical Office. Unfortunately, the pandemic didn't allow me to spend a few days in Italy chatting to dashing sailors, but thanks to the internet and the very friendly and fast-working people on the other end of the line, I soon found all the information I needed.

The ship is called the *Amerigo Vespucci*, named after the explorer and navigator. She is a very famous training ship still used by the Italian Navy today. Although built in 1930, she is inspired by eighteenth-century sailing ships, and with her three masts she's quite a sight. In 1962, an American aircraft carrier used light signalling to ask, 'Who are you?' And when the *Vespucci* identified herself, the American ship replied, 'You are the most beautiful ship in the world.'

I can't find out if the two ever met again and if this flirting ever led to something more substantial, or if they were just ships that passed in the night.

Sorry, I couldn't resist.

The *Amerigo Vespucci* makes many very long journeys that give the cadets on board a ton of sailing experience but also the adventure of a lifetime. In 1963, one of the young men embarking on this amazing experience was Robert Borra, who had just completed a course as a naval photographer. Because he finished at the top of his class, he was assigned to the most coveted position there was: the *Vespucci*, during one of her longest and most exciting trips, one that would take Robert across the ocean, over 11,000 miles.

Robert took lots of photos that were then sent to newspapers and magazines all over the world. He also took pictures when the boys said goodbye to the girls they had met on shore – really good photos, too.

But . . . the sailors were going off on an exciting trip, they were not going to war, there was no risk they'd be sunk by U-boats and, although it was a long journey, they would be back. And unless they found a girl in another harbour or the girl found a sailor on another ship, the parting lovers would one day meet again.

94

Secret agents used amazing walking-backwards spy shoes to confuse the Nazis

What you may have been told

Just look at these crazy shoes! They're back to front: the heel is where the toes should be and the toe is where the heel is and it hurts my brain! But they are actually quite brilliant because they were made during the Second World War by Allied spies. German soldiers would see footprints and think the wearer of the shoes was walking in the other direction.

The debunking

These crazy shoes and their even crazier story have been popular on social media for a very long time, but clearly there's something fishy about them. They're civilian shoes, so they look like they're supposed to be worn in public and they are very, very weird looking. So any secret agent planning to fool the enemy wearing these would have to avoid being seen by anyone before they got to do the forwards-walking-backwards thing. In which case they might as well not have bothered.

Besides it just being a strange story, the shoes also don't look like they were around in the thirties or forties at all. So what is going on here?

It was clear that the shoes were in a museum somewhere, as there was a glass cabinet with shoes in the background of the photo and, annoyingly, just the edge of what appeared to be a sign could be seen in the corner – most probably a sign that explained exactly what these shoes were all about. But no matter how much I looked, the shoes, the museum and the little sign remained out of reach.

So I used the most powerful research tool there is: I asked the internet.

I have quite a lot of followers on Twitter and some of my tweets reach hundreds of thousands of people so I just shared the picture and hoped someone would recognise it. Surely one person who saw it would remember seeing them in a museum somewhere?! I shared the image of the shoes a few times over the years but nobody ever managed to track them down until, at last, someone did.

Krystel Contreras, username OphisCode, found them and the whole mystery was finally solved. The shoes are exhibited in the Deutsches Schuhmuseum in Hauenstein. Yes, the German Shoe

Museum. I haven't been but from the website it looks like a fantastic museum with wonderful and fun exhibits.

Once the location of the shoes was found it was of course easy to look for more pictures and I could also ask the museum about them. Now knowing what I was looking for, I found another photo online in which I could finally read the little sign and, guess what, the shoes were not spy shoes used by secret agents during the Second World War. You're shocked and stunned, I'm sure.

The museum gave me the real story behind these shoes. A couple of decades ago, a certain Herr Wolf who worked for a shoe import firm got sick and tired of customers always complaining about the new collections; there was always something that wasn't right. So he had a couple of silly joke shoes made, perhaps to put on display in his office or to bring out every time someone found something to moan about. So the shoes are simply a wonderful example of that famous German humour you've heard so much about.

The spy story is of course a lot more exciting and it's no wonder people were interested in the mysterious background of the shoes. But although these shoes were commissioned by a German shoe salesman, at different times in history shoes *have* been made to confuse the enemy.

For instance, smugglers and bootleggers used shoes with soles that left footprints that appeared the wrong way, but they would only fool your average police officer or border guard because anyone who has a bit of experience in examining tracks knows there is a difference in pressure on the heel and the toes when a human is walking, and you can tell which is the front and back of a foot, regardless of what the print looks like.

But there are much more effective shoes that let you confuse your pursuers. Moonshiners in the 1920s had shoes with cow hooves under them, leaving very different prints. And possibly the coolest shoes I've seen are the 'decoy sneakers' used by the

British Special Operations Executive (SOE) during the Second World War. These were rubber barefoot casts that you tied under your regular shoes so that when you landed on a beach somewhere, any passing guard who might see your footprint would just assume it was a regular bather or local instead of someone wearing army boots.

You can see how this makes a lot more sense than having regular shoes that have weird soles or are completely made back to front. It takes seconds to tie the bare feet camouflage to your shoes and it takes even less time to take them off and dispose of them.

Another case closed.

95

The Iron Maiden and the Pear of Anguish were brutal medieval torture devices

What you may have been told

Everybody knows that during the Middle Ages, people used the most horrific instruments of torture imaginable. For even the smallest crime, you'd be stuck in the Iron Maiden, put on a rack, burned alive, have bits shoved up places you didn't want anything shoved up and worse. Maybe all at the same time.

The debunking

Like every normal person, I've been obsessed with medieval torture devices ever since I was a little girl.

What do you mean that's not normal? Surely all kids love hearing gruesome stories and shudder while looking at those horrific instruments during visits to old castles? There's a reason Roald Dahl is such a popular writer! All right, maybe not everybody has that weird fascination. I blame that old guide at the museum I used to visit.

I grew up in the Hague, where we have the Prison Gate, a wonderful museum that I went to several times when I was young and I loved it. Not only is it a fascinating and slightly spooky former prison with impressive rooms, execution swords and graffiti left by former inmates, but it also used to have really irresponsible tour guides who told absolute nonsense to the visitors. (This is of course no longer the case and if you ever find yourself in the area, visit the place.) There was this one older gentleman who would show us around and tell us all sorts of gruesome stories about the torture that happened there.

Later I learned that many of those stories were not true at all!

Of course, spreading fake history is really bad and that chap made a lot of people believe things that simply aren't true, but I have to admit that he knew exactly what young visitors wanted to hear. As the accompanying adults got paler and paler, we kids got redder and redder with excitement – the stories were disgusting, vile and terrifying . . . so we loved it and we spoke about this school outing for a long time afterwards. I bet it made some of us more interested in history.

There was a lot of torture in the Middle Ages and it is true that they had some very creative devices to work with. What I want to argue here is that some of the most famous 'medieval' torture devices are not medieval at all, and sometimes they were never even really used for torture! And yet you will still find them in museums and castles that often 'forget' to mention they may not be genuine.

So, let's look at two of the most popular ones, the Iron Maiden and the Pear of Anguish.

The Iron Maiden

Eiserne Jungfrau geschlossen.

Das heimliche Gericht mit der eisernen Jungfrau zu Nürnberg 1533.

Eiserne Jungfrau geöffnet.

You've seen this thing, if not in museums then in countless films and TV shows, and it certainly does speak to the imagination. The idea is that a victim is pushed into a human-shaped sort of standing coffin with spikes on the inside. When the lid is then shut, these spikes puncture the body in many different places, killing the prisoner or slowly making them bleed to death.

As you've probably guessed, the Iron Maiden was not a thing. Not during the Middle Ages, after it or ever. There may have been similar devices, but none that really looked or functioned like the one we are thinking of. People have been stuffed into boxes and containers with sharp pointy spikes on the inside since ancient times, which made it rather unpleasant for the standing victim to lean. But they were not skewered by many spikes inside a coffin.

There is only one real mention of the Iron Maiden as we know it being used in the distant past and that's in a book by Johann Philipp Siebenkees, written in 1793, in which he claimed it was used in 1515, but there's no real evidence for that and some historians think he just made it up, or at least used his imagination a bit too much. To be fair, he himself suggested it may all have just been a legend.

Either way, just a few years after it was mentioned in that book, an Iron Maiden mysteriously popped up out of nowhere and was put on display in Nuremberg. Soon the device became very popular and suddenly more of them were 'found' and put in museums and collections all over the world. It is quite telling that the original wooden body of the Iron Maiden at the Medieval Crime Museum in Rothenburg, Germany, was from the fifteenth or sixteenth century, but the spikes on the inside were from the early nineteenth century.

The Victorians read a story, got obsessed by it, and wanted to see this torture device for themselves. Museums and tourist attractions like having lots of visitors so they wanted these devices, and dodgy but smart salesmen started making fakes. And we all fell for it.

The Pear of Anguish

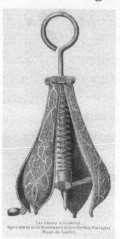

This is a sort of pear-shaped device with a screw on the end that allowed the parts of the pear to expand. It was inserted into a bodily orifice – yes, that one . . . yes, also that one and that other one – and then slowly opened up.

Well, luckily for our medieval friends, there's no evidence whatsoever of them being used or even existing before the 1600s, and the earliest mentions suggest it was used as a 'mechanical gag' by a thief during a heist. Which sounds unconvincing and impractical. I'm not sure it would even work but you'd also need to bring one for every person in the place you're robbing and then what, leave them behind? They sound like they would have been expensive to make. Why not just use a regular gag? They work, they're cheap and they don't need to be retrieved afterwards.

According to some researchers these devices can't even work as they are too weak to be opened once inside the human body to do any serious damage.

After this one early mention, we don't really hear about them till . . . the Victorian era. And even then only as something to put in someone's mouth, that functioned by expanding automatically with a spring when inserted and then closed again with the screw, not the other way around.

So although some of them are genuinely old, none is medieval. If any are real and not simply copies of what we imagine this torture instrument to be, they could have been used for anything. Something medical perhaps, or maybe they had a very mundane function, like sticking some glowing coal inside to warm some shoes. We don't know.

All we really know is that one was supposedly used as a gag in a dodgy story and then the Victorians put one in an exhibit and started writing about it, someone came up with the idea of them being inserted into not-just-the-mouth and everybody got suspiciously excited about that claim for decades to come. What a bunch of pervy ancestors.

These and some of the other devices suspected of not being very medieval often have a few things in common that you may have already noticed. They weren't very practical, they often involve sex, they all became very popular in the nineteenth century and people flocked to museums that had these artefacts, which resulted in smart fraudsters making fakes that we're still paying to look at today.

People want to believe these stories because most of us are a morbid bunch and the Middle Ages are the perfect scapegoat for everything awful. People being tortured all over the place for the most harmless little misdemeanours with gruesome devices simply fits the shared dystopian image we have of that era and historians have been struggling to combat this bias for decades. Ironically, what we project on to that old, long-gone world is in many cases the result of the imagination of someone in a time much closer to ours.

96

During the Middle Ages, people drank beer instead of water

What you may have been told

During the Middle Ages, water was filthy and disgusting because everybody just chucked their waste into the closest river and this polluted all the water sources nearby. So nobody drank water, ever; instead they drank beer, all day, every day, even the children. Which of course meant our medieval ancestors were permanently drunk.

The debunking

I've already written about how the Middle Ages were not that filthy and that the idea of people just dumping their waste all over the place isn't quite true. As cities became busier and more built-up things did get out of hand and sometimes, yes, rivers, canals and other water sources did become polluted. Which, of course, is still the case today. But the people then were not stupid, or at least, not as stupid as some individuals seem to think they were.

Although they didn't know about bacteria and microbes, our ancestors knew that it was not a good idea to drink from dirty-looking, smelly standing water with bugs, poo or dead animals floating in it. This is something humans have known since the dawn of time and even if they didn't, it wouldn't take long for you to figure out that if you drank from a dodgy source of water you'd spend the next couple of days shut in the outhouse empty-ing your guts and/or being very dead.

I think we modern people in most developed countries don't realise how important clean water was to our ancestors because we're so used to having only very clean water piped to our houses. Even if we do drink something we shouldn't have, it's usually something doctors can sort out for us. But if you made the mis-take of dipping your mug in the wrong puddle just a few genera-tions ago it could literally kill you. So people have been trying to keep their drinking source as clean as possible and away from waste for a very, very long time.

And there were more drinking sources than you may think. We all imagine a well in the village square that everybody used but until towns and cities became overpopulated and yards and gar-dens started disappearing, it was not uncommon in some parts of medieval Europe for houses, even those of peasants and farmers, to have their own water source. It doesn't work everywhere, of course, but here in the Netherlands digging a hole is sometimes all you need to do to get to clean drinking water.

Even if there were only a few wells, people made sure they were well protected by laws forbidding animals to be allowed near them and someone was often appointed to keep the area around them clean. Industries, such as tanners, were not generally permitted to do their work near sources of drinking water and when they made a mess they would be heavily fined.

We also know that people have been making water safe to drink with settling tanks, sieves, filters and by boiling for a very long time, so it is really quite obvious that during the Middle Ages (and before and after) a lot of effort and care was put into having lots of clean water.

Besides it being tasty and free, water was also seen as some-thing special, a gift from nature and thus God. It came from deep within the earth but also the sky and, in some cases, people who wanted to show off how pious they were would only drink water, or at least claim they did. There are lots of medieval stories that mention people drinking water and monks being so devout that they preferred water over beer (yeah, sure).

We know people drank water, and lots of it. Towns and communities were settled near and around fresh water sources; it was the most important necessity, not just for drinking either. As the fifteenth-century architect Leon Battista Alberti wrote,

> *Since a city requires a large amount of water not only for drinking, but also for washing, for gardens, tanners and fullers, and drains, and – this is very important – in case of sudden outbreak of fire, the best should be reserved for drinking, and the remainder distributed according to need.*

This whole idea that a village or town didn't need clean drinking water just makes no sense and is mostly based on people assuming that complaints and records about when things did go wrong were the norm instead of exceptional situations that infuriated people. Interestingly enough, when you read these complaints they sometimes turn out to be about the same individuals or a particular industry, so instead of everybody making a mess it was just one family or one shop. Which again is similar to what still happens today; newspapers regularly tell us about families being antisocial.

Imagine if future historians assume that, just because big industries pollute our lakes and rivers, and there are some places in developed countries today where the water from the tap is polluted, that this was a common thing in the early twenty-first century and we were fine with it . . . have you heard about all the raw sewage being dumped in UK lakes and rivers, and do the words Flint, Michigan, ring a bell?

So what about all the beer drinking?

Yes, during the Middle Ages (and quite a lot of eras that followed) people did drink a lot of beer, ale and, my favourite, mead, which is a kind of fermented honey. Ale was made by fermenting grain, water and yeast; beer was made with hops. By the way, beer or ale brewing also works better with clean water. An important detail here is that when making ale they generally didn't boil the water, so the idea that it would be safer to drink because of the boiling also makes no sense.

Even if the water was boiled, like when they made beer, it perhaps wouldn't have helped much if the brew then fermented for days in often less-than hygienic situations, as most brewing was done at home.

But yes, they drank it during the day and, yes, the children drank it too. This was because generally it tasted nicer than or at least different from water, and variety is the spice of life. But it was also full of nutrients, carbohydrates, proteins and calories. As my very drunk friends at the pub kept telling me, a pint is like a liquid sandwich. Which is great if you're a modern-day barfly but even greater if you're a medieval labourer who really needs his energy drink.

Luckily or unfortunately, depending on your perspective, the beer and ale they drank most of the time had very little alcohol in it. Nobody really knows what the percentage was but it was made from one of the later batches of a brew, which meant it had a lower alcohol percentage than the earlier batches, so it would have been quite challenging to get drunk on it. That's why it is sometimes called small, weak or table beer and it can perhaps be compared to what we now call 'light' beers.

Which explains why everybody was not permanently boozed. As happens a lot when I tell people these things, you might wonder why on Earth you believed the myth in the first place (if you did). Why is this old chestnut of a story so difficult to get rid of? It's such an established idea that you'll even find the claim being made in museums, school textbooks and history books by renowned and quite prestigious scholars. I guess it's because we like it as it relates to something that many of us like, a lot: drinking. And of course we already assume that the medieval times were grubby and backwards, so we are predisposed to believe it.

97

Hitler invented the motorway

What you may have been told

Hitler was a nasty piece of work but everybody knows that he invented the motorway, the autobahn. It was a huge project which practically eradicated mass unemployment in Germany, which we have to give him credit for, like it or not. As Uncle Günther used to say, 'At least he built the autobahn.'

The debunking

NEIN. He did not.

For starters, he of course did not invent the motorway. There are several contenders for the world's first motorway: there was one in New York and one in Italy before Hitler even came to power. The Italian one was called the *autostrada*, which I only mention because it is a very nice word to use, *capisce*?

So, I hear you think, surely he still was the guy who brought the motorway to Germany, who started the construction of the autobahn?

NEIN.

The first bit of motorway in Germany that sort of could be – as it was a bit short – called an autobahn was opened to the public in 1921 and a longer one (definitely a proper motorway) was opened in 1932. The Nazis didn't take power in Germany till 1933 and the motorway that was opened to the public that year had mostly been under construction since 1931, before Hitler had any say in it. We can credit the Weimar Republic government for that, specifically Konrad Adenauer, then mayor of Cologne, later the first chancellor of West Germany.

Of course, when things eventually went his way, Hitler started to build a lot more motorways, lots and lots of them. He didn't invent or even start the autobahn project but he did make it seem like it was all his idea, which I guess we have to admit was kind of smart, in a devious, lying sort of way. When the construction of the first section of autobahn under Nazi rule began, he put on a ground-breaking ceremony at which he was present. There was a lot of media, all his Nazi mates showed up in their fancy outfits (not designed by Hugo Boss), a band played music and so on. And every time a new autobahn project was started they did the whole Nazi ceremony thing with a ton of publicity again. Soon a lot of people started to believe they were all his idea. The fact that the Nazi party was originally against the idea of motorways before they came to power was quickly shoved under the carpet.

The pre-Nazi four-lane autobahn was even officially demoted and suddenly called a country road. Hitler was actively trying to cover up the history of the autobahn, replacing it with one that made it look like he started the whole thing. People who dared to publicly mention that the autobahn was not Hitler's idea could expect angry letters from Fritz Todt, the man responsible for building them, with less than subtle warnings. And the Nazi propaganda machine did such a good job of this that many believe their fairy tale to this day.

The motorways were huge projects that created a lot of jobs . . . but they'd already been doing that before the Nazis got involved. And even though lots of roads were built, this still only provided jobs to less than 5 per cent of the millions of unemployed in Germany. It was in the arms industry where most unemployed Germans finally found work – that, or being a soldier getting blown to bits.

The autobahn was also a bit useless during the Nazi era – motorways remained empty during most of the 1930s and 1940s as very few Germans could actually afford a car. Hundreds of thousands had already paid, often in instalments, for their very own Volkswagen, but never got one because of the war. I think my grandparents were among them as I found a little Volkswagen stamp book in their house. I wonder if they kept it in the vain hope that one day they'd still be able to get their car.

Ironically, the first time the autobahn in Germany was used by a lot of traffic may have been when the Allied troops entered the country to give the Nazis a good kicking. The liberators were quite enthusiastic about the motorways.

As a little patriotic side note, the next to start building motorways were the Dutch.

98

When knights went on crusade they put chastity belts on their wives

What you may have been told

Insecure sad little lords who could not trust their wives when they went slaughtering unbelievers in the Holy Land during crusade season, made them – the wives, not the unbelievers – wear metal underpants with a padlock on them so they couldn't have a bit of naughty fun with a stable boy.

The debunking

The story may have originated with a possible Roman tradition of a newly wedded couple wearing belts of fabric knotted together, which of course would be enormously frustrating during your wedding night, and potentially make things feel a bit awkward.

Something like this may have inspired the illustrator of Konrad Kyeser's fifteenth-century military manual *Bellifortis* to draw one and describe it as the hard iron breeches the women of Florence wore. Which to me sounds like either a crude joke about the prudishness of the women there, just a bit of random silliness or, accepting the very remote chance of them having been real, that they were actually some sort of rape-protection device – something to help women, not their husbands. In many early depictions of the belts in art you can spot the key that unlocks the device nearby, within reach of the woman, allowing her to decide who'd get access, which wasn't always the husband.

Women controlling or fooling their husbands while having a dashing chap on the side has been a popular subject of humour for centuries. But although chastity belts are a popular artistic subject, I still think they never really existed. Let me explain why.

Firstly, the idea is ridiculous. Wearing a metal device like that for weeks, even months, will cause severe damage to your skin, even when you put soft fabric inside. It would be worn under clothes, with sweat it would get rusty, there are other kinds of bodily fluids . . . yes, icky.

Imagine what awaits husband dearest when he returns home – a very annoyed wife with rashes, wounds, nasty smells, an infection and, oh, she may also be a bit dead because of all that. Besides, locks are not that difficult to pick; never underestimate the ingenuity of a man and woman who want to do some hanky panky . . . The padlock that can guarantee to stop passion has not yet been invented. And I bet that if anyone really had a chastity belt made, the lock maker would be a fool if he did not secretly make a spare key he could sell to the lady or her admirer behind the husband's back.

So although they've been written about since the very end of the Middle Ages, they seem to have mostly been a joke, metaphorical or symbolic, part of naughty stories, but no real medieval version has ever been found. What we have here is a recipe that those Victorians found predictably impossible to resist: the Middle Ages, pain, sex, kinky toys, infidelity and an era they imagined to be so backwards that it made them feel superior. And once more, as these items became popular, mysteriously they started appearing all over the place, being bought by museums and collectors.

Modern science, which allows us to figure out how old metal objects really are, has resulted in quite a bit of embarrassment when museum exhibits turn out to be quite a lot younger than was long assumed. Staff at the Musée de Cluny were sad to find out that the chastity belt they thought belonged to Catherine de' Medici (1519– 89) was made in the nineteenth century, and the British Museum removed one from its exhibit that it thought was medieval but also turned out to be Victorian.

Once more, something that we projected on to our medieval ancestors actually says more about us and our great-grandparents, because chastity belts did become a real thing in more recent times. The Victorians were obsessed with them as anti-masturbation tools for (mostly) boys and today they seem to be quite popular for the exact opposite reason in the BDSM scene.

So, yet again it seems we can blame our favourite scapegoat when it comes to teaching the world nonsense about the past . . . the Victorians!

99

The flush toilet was invented by Thomas Crapper

What you may have been told

The flush toilet was invented by Thomas Crapper, which is of course why his last name is now connected to, you know . . . well . . . that.

The debunking

Mr Crapper was a very impressive gentleman who invented a lot of things that made our lives a bit easier. He patented manhole covers, pipe joints, the floating ballcock (careful googling that one), the U-bend and a few more things.

His life is also a sort of rags-to-riches story: he came from humble beginnings but eventually owned his own company that even installed plumbing and lavatories for the royal family. He was very passionate about convincing people they needed proper plumbing and functioning indoor toilets, and not just because he sold them. But one of the things he didn't patent was the flush toilet, and that's because he didn't invent it.

Toilets and even indoor plumbing have been around for thousands of years. For instance, archaeologists think that small side rooms in the Neolithic houses of the tiny settlement of Skara Brae on the Orkney Islands in Scotland may have been toilets as they had a connection to underground drains used to get rid of wastewater. And how do you get rid of waste? You empty some water into the hole after it. So Orcadians were very likely doing that 5,000 years ago!

We also have examples of flush toilets from the Indus Valley civilisation, the Minoans on Crete, the Hittites, ancient Greeks and so on. People have been flushing their icky stuff down holes for literally thousands of years. So while our hero Thomas helped make the flush toilet much more popular through good publicity and by being a brilliant businessman, he cannot be credited for it unless he had a time machine, and he didn't patent one of those either.

I can hear you thinking: 'They probably mean the nice proper flushing toilet we have today then, not some hole in the ground you had to chuck a bucket of water in after you did your business.' Well, besides some of these ancient toilets being connected to sewers with permanently running water and, of course, having actual seats, even the toilet that works mechanically, flushing when something is pulled or pushed, existed before Thomas was even born.

Clifford's Tower in York, an impressive thirteenth-century building, has a flush toilet, or garderobe as they used to call them. This lavatory was built for King Henry III and besides the regular old wooden seat with a hole in it and a chute underneath that would take your waste away to outside the castle, it also had a sort of spout that would flush the toilet with water from a rainwater-filled cistern on the roof. I'm not sure what kind of technology was involved. Presumably there was a way to stop and start the downpour which would have to be sturdy or the entire cistern would empty in no time. Either way, it was a flush toilet that involved more than just manually emptying a jug of water down a hole.

If you are still not convinced, there's another contender. In the sixteenth century, Sir John Harington of Kelston, Somerset, built a toilet with a mechanism that would flush the waste away with water if you pulled a cord. He liked designing fountains and as he was Queen Elizabeth I's godchild he spent a lot of time at court. The queen rather liked him because apparently he didn't care much about what kind of behaviour was expected of him and he just said whatever he felt like saying instead of playing all the political games and caring about proper etiquette. So, in other words, he was a rebel, a bit of a troublemaker.

In between upsetting all the ladies-in-waiting and being banished from court, he took the time to write a book called *Metamorphosis of Ajax*, in which he not only described a flush toilet system, he even added a clear drawing of how it worked. As far as we know, it didn't result in lots of people installing these in their houses but we know the queen got one set up in Richmond Palace. It was quite cumbersome, involved a lot of maintenance and didn't work that well, but it was still a mechanical flush toilet.

By the time Mr Crapper finally entered the toilet market, there were already public toilets using the flush system. For instance, the ones installed for the Great Exhibition in the Crystal Palace in London's Hyde Park were causing quite some excitement in 1851. Many visitors – 827,280 in total – used them, and all paid a penny for the honour. (And I know you want me to say that this is where 'to spend a penny' comes from, but there's no real evidence for that either, and the phrase can't be found on record anywhere till the 1940s. Sorry.)

So Mr Crapper did a lot to improve toilets but the main reason so many people still think he invented them is because of his marketing, popularity and, well, his name. But no, it is not where we get the word crap from either. I can't help but wonder if his ghost is relieved or disappointed by that. The word crap has been around since the Middle Ages, although it meant something else back then and wasn't really used for human waste till much later, but still long before Mr Crapper became a household name.

But there's another reason we've fallen for it for such a long time and there's an actual guilty party here: an agent of mischief, a fake history spreader! In 1969, Wallace Reyburn published *Flushed with Pride: The Story of Thomas Crapper*, which was far from a serious biography but was still based on the real man, and may have confused a lot of people.

In conclusion, Mr Crapper was an impressive chap who did a lot to make the flush toilet more popular and a common part of our daily lives, which we should be grateful for. But he didn't invent the flush toilet nor is his name the reason we say crap.

100

A baby falling out of a window was rescued by the same man twice

What you may have been told

In 1930s Detroit, a street cleaner by the name of Joseph Figlock was just doing his work when suddenly a baby fell from an open window, right on Joseph's head! Both Joseph and the baby survived.

The next year, while he was again cleaning the same street, the same child fell from the same window and again Joseph broke the kid's fall and thus saved his life. What are the odds?!

The debunking

Yeah, what are the odds . . .

I'm truly a moron when it comes to numbers and statistics but I reckon that the odds of this story having happened as described above are astronomical. The story is not quite as it's being told, and not just on Twitter and Facebook by the way; this myth has also been repeated in quite a few books.

The extra annoying part of this fake history is that at its core, there is a true story that was already amazing and already contained some really incredible luck, but I guess it was not sensational enough and someone had to dial it up even more. So, let's get to the real story.

In 1938, Department of Public Works employee Joseph Figlock was sweeping an alley in Detroit at ten in the morning when two-year-old David Glenn Thomas, who had been playing too near an open window in his fourth-floor apartment, fell out and hit Joseph on the head and shoulders. Joseph wasn't injured but little David was badly wounded and had to be taken to hospital. Luckily he survived, thanks to Joseph being his involuntary catcher.

We know this happened as the police and hospital got involved. We know the name of the child and the address (77E Canfield Avenue), thanks to the article published in the *Detroit Free Press* a day later, with a photo of Joseph. When he was interviewed by the reporter, Joseph mentioned that this was the second time something like that had happened to him. A year earlier, a baby girl had fallen from a window and had also hit him on the head, again saving her life.

I can't find any mention of this first occasion in old newspapers and Joseph or the reporter may even have made it up, but we have no reason to really doubt it.

You may find it odd that it was raining babies in Detroit back then but it was something that did happen occasionally. I've found a few other cases in the archives, and it is not that strange. American apartment blocks back then had (and still have) those famous fire escapes that people often used (and still do) as an improvised balcony. A place to sit, read, sing a duet with Maria, sleep during heatwaves or let your kids play. There were also lots of windows and young children have a pesky habit of getting into lots of trouble when you take your eye off them for one tenth of a second. (Honourable mention to Lena Gauthier, who saw her two-year-old son fall out of a window while she was on the street outside and somehow managed to catch him while she was already holding her seven-month-old daughter!)

So children did fall from buildings and, at least in the cases I found, luckily they all survived. There were probably a lot more cases that didn't even get a mention in the newspaper, and not all with a happy ending either.

So we have this excellent anecdote of an accidental rescue that is true, and an earlier incident that is probably true but is impossible to prove. This is a great story with already incredible odds. Yes, a street cleaner who walks through the city every day, for years, has higher odds of having a child fall on him than most other people, but it's still quite amazing.

But someone decided it was not amazing enough. Or maybe they were just too dumb to understand the story, or it was a typo – we will never know why this unknown idiot changed the story and made Joseph catch the same child twice in the same street.

Can you even imagine if that was true? Besides the odds being insane, how would the world have judged the child's mother? So you let your kid fall out of the window TWICE?!

101

This is an amazing Art Nouveau villa in Bucharest

What you may have been told

This photo shows the most amazing Art Nouveau villa you can imagine. Isn't it captivating? The flowing lines make it look as if it was made by Mother Nature herself and the large, stunning window above the door gives us a hint of what must be an absolutely gorgeous interior. The building is somewhere in Bucharest.

The debunking

The picture is wonderful, this mysterious villa is a superb example of Art Nouveau architecture and yes, I too would love to visit it. But it doesn't exist.

It was created by an artist using artificial intelligence software called Midjourney. Giving this tool several keywords and commands results in it creating an image for you. It is very popular and the creations made with it are flooding the internet. Sometimes the results are silly or weird, but they can also look amazing and very convincing. Which of course makes my job as a Fake History Hunter a bit more difficult.

A non-existent building is easily debunked, but if the photo had been made to look old and the claim was that the building had been destroyed in the Second World War, it would have become a lot harder to prove it wasn't real, even if architects, experts and specialists can tell it can't be a real building.

If you want to spread misinformation, AI can help you with that – but in this case that was not the creator's intention.

The picture was made by Thierry Lechanteur, an artist from Belgium who combines traditional photography with digital manipulation. People have of course been altering photos since photography has existed, but thanks to Photoshop and AI there are now a lot of new and impressive options available, not just to experienced creators, but also to the general public.

Lechanteur tries to bring a dream world to life and has embraced AI as a new tool but is always honest and upfront about using it. When he shares his creations he mentions how they were made, and he doesn't pretend the buildings and cityscapes he made are real. Currently he's even working on a special exhibition about Art Nouveau where he hopes visitors will start to think about the advantages but also dangers of using AI for art.

But of course, someone saw his picture, shared it online and 'forgot' to mention that the house was not real, that it was an AI creation. And, rudely, they also forgot to mention the artist.

The building speaks to the imagination; people fell in love with it, wanted it to be real and shared it without fact-checking it first. And sometimes they get a bit angry when I tell them the true story. It is ironic that the artist who is working on an exhibition about how controversial AI art is had one of his works go viral for all the wrong reasons.

Of course, the real problem here is the number of social media accounts who don't care, who just steal the picture from somewhere (often Reddit), share it and rake in the likes and shares. And architecture is an easy target, as many people are bored with modern designs and the concrete jungles our cities have become. They long for romantic old buildings, magical villas, richly decorated houses . . . they prefer the architecture of the past, even if sometimes this past never really existed.

In the olden days, when we saw paintings we knew we were looking at something totally made up. Then photography and film were invented, and although we've known that what we see has been altered and changed and is often fake, we still seem to find it difficult to be sceptical of images that look like photos. I guess that is one of the good sides of AI: maybe now, finally, everybody will realise that we can't trust our eyes and have to be sceptical of every image shown to us.

There's nothing wrong with AI art, besides the ongoing ethical debate about whether it's OK for AI to use art made by others to create something new, but anyone should be free to create their fantasy images with AI. But I don't understand why people feel the need to pretend it's real. Just share it as AI! The building won't be any less gorgeous because of it.

Go google it

This is a list of myths and misconceptions that I didn't get to write about in this book but still wanted to share with you. None of the claims below are true, they're all fake history . . . or are they? Maybe I'll write about them in another book, but till then, as people on social media say when they can't be bothered to explain something: go google it!

- The monster in Mary Shelley's book is called Frankenstein.
- Sherlock Holmes said, 'Elementary, my dear Watson.'
- Roman galleys were rowed by slaves.
- The palace of Versailles was a filthy place where everybody did their business in corners and nobody cared.
- Romans cleaned their teeth with urine.
- Medieval food was bland.
- Cleopatra was Black.
- The last song the band played on deck as the *Titanic* sank was 'Nearer My God to Thee'.
- Tall gates kept third-class passengers on the *Titanic* from reaching the deck as she sank.
- Neanderthals were brute, dumb savage creatures; *Homo sapiens* were much more advanced.
- Nobody got old during the Middle Ages.
- Columbus was the first European to visit the Americas.
- George Washington had wooden teeth.
- There was a female pope, and her name was Joan.

- Before she sank everybody thought the *Titanic* was unsinkable.
- The phrase 'sleep tight' is a reference to how tight the ropes supporting a mattress were.
- The Great Fire of London stopped the Great Plague.
- Jesus was born on 25 December.
- Julius Caesar was born by Caesarean section.
- The Dutch bought Manhattan island from Native Americans for 24 dollars' worth of beads.
- The radio-play *War of the Worlds* caused mass panic among people who thought it was real.
- During the Middle Ages the regional ruler was permitted to sleep with the peasants' brides on their wedding night.
- Feminists burned lots of bras.

Afterword: How to hunt fake history

Finding and hunting fake history can be quite tricky, but here are a few tips that can help you figure out if something shared online is true or not.

Quotations

When you spot a quote that you don't trust, figuring out if that funny or smart thing was really said or written by that funny or smart famous historical figure can involve a lot of research. You might have to go through everything they ever said or wrote! But thankfully others have often already done that work for us.

So, when you spot a quotation online that you don't trust, you can look for it by going to:

- www.quoteinvestigator.com
- www.wikiquote.org

Or look them up in one of these books:

- *The New Yale Book of Quotations*, edited by Fred R. Shapiro
- *Hemingway Didn't Say That*, by Garson O'Toole

If you can't find the quotation after looking there, your suspicions are probably justified. Just because you find them on websites that are dedicated to sharing quotes or because they're shared online with a picture does not mean quotes are properly attributed. A quote is only real when it can be proven that the person who's connected to it actually wrote or said it before anyone else.

If the sites and books above can't help you and you still really want to figure out if the quotation you found is genuine, you can look for more detailed and reliable sources. For example, some famous historical figures have books and websites dedicated to them and everything they did and didn't say.

A few I've used are:

- *Churchill by Himself*, edited by Richard Langworth
- www.winstonchurchill.org
- www.darwinproject.ac.uk
- www.oscarwildesociety.co.uk
- www.marktwainstudies.com

And if you're still stuck, then you can ask me on Twitter or send a nice polite email to the Quote Investigator.

Pictures

If you see a picture and you don't trust the description, you'll have to do a bit of detective work.

It's of course easier if you have decades of research and image analysis experience because you'll be able to just look at a photo and know that it's not really from the 1920s but actually from the 1930s, for instance. You'll notice the fashion, the hairstyles, the way the photo was taken, the age of the architecture and so on, and be able to sense that something's not quite right. But if you don't, or if you need to prove to others that it's wrong, then the easiest and fastest way to find out the story behind a photo is by putting it through an internet search engine. Quite a few of the ones you probably already use have a reverse-image option.

Here are some of the ones I use:

- www.tineye.com
- www.google.com/imghp

- www.yandex.ru/images
- www.bing.com/images

All you have to do is drag the suspicious photo into the search option and these engines will look for it everywhere on the internet. I use all four of them because they all have different results and different qualities. Bing, for example, has a wonderful extra tool that recognises words in an image and turns it into copyable text. So when I had to research a crime committed in Paris in 1903, I could take screenshots of old French newspapers, let Bing lift the words off the images and use Google to translate them into English.

There are also a few other tools and applications for mobile devices but I don't own any of those, not even a mobile phone, so I can't advise you on this.

Most important for our research here, though, is that these websites can help us find the oldest upload of the picture. After all, the odds of the person who originally put the photo on the internet knowing more about it are pretty good.

Also extremely helpful is that these engines can find the biggest version of the photo on the internet. Not only may this lead us to someone who owns the original image but it also allows us to study it in more detail. This is how I first realised that the photo of Bertha Benz from 1880 might not be genuine ... a much bigger copy of the picture showed me that her sons were wearing modern shoes!

Often these searches will lead you to a photo-stock company website; they can be quite a goldmine of information when it comes to old images. But be careful – they also sometimes have incorrect descriptions and don't care about correcting them (I've tried).

Sometimes the investigation will take you to websites that have long gone from the internet. It can be terribly frustrating to find a mention on the internet of the subject you're investigating but then discover an empty page when you click on the link. The internet is getting old, we're getting old, and websites come and go.

Luckily there is a website that has been archiving hundreds of billions (yes, really!) of web pages for many years and you can check its archive online. The website is the Internet Archive, www.archive.org, and it is a lifesaver for researchers. If you're lucky, you'll see the blog, article or tweet that you thought was gone forever. It can also be a bit embarrassing, of course, as you'll discover when you can't resist looking up your first website or that profile you had on that poetry forum during your teenage years. But seriously, for research, this website is a gift from heaven.

Besides having an archive of old web pages you'll also find millions of books, audio recordings, videos, images and software on there, which is a great solution if you can't afford to buy lots of books or if the one you're looking for is no longer available or is hidden in some library a long way away. I have a ridiculously large library at home, with way too many books – it's another addiction of mine – so I'm glad I got to look up some of the things for the book you're reading on the Internet Archive instead of having to buy yet another book and wait for it to be shipped to my home.

But when it comes to finding the actual origin of a photo, the best sources are, of course, museums and archives. Many these days have wonderful online archives as well, so make sure you check those out. The best thing about them is that lots of experts and knowledgeable people tend to work there. So sometimes you just have to be a bit forward and contact them. More than once a myth has been busted by me contacting the people who work where the image is kept. Thousands of people, perhaps even millions, have been arguing about the truth behind a photo while all it took to solve the mystery was one call to a lovely lady at a desk somewhere who easily found the picture in a filing cabinet with the original description.

Claims

Proving claims wrong is tricky and it is even harder to write instructions and tips for that. I'm afraid that this just involves a lot of research, googling, reading books, talking to experts and so on.

But one tip I can give you is that a random blog, some website, a TikTok or YouTube video is completely worthless if it doesn't back up a story with actual sources. If you find an article or if someone you're debating with shares one to try to prove you wrong, go straight to the bottom of the page or to the description of the video and look for references.

Where did they get this information from?

How do we know they're not just making it up?

Shakespeare was an alien?

Really?

Great, where is the proof?

Try to see every claim like a criminal investigation: you need witnesses, records, books written by experts, museum collections and so on. Google is great but if all you've got is the first couple of search results, you're not going to be very convincing. Where did they get their information from?

I must admit, I've been quite surprised at how often people can't back up what they claim and I think schools should perhaps spend a little more time teaching kids how to research what they're being told and find out the truth.

I know; nobody wants young people to be stubborn, nosy and ask too many questions. It is not going to make it any easier to bring up children or teach them at school if you encourage them not to blindly trust everything they're being told. But if we give them the tools, knowledge, ability and permission to ask critical questions and fact-check their parents, teachers and peers, I am convinced we'll end up with a better world. These days, when technology means there are so many impressive-looking videos, professionally Photoshopped images and such a torrent of misinformation, it is especially important that everybody learns not just how to fact-check what they're being told but also how to disprove fake history and fake news and prove their own claims.

Which is why I am extremely proud when I'm told by teachers that they use some of my debunking in their classrooms!

Finally, a few words about Wikipedia

Everybody knows that Wikipedia can easily be altered by anyone and is totally untrustworthy. Even the co-founder says so. There is misinformation on there, of course there is. But the fact is that this website is still more valuable, more neutral and provides more sources and references than pretty much all random blogs and articles people drag into the debate after they laugh at you for using Wikipedia.

Yes, anyone can alter the articles, but it's not as easy as people think. If I decide to change the page about Miss Universe to make it look like I won it three years in a row, it will be changed back before I finish my bottle of mead.

But Wikipedia is a very transparent website: on every page you can see the revision history, who's been altering it, how, why and so on. In my experience, overall, what I've found on Wikipedia has proved to be pretty reliable. Still, people should treat it for what it is: an online reference website. You can find articles on everything and they almost all have lots of lovely sources, references and links that can help you further with your investigation. Most historians, journalists, students, researchers, educators, scholars and academics I know start their research with Wikipedia and are not afraid to admit it.

But, and this is important, while this free encyclopaedia can be your first step, it shouldn't be your last. Begin there, look up the basic stuff, note the book titles, the names of experts, follow the links and go from there.

Acknowledgements

There are too many people I have to thank for helping me put this book together. Besides family, friends and pets who supported me, there are of course my wonderful followers on Twitter and countless historians, bloggers, researchers and so on, who made a contribution.

Special thanks to my 'brothers in arms': fellow debunkers like *HoaxEye*'s Janne Ahlberg, Quote Investigator Garson O'Toole, PicPedant, Inviting History's Anna Gibson, the BS Historian, Ernst Dommershuijzen and others.

Sources

The primary publications, articles and programmes that I used to find and check information for each chapter are listed below, and where appropriate the list includes details of any further resources such as archives, institutions and museum objects that I found helpful during my research.

1. Napoleon Bonaparte shot the nose off the Sphinx

Baumgarten, Siegmund Jakob, Beer, Ferdinand Wilhelm and Semler, Johann Salomo, *A Supplement to the English Universal History* . . . (E. Dilly, 1760)

Greener, Leslie, *The Discovery of Egypt* (Viking Press, 1967)

Heyman, Johannes and Egmond van der Nijenburg, Johannes Aegidius van, *Travels Through Part of Europe, Asia Minor, the Islands of the Archipelago; Syria, Palestine, Egypt, Mount Sinai, &c* . . . (L. Davis and C. Reymers, 1759)

Mayer, Luigi, *Views in Egypt, from the original drawings* . . . (T. Bensley for R. Bowyer, 1805)

Zivie-Coche, Christiane, *Sphinx: History of a Monument* (Cornell University Press, 2004)

Other helpful resources: Anti-Defamation League (www.adl.org); Tom Holmberg's *The Napoleon Series* website (www.napoleon-series.org); Voices of Democracy (www.voicesofdemocracy.umd.edu)

2. Hugo Boss designed the Nazi uniforms

Köster, Roman, *Hugo Boss, 1924–1945: die Geschichte einer Kleiderfabrik zwischen Weimarer Republik und 'Drittem Reich'* (Herbig, 2011)

Leigh Davis, Brian and Turner, Pierre, *German Uniforms of the Third Reich 1933–1945* (Blandford Press, 1987)

Timm, Elisabeth, 'Hugo Ferdinand Boss (1885–1948) und die Firma Hugo Boss. Eine Dokumentation' (1999), www.metzingen-zwangsarbeit.de/hugo_boss.pdf

3. Marie Antoinette said 'Let them eat cake'

Bernier, Olivier, *Secrets of Marie Antoinette: A Collection of Letters* (Fromm International, 1986)

Fraser, Antonia, *Marie Antoinette: The Journey* (Orion, 2010)

Shapiro, Fred R. (ed.), *The New Yale Book of Quotations* (Yale University Press, 2021)

Xuanling, Fang., et al., *The Book of Jin* (China: 648)

Other helpful resources: Anna Gibson's *Inviting History* website (www.invitin ghistory.com)

4. That famous person said that smart thing

Churchill, Winston S., *Churchill by Himself: In His Own Words*, ed. Richard M. Langworth (Ebury Press, 2012)

Langworth, Richard M., *Winston Churchill, Myth and Reality: What He Actually Did and Said* (McFarland, 2017)

O'Toole, Garson, *Hemingway Didn't Say That: The Truth Behind Familiar Quotations* (Amazon Publishing, 2017)

Shapiro, Fred R. (ed.), *The New Yale Book of Quotations* (Yale University Press, 2021)

Other helpful resources: International Churchill Society (www.winstonchurch ill.org); Collected Papers of Albert Einstein (www.einsteinpapers.press. princeton.edu); Oscar Wilde Society (www.oscarwildesociety.co.uk); Wikiquote (https://en.wikiquote.org/wiki/Main_Page)

5. *Star Trek* showed the first interracial kiss on television in 1968

'Beeldromance', *Pension Hommeles*, dir. Erik de Vries, written by Annie M.G. Schmidt (5 January 1959)

Brady, Kathleen, *Lucille: The Life of Lucille Ball* (iUniverse, 2011)

Shatner, William and Fisher, David, *Up Till Now* (Pan Macmillan, 2009)

Tawney, Raj, 'Was I Love Lucy Ahead of Its Time?' *Emmys* (22 March 2019), www.emmys.com/news/online-originals/was-i-love-lucy-ahead-its-time

'TV Listings Past and Present: November 22, 1968', *TV Tango* (www. tvtango.com/listings/1968/11/22)

6. *EastEnders* showed the first same-sex kiss on television in 1989

Bourne, Stephen, *Playing Gay in the Golden Age of British TV* (History Press, 2019)

Davies, John, 'Sex and the BBC', *Prospero* 4 (August 2021): 8–9

Felton, James, *Sunburn: The Unofficial History of the Sun Newspaper in 99 Headlines* (Sphere, 2020)

'History of the BBC: LGBTQ+ Timeline', BBC (2023), www.bbc.com/historyofthebbc/lgbtq/lgbtq-timeline

Martin and Lewis – The Kings of Bromance (Tribute), uploaded by haronidu23 (31 January 2012), www.youtube.com/watch?v=ROfhjEBKkUc

O'Connor, John, 'PBS Capitalizes on Imported "Classic Theater"', *New York Times*, 5 October 1975

7. Vikings had horns on their helmets

'Britain's first ever Viking helmet discovered', Preston Park Museum and Grounds (2020), https://prestonparkmuseum.co.uk/preston-park-museum-britains-first-ever-viking-helmet-discovered.

Doepler, Carl Emil, *Der Ring des Nibelungen* (Berlin Kunstdruck und Verlags-Anstalt, 1889)

Frank, Roberta, 'The Invention of the Viking Horned Helment', *International Scandinavian and Medieval Studies in Memory of Gerd Wolfgang Weber* (Parnaso, 2000)

Gritton, Jim, 'Wagner and the Trope of the Horned Helmet', 2017 (www.researchgate.net/publication/335219184_Wagner_and_the_Trope_of_the_Horned_Helmet)

Mueller-Vollmer, Tristan and Wolf, Kirsten, *The Vikings: Facts and Fictions* (ABC-CLIO, 2018)

Vandkilde, Helle et al., 'Anthropomorphised warlike beings with horned helmets: Bronze Age Scandinavia, Sardinia, and Iberia compared', *Praehistorische Zeitschrift* 97/1 (2022): 130–58, https://doi.org/10.1515/pz-2021-2012

Other helpful resources: Jimmy Johnson, The Welsh Viking (www.youtube.com/c/TheWelshViking); National Museum of Denmark (https://en.natmus.dk)

8. People ate potatoes in the Middle Ages

Crosby, Alfred W., *The Columbian Exchange* (Praeger, 2003)

Reader, John, *Potato: A History of the Propitious Esculent* (Yale University Press, 2009)

9. The word 'hangover' originated from passed-out drunks leaning on a rope

Balzac, Honoré de, *The Magic Skin*, trans. Katharine Prescott Wormeley (Roberts Brothers, 1888)

Dickens, Charles, *The Posthumous Papers of the Pickwick Club* (Chapman and Hall, 1887)

Orwell, George, *Down and Out in Paris and London* (Arcturus, 2021)

Walton, Geri, 'Four Penny Coffins, Penny Sit-ups, and Two Penny Hangovers' (12 March 2018), www.geriwalton.com/victorian-four-penny-coffins-penny-beds-homelessness

Other helpful resources: Online Etymology Dictionary (www.etymonline.com/word/hangover#etymonline_v_1443)

10. Santa wears red because of Coca-Cola

Bowler, Gerry, *Santa Claus: A Biography* (McClelland & Stewart, 2011)

English, Adam C., *The Saint Who Would Be Santa Claus: The True Life and Trials of Nicholas of Myra* (Baylor University Press, 2014)

Guinn, Jeff, *The Autobiography of Santa Claus* (Penguin, 2006)

Saint Nicholas and Santa Claus (Charles River Editors, 2019)

Other helpful resources: Public Domain Review; Coca-Cola archives; *Saturday Evening Post* archives

11. Germany invented the concentration camp

Pitzer, Andrea, *One Long Night: A Global History of Concentration Camps* (Little, Brown, 2017)

12. A narrow doorway stopped monks in Portugal getting fat

'Guião de visita', Mosteiro Alcobaça (undated), www.mosteiroalcobaca.gov.pt/data/at621_an1_pt.pdf

'Monastery of Alcobaça', UNESCO World Heritage Convention (undated), https://whc.unesco.org/pg.cfm?cid=31&id_site=505

13. The FBI coined the term 'serial killer' in the 1970s

'Cinema Royal', *Algemeen Handelsblad* (27 February 1927), www.delpher.nl/nl/kranten/view?query=seriemoordenaar&coll=ddd&sortfield=date&identifier=ddd:010657985:mpeg21:a0262&resultsidentifier=ddd:010657985:mpeg21:a0262&rowid=1

Gennat, Ernst, 'Die Düsseldorfer Sexualverbrechen', in *Kriminalistische Monatshefte* (1930).

Ressler, Robert K. and Shachtman, Tom, *Whoever Fights Monsters: My Twenty Years Tracking Serial Killers for the FBI* (St Martin's Press, 1992)

Rule, Ann, *Kiss Me, Kill Me* (Pocket Star, 2004)

Waller, S. and Allhoff, F. (eds), *Serial Killers: Philosophy for Everyone* (Wiley-Blackwell, 2011)

Vronsky, Peter, *Serial Killers: The Method and Madness of Monsters* (Berkley, 2004)

14. The word honeymoon comes from giving the married couple a month's supply of mead

Heywood, John, *A dialogue conteinyng the nomber in effect of all the prouerbes in the englishe tongue compacte in a matter concernyng two maner of mariages, made and set foorth by John Heywood* (Thomas Berthelet, 1546), Oxford Text Archive, http://hdl.handle.net/20.500.12024/A03168

'honeymoon, n.', *Oxford English Dictionary*, OED Online (Oxford University Press, 2022), www.oed.com/view/Entry/88181

Krünitz, Johann Georg, *Oeconomischen Encyclopädie* (Ernst Litfaß, 1858)

Pulleyn, William, *The Etymological Compendium, Or, Portfolio of Origins and Inventions . . .* (T. Tegg, 1830)

Winder, Robert, *Bloody Foreigners* (Little, Brown, 2010)

15. The famous 1920s actress Clara Bow was a Nazi

Stenn, David, *Clara Bow: Runnin' Wild* (Cooper Square Press, 2000)

'Ancient Cross Defies Jinx Day', *Los Angeles Times*, 13 April 1928, p. 27, www.newspapers.com/clip/24782276/clara-bow-wears-ancient-good-luck

Other helpful resources: Revue des Monats; *Photoplay*

16. Coca-Cola used Nazi slogans and symbols in its German adverts

'The evolution of the Coca-Cola logo: 2011–2013,' *The Martin Guide to Coca-Cola Memorabilia* (undated), www.earlycoke.com/evolution-of-the-coca-cola-logo

'History of Coca-Cola Advertising Signs', The Coca-Cola Company (undated), www.coca-colacompany.com/company/history/history-of-coca-cola-advertising-slogans

Other helpful resources: Ethical Consumer (www.ethicalconsumer.org/company-profile/coca-cola-company); Sanderswood (www.sanderswood.com); Scott Joyce Photography (https://scottjoycephotography.net)

17. This dog was sent to prison for murdering a cat

'Mrs Pincho Clears Record of Her Dog', *New York Times* 14 January 1926

Other helpful resources: Eastern State Penitentiary (www.easternstate.org); Pennsylvania State Archives; Tyler Stump's *Another Century* blog (https://anothercenturyblog.wordpress.com/about)

18. A soldier carried a donkey across a minefield during the Second World War

Condado-Madera, Emilio, *Histoires de l'Histoire de la légion* (Publibook/ Société des écrivains, 2010)

Lianos, Constantin, 'L'ânon Bambi', **Monsieur Légionnaire**, 18 October 2016, www.monsieur-legionnaire.org/notre-actualite/19-monsieur-legionnaire/61-l-anon-bambi

Porch, Douglas, *The French Foreign Legion: A Complete History of the Legendary Fighting Force* (Skyhorse, 2010)

Other helpful resources: Veterans of the French Foreign Legion Antwerp Department; British Royal Society for the Prevention of Cruelty to Animals (www.rspca.org.uk); Foreign Legion Info (http://foreignle gion.info)

19. This woman made a dramatic dash for freedom at a Berlin border crossing

'Hun Laatste Ontmoeting', *De Tijd de Maasbode* (17 January 1964), www. delpher.nl/nl/kranten/view?query=%22hun+laatste+ontmoeting% 22+film&coll=ddd&sortfield=date&page=1&facets%5Bperiode% 5D%5B%5D=1%7C20e_eeuw%7C1960-1969%7C&identifier=ddd: 011233316:mpeg21:ao118&resultsidentifier=ddd:011233316:mpeg21: ao118&rowid=4

'*Oggi a Berlino*', *International Movie Database*, www.imdb.com/title/tt0056304

20. The bird-beak plague doctor mask is medieval

Black, Winston, *The Middle Ages: Facts and Fictions* (ABC-CLIO, 2019)

Lucenet, Monique, 'La peste, fléau majeur', Université Paris Cité (undated), www.biusante.parisdescartes.fr/histoire/medica/presentations/peste.php

Muratori, Lodovico Antonio, *Del governo della peste, e delle maniere di guard-arsene, trattato di Lodovico Antonio Muratori . . .* (Bartolomeo Soliani, 1714)

Saint-Martin, Michel de, *Moiens faciles et eprouvez, dont M. de Lorme . . . s'est servi pour vivre près de cent ans* (Marin Yvon, 1683)

Tibayrenc, Michel (ed.), *Encyclopedia of Infectious Diseases: Modern Methodologies* (Wiley, 2007)

21. This Second World War photo shows a German soldier using a mobile phone

Bohéma, TV series, Česká Televize (2017)

'*Bohéma*', International Movie Database, www.imdb.com/title/tt6284192

Other helpful resources: Richard Tanton's Flickr collection (www.flickr.com/photos/tantonr/27341797601/)

22. Toddler François Bertillon was arrested and had a mugshot taken

'Alphonse Bertillon', Artnet, www.artnet.com/artists/alphonse-bertillon

Bertillon, Suzanne, *Vie d'Alphonse Bertillon* (Éditions Gallimard, 1941)

Clark, Terry Nichols, *Prophets and Patrons: The French University and the Emergence of the Social Sciences* (Harvard University Press, 1973)

Fisher, Jim, 'Alphonse Bertillon: The Father of Criminal Identification' (2008), https://web.archive.org/web/20201201212727/https://jimfisher.edinboro.edu/forensics/bertillon1.html

Hoobler, Thomas and Hoobler, Dorothy, *The Crimes of Paris: A True Story of Murder, Theft, and Detection* (Little, Brown, 2009)

'Portrait Présumé de George et François Bertillon', MutualArt, www.mutualart.com/Artwork/Portrait-Presume-de-George-et-Francois-B/B08E569FA7726181

Other helpful resources: Rémi Mathis on Twitter (https://twitter.com/remimathis); www.ancestry.com

23. Members of the media, doctors and nurses were hanged in public in Nuremberg in 1945

Helpful resources: H.S. Pshenichny Central State Film and Photographic Archives of Ukraine (https://tsdkffa.archives.gov.ua); United States Holocaust Memorial Museum (www.ushmm.org)

24. The first depiction of Jesus is in a museum in Cairo

Beck, Roger B. et al., *A History of World Societies* (Bedford/St Martin's, 2014)

Ice Cube, 'Earliest found painting of Jesus . . .', Twitter (7 June 2020), https://twitter.com/icecube/status/1269589523563868160

Sadek el Gendi, Sherin Hassan, 'Different Attitudes of Jesus Christ in Coptic Art' (2013), https://cguaa.journals.ekb.eg/article_32586.html

Taylor, Joan E., *What Did Jesus Look Like?* (Bloomsbury, 2018)

25. Victorian prostitutes used tiny candles to time their clients

Ponson du Terrail, Pierre-Alexis, *Le dernier mot de Rocambole* (Dentu, 1867)

Other helpful resources: Dagblad van Zuidholland en 's Gravenhage (1886); Deutsches Historisches Museum

26. Medieval people all had terrible teeth

Anderson, T., 'Dental treatment in Medieval England', *British Dental Journal* 197/7 (October 2004): 419–25

Cybulskie, Danièle, *Life in Medieval Europe: Fact and Fiction* (Pen & Sword, 2019)

Gerald of Wales (Giraldus Cambrensis), *The Journey Through Wales and the Description of Wales*, ed. Betty Radice, trans. Lewis Thorpe (Penguin, 1978)

Green, Monica, *The Trotula: An English Translation of the Medieval Compendium of Women's Medicine* (University of Pennsylvania Press, 2002)

Medieval hygiene: Did people have bad teeth in medieval times? (I use a twig!), Modern History TV (18 April 2019), www.youtube.com/watch?v= fcVwcvWePhU

Montanari, Massimo, *Medieval Tastes: Food, Cooking, and the Table* (Columbia University Press, 2015)

Ordronaux, John, *Regimen sanitatis Salernitanum* (Lippincott, 1870), https:// archive.org/details/codehealthschoooosalegoog/page/n57/mode/1up

27. These windows were made so people could still buy wine during the Black Death

Corsini, Diletta and Giordano, Lucrezia, *Wine Windows in Florence and Tuscany* (Edizioni BDV, 2021)

Other helpful resources: Buchette del Vino, Associazione Culturale (https:// buchettedelvino.org)

28. This is a photo of the first Black American female lawyer, Charlotte E. Ray

Clay Smith Jr, J., *Emancipation: The Making of the Black Lawyer, 1844–1944* (University of Pennsylvania Press, Incorporated, 1999)

Other helpful resources: National Marian Anderson Museum (http://mari anandersonhistoricalsociety.weebly.com)

29. A nineteenth-century princess and a countess had a topless duel

Cohen, Richard, *By the Sword: Gladiators, Musketeers, Samurai Warriors, Swashbucklers, and Olympians* (Simon & Schuster, 2010)

Hopton, Richard, *Pistols at Dawn: A History of Duelling* (Portrait, 2007)

Matthey, Ignaz. 'The Mythologisation of Duelling by Women' (2019), www.academia.edu/56569598/THE_MYTHOLOGISATION_OF_DUELLING_BY_WOMEN

Other helpful resources: Le Figaro; *La Liberté*

30. This beautiful French house was built in 1509

Helpful resources: Gérard Roger; *Le Journal de l'Orne* (https://actu.fr/le-journal-de-l-orne/); Médiévale . . . Remparts de Normandie (http://remparts-de-normandie.eklablog.com/#:~:text=LES%20REM-PARTS%20DE%20SAINTE%2DCROIX%2DS%2FORNE%20(Orne)&text=%22%20L'%C3%A9difice%20dans%20sa%20forme,deux%20familles%20seigneurs%20de%20Putanges); Commune-Mairie, Monuments historiques à Argentan; Monumentum (https://monumentum.fr)

31. Thomas Edison invented the lightbulb

Freeberg, Ernest, *The Age of Edison: Electric Light and the Invention of Modern America* (Penguin, 2014)

Friedel, Robert and Israel, Paul with Finn, Bernard S., *Edison's Electric Light: The Art of Invention* (Rutgers University Press, 1986)

Morris, Edmund, *Edison* (Random House, 2019)

32. An angry maharaja used ten Rolls-Royces to clean the streets because of a rude salesman

Facts & Fallacies (Reader's Digest, 1988)

Whiting, John D., 'Diary in Photos, 1934–1939', www.loc.gov/resource/ppmsca.17411/?sp=17

Yadav, Harish. *Incredible But True* (Pustak Mahal, 1993)

Other helpful resources: Corporate Heritage and the Rolls-Royce Heritage Trust (www.rolls-royce.com/about/heritage-trust.aspx)

33. Napoleon was short

Antommarchi, Francesco A., *The Last Days of Napoleon: Memoirs of the Last Two Years of Napoleon's Exile* (H. Colburn, 1826)

Bell, David Avrom, *Napoleon: A Concise Biography* (Oxford University Press, 2015)

Knapen, J.E.P., Blaker, N.M. and Van Vugt, M., 'The Napoleon Complex: When Shorter Men Take More', *Psychological Science* 29/7 (2018): 1134–44

Lugli, A. et al., 'The Medical Mystery of Napoleon Bonaparte: An Inter-disciplinary Exposé', *Advances in Anatomic Pathology* 18/2 (March 2011): 152–8

Steckel, Richard H. and Floud, Roderick (eds), *Health and Welfare During Industrialization* (National Bureau of Economic Research, 1997)

34. Newton came up with his theory of gravity when an apple fell on his head

Disraeli, Isaac and Disraeli, Benjamin, *Curiosities of Literature* (F. Warne, 1881)

'Isaac Newton's Apple Tree', National Trust (undated), web.archive.org/web/20220105091448/https://www.nationaltrust.org.uk/woolsthorpe-manor/features/the-story-of-our-apple-tree-at-woolsthorpe-manor

Ronsmans, Herwig, 'De appelboom van Newton – Historische Bronnen' (2018), https://mira.be/sites/default/files/bijlages/artikels/2018-10/Newton_appelboom.pdf

Stukeley, William, *Memoirs of Sir Isaac Newton's Life* (handwritten, 1752), https://ttp.royalsociety.org//ttp/ttp.html?id=1807da00-909a-4abf-b9c1-0279a08e4bf2&type=book

35. Nero fiddled while Rome burned

Barrett, Anthony A., *Rome Is Burning: Nero and the Fire That Ended a Dynasty* (Princeton University Press, 2020)

Gyles, Mary Francis, 'Nero Fiddled While Rome Burned', *Classical Journal* 42/4 (1947)

Tacitus, *The Annals of Tacitus*, trans. Alfred John Church and William Jackson Brodribb (Macmillan, 1884), Book 15, www.faculty.fairfield.edu/rosivach/cl116/tac.%20ann.%2015.38-43.htm

36. The Roman vomitorium was a room for vomiting

Bontty, Monica M., *Ancient Rome: Facts and Fictions* (ABC-CLIO, 2020)

Davenport, Cillan and Malik, Shushma, 'Mythbusting Ancient Rome – the truth about the vomitorium', *Conversation* (19 January 2017), https://theconversation.com/mythbusting-ancient-rome-the-truth-about-the-vomitorium-71068

McDaniel, Spencer, *Tales of Times Forgotten*, blog, https://talesoftimesforgotten.com

37. Staircases in castles go clockwise so defenders have an advantage during fighting

Guy, Neil, 'The Rise of the Anti-clockwise Newel Stair', *Castle Studies Group Journal* 25 (2011–12): 113–74

38. The nursery rhyme 'Ring a Ring o' Roses' is about the plague

Black, Winston, *The Middle Ages: Facts and Fictions* (ABC-CLIO, 2019)

Greenaway, Kate, *Mother Goose* (George Routledge and Sons, 1881)

Opie, Iona and Opie, Peter, *Oxford Dictionary of Nursery Rhymes* (Oxford University Press, 1997)

Wilton, David, *Word Myths: Debunking Linguistic Urban Legends* (Oxford University Press, 2004)

Other helpful resources: Gary Martin's *The Phrase Finder* (www.phrases.org.uk/gary-martin.html)

39. The two-finger gesture dates back to medieval archers at Agincourt

Cooper, Stephen, *Agincourt: Myth and Reality 1415–2015* (Pen & Sword Military, 2014)

Curry, Anne, *The Battle of Agincourt: Sources and Interpretations* (Boydell Press, 2000)

Wavrin, Jean de, *A Collection of the Chronicles and Ancient Histories of Great Britain, Now Called England*, trans. William Hardy and Edward L.C.P. Hardy (HMSO, 1887)

40. Lady Godiva rode a horse in the nude because of taxes

Donoghue, Daniel, *Lady Godiva: A Literary History of the Legend* (Wiley, 2008)

Haviland, David, *The Not-So-Nude Ride of Lady Godiva: & Other Morsels of Misinformation from the History Books* (Penguin, 2012)

Lacey, Robert, *Great Tales from English History: Cheddar Man to DNA* (Little, Brown, 2011)

Roger of Wendover, *Rogeri de Wendover Chronica* (Sumptibus societatis, 1841)

41. The Victorians had vampire hunting kits

Ferguson, Jonathan, 'The "vampire killing kit"', Royal Armouries (undated), web.archive.org/web/20220507203559/https://staging.royalarmouries.org/stories/our-collection/object-of-the-month-october-the-vampire-killing-kit

Hogg, Anthony, '6 Reasons Why You Shouldn't Buy an "Antique" Vampire Killing Kit', *Vamped* (31 October 2014), https://vamped.org/2014/10/31/6-reasons-why-you-shouldnt-buy-an-antique-vampire-killing-kit

42. Einstein flunked maths

Isaacson, Walter, *Einstein: His Life and Universe* (Simon & Schuster, 2008)

Perillán, José G., *Science Between Myth and History: The Quest for Common Ground and Its Importance for Scientific Practice* (Oxford University Press, 2021)

43. Ancient and medieval statues and buildings were always white or unpainted

Brinkmann, Vinzenz, *Bunte Götter* (Hirmer, 2010)

Dimitriou, Penelope, 'The Polychromy of Greek Sculpture: to the Beginning of the Hellenistic Period', dissertation (Columbia University, 1951)

44. In the Middle Ages millions of women were accused of witchcraft and burned at the stake

Black, Winston, *The Middle Ages: Facts and Fictions* (ABC-CLIO, 2019)

Kieckhefer, R., *Magic in the Middle Ages* (Cambridge University Press, 1989)

Leeson, Peter T. and Rus, Jacob W., 'Witch trials', *Economic Journal* 128 (2017), www.peterleeson.com/Witch_Trials.pdf

Levack, B.P., *The Witch-Hunt in Early Modern Europe*, fourth edition (Routledge, 2016)

45. The Nazi salute has Roman origins

Allert, Tilman, *The Hitler Salute: On the Meaning of a Gesture* (Henry Holt and Company, 2009)

Winkler, Martin M., *The Roman Salute: Cinema, History, Ideology* (Ohio State University Press, 2009)

46. Vikings were 'buried' at sea on a burning ship

Aḥmad ibn Faḍlān, *Mission to the Volga*, trans. James E. Montgomery (New York University Press, 2017)

Sigurðsson, Jón Viðar, *Scandinavia in the Age of Vikings* (Cornell University Press, 2022)

Sjøvold, Thorleif, 'A Royal Viking Burial', *Archaeology* 11/3 (September 1958): 190–9

Winroth, Anders, *The Age of the Vikings* (Princeton University Press, 2016)

47. The Bayeux Tapestry is a tapestry (and Harold was shot in the eye by an arrow)

Bridgeford, Andrew, *1066: The Hidden History of the Bayeux Tapestry* (Fourth Estate, 2004)

Oxford Dictionary of English, ed. Angus Stevenson (Oxford University Press, 2010)

Wright, Arthur Colin, *Decoding the Bayeux Tapestry: The Secrets of History's Most Famous Embroidery Hidden in Plain Sight* (Pen & Sword, 2019)

Other helpful resources: La Tapisserie de Bayeux museum (www.bayeuxmuseum.com/en/the-bayeux-tapestry)

48. Nelson's last words were 'Kiss me, Hardy'

Beatty, William, *Authentic Narrative of the Death of Lord Nelson* (T. Davison, 1808)

Coleman, Terry, *The Nelson Touch: The Life and Legend of Horatio Nelson* (Oxford University Press, 2004)

'The Death of Nelson', Royal Museums Greenwich (undated), www.rmg.co.uk/stories/topics/what-were-nelsons-last-words

Pocock, Tom, *Horatio Nelson* (Pimlico, 1994)

Southey, Robert, *Southey's Life of Nelson* (Macmillan, 1890)

49. Hundreds of books were left floating in the street after the Paris flood of 1910

Fitzsimons, Nick, Twitter (19 August 2014), https://twitter.com/NickFitz/status/501719493216043009

Jackson, Jeffrey H., *Paris Under Water: How the City of Light Survived the Great Flood of 1910* (Palgrave Macmillan, 2010)

'Library books floating in Paris?', *HoaxEye* (12 March 2017), https://hoaxeye.com/2017/03/12/library-books-floating-in-paris

50. Carrots were made orange by the Dutch in homage to their royal family

Greene, Wesley, *Vegetable Gardening the Colonial Williamsburg Way* (Rodale Books: 2012)

Stolarczyk, John and Janick, J., 'Carrot: History and Iconography', *Chronica Horticulturae* 51/2 (2011): 13–18

51. Carl Benz invented the car

'Automobile Department', *The Hub* 43/1 (April 1901): 28

'The dispute about the "birthday" of the modern automobile', Deutsches Patent- und Markenamt (22 December 2014), web.archive.org/web/20170102082130/https://www.dpma.de/service/klassifikationen/ipc/ipcprojekt/einekurzegeschichtedesautomobils/geburtstagdesautos/index.html

'Dr Carl Benz Car Museum', Mercedes-Benz (undated), www.mercedes-benz.com/en/art-and-culture/museum/dr-carl-benz-car-museum

Fersen, Olaf von, *Ein Jahrhundert Automobiltechnik* (Springer, 1986)

Kurinsky, Samuel, 'Siegfried Marcus: An Uncredited Inventive Genius', Hebrew History Federation, Fact Paper 32-I (undated), https://hebrewhistory.info/factpapers/fp032-1_marcus.htm

Leonardo da Vinci, *Codex Atlanticus* (1478–1519), https://codex-atlanticus.ambrosiana.it

Seiffert, Reinhard, *Die Ära Gottlieb Daimlers* (Vieweg & Teubner Verlag, 2009)

52. This is a photo of Bertha Benz and her sons during the first ever car trip in 1888

'The dispute about the "birthday" of the modern automobile', Deutsches Patent- und Markenamt (22 December 2014), web.archive.org/web/20170102082130/https://www.dpma.de/service/klassifikationen/ipc/ipcprojekt/einekurzegeschichtedesautomobils/geburtstagdesautos/index.html

'Dr Carl Benz Car Museum', Mercedes-Benz (undated), www.mercedes-benz.com/en/art-and-culture/museum/dr-carl-benz-car-museum

Other helpful resources: Mercedes-Benz Classic archive (https://mercedes-benz-publicarchive.com/marsClassic/en/instance/ko/Contact.xhtml?oid=4912972)

53. In the Middle Ages, nobody except the clergy could read

Briggs, Charles F., 'Literacy, reading, and writing in the medieval West', *Journal of Medieval History* 26/4 (December 2000): 397–420

Goina, Mariana, 'The Uses of Pragmatic Literacy in the Medieval Principalities of Moldovia and Wallachia', PhD thesis (Department of Medieval Studies of the Central European University, 2009)

Lacey, H.E., 'Pragmatic Literacy and Political Consciousness in Later Medieval England', *Cahiers Électroniques d'Histoire Textuelle du Laboratoire de Médiévistique Occidentale de Paris* 5, University Paris 1 Panthéon-Sorbonne (2012): 19–35

Rogers, Nicola, 'Writing and Literacy in the Medieval Period: an Insight Report', York Archaeological Trust for Excavation and Research (2017)

Other helpful resources: York Archaeology (www.yorkarchaeology.co.uk)

54. The first ever video or computer game was *Pong*

Copeland, B. Jack, *Turing: Pioneer of the Information Age* (Oxford University Press, 2014)

Link, David, 'Programming ENTER: Christopher Strachey's Draughts Program', *Resurrection* (Winter 2012/13): 23–31

Smith, Alexander, *They Create Worlds, Vol. I: 1971–1982* (CRC Press, 2019)

Smith, Alvy, 'The Dawn of Digital Light', *IEEE Annals of the History of Computing* 38/4 (2016): 74–91

Turing, Dermot, *Alan Turing Decoded: The Man They Called Prof* (History Press, 2021)

55. The Great Wall of China is the only human-made object visible from space

Atkinson, Nancy, 'Can You See the Great Wall of China From Space?', *Universe Today* (5 June 2013), www.universetoday.com/25364/can-you-see-the-great-wall-of-china-from-space

'China's Wall Less Great in View from Space', NASA (5 September 2005) www.nasa.gov/vision/space/workinginspace/great_wall.html

Córdoba, S. Sanz Fernández de, '100km Altitude Boundary for Astronautics', FAI Astronautic Records Commission (21 June 2004), www.fai.org/page/icare-boundary

Hvistendahl, Mara, 'Is China's Great Wall Visible from Space?', *Scientific American* (21 February 2008)

Stukeley, William et al., *The Family Memoirs of the Rev. William Stukeley, M.D.* (Surtees Society, 1882)

Other helpful resources: Heavens Above (www.heavens-above.com)

56. Medieval people thought the world was flat

Black, Winston, *The Middle Ages: Facts and Fictions* (ABC-CLIO, 2019)

Dante Alighieri, *Inferno*, trans. Allen Mandelbaum (University of California Press, 1980)

Falk, Seb, *The Light Ages: The Surprising Story of Medieval Science* (W.W. Norton, 2020)

Glick, Thomas F., Wallis, Faith and Livesey, Steven John, *Medieval Science, Technology, and Medicine: An Encyclopedia* (Routledge, 2005)

Gould, Stephen Jay, 'The Late Birth of a Flat Earth', in *Dinosaur in a Haystack* (Harvard University Press, 1995)

Russell, Jeffrey Burton, *Inventing the Flat Earth* (Praeger 1991)

57. In the Middle Ages, everyone emptied chamber pots into the street, often from windows

Brant, Sebastian, *Das Narrenschiff* (Jakob Locher, Johann Bergmann von Olpe, 1494), https://digital.staatsbibliothek-berlin.de/werkan sicht?PPN=PPN848961617&view=picture-double&DMDID=& PHYSID=PHYS_0155

Ciecieznski, N.J., 'The Stench of Disease: Public Health and the Environment in Late-Medieval English towns and cities', *Health, Culture and Society* 4/1 (2013): 92–104

Cybulskie, Danièle, *Life in Medieval Europe: Fact and Fiction* (Pen & Sword, 2019)

Havlíček, Filip, Pokorná, Adéla and Zálešák, Jakub, 'Waste Management and Attitudes Towards Cleanliness in Medieval Central Europe', *Journal of Landscape Ecology* 10/3 (2017): 266–87

Jørgensen, Dolly, 'City Sanitation Regulations in the Coventry Mayor's Proclamation of 1421', *Arcadia* 8 (2012), www.environmentandsociety.org/ arcadia/city-sanitation-regulations-coventry-mayors-proclamation-1421#:~:text=Keeping%20Coventry's%20river%20flowing%20 was,structures%2C%20such%20as%20crafting%20equipment

Jørgensen, Dolly, 'The Medieval Sense of Smell, Stench and Sanitation' (August 2014), https://dolly.jorgensenweb.net/the-medieval-sense-of-smell-stench-and-sanitation

Mitchell, Piers D., *Sanitation, Latrines and Intestinal Parasites in Past Populations* (Routledge, 2015)

Oosten, R.M.R. van., 'The "Great Sanitary Awakening" Questioned: Is There a Solid Argument in Favour of the "Filthy Medieval City" Hypothesis?', *Medieval and Modern Matters* 5 (2014): 95–116

58. Queen Elizabeth I bathed once a year 'whether she needed it or not'

Borman, Tracy, *Elizabeth's Women: Friends, Rivals, and Foes Who Shaped the Virgin Queen* (Random House, 2010)

Borman, Tracy, *The Private Lives of the Tudors* (Grove Atlantic, 2016)

Freud, Sigmund, *Jokes and Their Relation to the Unconscious* (Franz Deuticke, 1905)

Furnivall, Frederick, *The Babees' Book: Medieval Manners for the Young*, trans. Edith Rickert and L.J. Naylor (Chatto & Windus, 1923)

Goodman, Ruth, *How to Be a Tudor: A Dawn-to-Dusk Guide to Tudor Life* (Penguin, 2015)

Howes, David, Classen, Constance and Synnott, Anthony, *Aroma: The Cultural History of Smell* (Routledge, 1994)

Meyer, G.J., *The Tudors: The Complete Story of England's Most Notorious Dynasty* (Delacorte Press, 2010)

Mortimer, Ian, *The Time Traveller's Guide to Elizabethan England* (Random House, 2012)

Thurley, Simon, *Houses of Power: The Places that Shaped the Tudor World* (Transworld, 2017)

Thurley, Simon, *Whitehall Palace: An Architectural History of the Royal Apartments, 1240–1698* (Yale University Press, 1999)

Watkins, Susan, *In Public and in Private: Elizabeth I and Her World* (Thames & Hudson, 1998)

Wright, Lawrence, *Clean and Decent: The Fascinating History of the Bathroom and the Water-Closet* (Penguin, 2000)

59. The phrase 'Upper crust' comes from the rich getting the top of the bread (the poor got the bottom)

Badcock, John, *Slang, a Dictionary of the Turf, the Ring, the Chase, the Pit, of Bon-ton, and the Varieties of Life . . . Interspersed with Anecdotes and Whimsies* (T. Hughes, 1823)

Furnivall, Frederick, *The Babees' Book: Medieval Manners for the Young*, trans. Edith Rickert and L.J. Naylor (Chatto & Windus, 1923)

Russell, John, *The Boke of Nurture . . .* ed. Frederick Furnivall (John Charles & Son, 1867)

Singman, Jeffrey L., *Daily Life in Medieval Europe* (Greenwood, 2008)

Wilton, David, *Word Myths: Debunking Linguistic Urban Legends* (Oxford University Press, 2004)

60. A long beard killed its owner

Gelling, Natasha, 'The World's Longest Beard Is One Of The Smithsonian's Strangest Artifacts', *Smithsonian* (19 November 2014), www.

smithsonianmag.com/smithsonian-institution/smithsonian-home-worlds-longest-beard-180953370

Other helpful resources: The Hans Langseth website (www.hanslangseth.com)

61. Queen Elizabeth II bowed to Emperor Haile Selassie

'Haile Selassie and Queen Elizabeth II', *HoaxEye* (31 March 2019), https://hoaxeye.com/2019/03/31/haile-selassie-and-queen-elizabeth-ii/

'Queen Greets Haile Selassie', British Pathé (1954; uploaded 13 April 2014), www.youtube.com/watch?v=46l17LlB6-M

'State visits paid by the Queen with the Duke of Edinburgh', Royal Archives (undated), www.royal.uk/sites/default/files/media/state_visits_paid_by_the_queen_with_the_duke_of_edinburgh_2.pdf

'A Wing on the Palace', *TIME* (12 February 1965)

Other helpful resources: LIFE magazine

62. Medieval Europeans were filthy and had to be taught about basic hygiene and soap by the Moors

Angelakis, Andreas N. and Rose, Joan B. (eds), *Evolution of Sanitation and Wastewater Technologies Through the Centuries* (IWA Publishing, 2014)

Archibald, Prof. Elizabeth, 'Baths of Bliss in the Middle Ages: Fact and Fiction', lecture (2014), www.youtube.com/watch?v=bTh2O5jYmFY

Caesar, Julius, *Caesar's Gallic War*, trans. W.A. McDevitte and W.S. Bohn (Harper & Brothers, 1869)

Collins, Roger, *Visigothic Spain 409–711* (Wiley, 2008)

Constable, Olivia Remie, *To Live Like a Moor: Christian Perceptions of Muslim Identity in Medieval and Early Modern Spain* (University of Pennsylvania Press, 2017)

Dam, Fabiola van, *The Medieval Public Bathhouse: Phenomenon, Metaphor, Stage of the World* (Uitgeverij Verloren, 2020)

Daniel of Beccles, *The Book of the Civilised Man: An English Translation of the Urbanus Magnus of Daniel of Beccles*, ed. Fiona Whelan et al. (Taylor & Francis, 2019)

Goodman, Ruth, *How to Be a Tudor: A Dawn-to-Dusk Guide to Tudor Life* (Penguin, 2015)

Guizzi, Giulio, *Cleaning and Sanitation: a Global History* (Edizioni LSWR, 2016)

Hanawalt, Barbara A., *The Ties that Bound: Peasant Families in Medieval England* (Oxford University Press, 1986)

Jervis, Ben and Kyle, Alison (eds), *Make-do and Mend: Archaeologies of Compromise, Repair and Reuse* (British Archaeological Reports Oxford, 2012)

Jiménez, Javier, 'The continuity of Roman water supply systems in Post-Roman Spain: The case of Valentia, a reliable example?', *Arkeogazte* 1 (January 2011): 125–44

Pliny the Elder, *Naturalis Historia* (*c.* AD 77)

'Profile: The Nation of Islam', The Anti-Defamation League (2021), www.adl.org/resources/profile/nation-islam

Singman, Jeffrey L., *Daily Life in Medieval Europe* (Greenwood, 2008)

'Soap and washing: Did they have soap in medieval times?', Modern History TV (5 June 2019), https://youtu.be/j30HOdWJ5gE

Sowina, Urszula, 'Water supply of the Late Medieval and Early Modern town in the Polish lands', *Fasciculli Archaeologiae Historicae* 24 (2011): 11–18

Tacitus, *De origine et situ Germanorum* (*c.* AD 98)

Trotula de Ruggiero, *De Ornatu Mulierum* (12th century)

Underwood, Douglas, *(Re)using Ruins: Public Building in the Cities of the Late Antique West, A.D. 300–600* (Brill, 2019)

Other helpful resources: Dr Eleanor Janega's *Going Medieval* website (https://going-medieval.com)

63. The first time women wore shorts they caused a car crash

Useful resources: City of Toronto Archives (www.toronto.ca/city-government/accountability-operations-customer-service/access-city-information-or-records/city-of-toronto-archives/)

64. A man tested American football helmets by bashing his head into a wall

'Air Eddies', *Flight International* (6 April 1912), https://archive.org/details/Flight_International_Magazine_1912-04-06-pdf/page/n9/mode/2up

Brown, Timothy P., 'Early Testing of Helmets and Protective Cups', *Football Archaeology* (24 January 2021), www.footballarchaeology.com/p/early-testing-of-helmets-and-protective-cups

Grothe, Solveig, 'Mit dem Kopf durch die Wand', *Spiegel* (26 March 2016), www.spiegel.de/geschichte/augenblick-mal-mit-dem-kopf-durch-die-wand-a-1083385.html

Other helpful resources: 'Flying Helmet, Warren Safety Helmet: Royal Flying Corps', Imperial War Museum, www.iwm.org.uk/collections/item/object/30091141

65. Paris Hilton invented the selfie

Hannavy, John (ed.), *Encyclopedia of Nineteenth-Century Photography* (Taylor & Francis, 2013)

Meehan, Sean Ross, *Mediating American Autobiography: Photography in Emerson, Thoreau, Douglass, and Whitman* (University of Missouri Press, 2008)

Other helpful resources: Photography 1839–1937 exhibition, 1937, The Museum of Modern Art, New York (www.moma.org/calendar/exhibitions/2088); Robert Cornelius, [*Self-portrait*], photograph, 1839, Library of Congress (www.loc.gov/pictures/item/2004664436/)

66. Wojtek the bear was enlisted into a Polish unit in the Second World War but switched sides and joined the Germans

Bär, dir. Pascal Floerks (2014), www.youtube.com/watch?v=C3ZVWQBVZWU

Kringiel, Daniel, 'The Nazis' Furriest Enemy', *Spiegel* (13 July 2012)

Wojtek: The Bear That Went to War, BBC Two (30 December 2011), www.bbc.co.uk/programmes/b018jhfr

Other helpful resources: Pascal Floerks's website (www.floerks.de); Filmakademie Baden-Württemberg GmbH (www.filmakademie.de); image of the badge of the 22nd Artillery Support Company, 2nd Polish Corps, 1944, Imperial War Museum (www.iwm.org.uk/collections/item/object/205026421)

67. This is the guillotine blade that killed Marie Antoinette

Pilbeam, Pamela, *Madame Tussaud: And the History of Waxworks* (Bloomsbury Academic, 2006)

Tussaud, Marie, *Madame Tussaud's Memoirs and Reminiscences of France, Forming an Abridged History of the French Revolution* (Saunders and Otley, 1838)

68. The Minions from *Despicable Me* were based on photos of Nazi experiments on children

Helpful resources: Royal Navy Submarine Museum (www.nmrn.org.uk/visit-us/submarine-museum); National Museum of the Royal Navy (www.nmrn.org.uk); The Historical Diving Society (www.thehds.com); The Diving Museum (www.divingmuseum.co.uk.)

69. The White House was painted white to cover up damage after the British set fire to it

Barnhart, David K. and Metcalf, Allan, *America in So Many Words: Words That Have Shaped America* (HarperCollins, 1999)

Jennings, Paul, *A Colored Man's Reminiscences of James Madison* (George C. Beadle, 1865)

Vogel, Steve, *Through the Perilous Fight* (Random House, 2014)

Other helpful resources: The White House Historical Association (www.white housechistory.org)

70. The Tudors used spices to cover up the taste of bad meat

Bryson, Bill, *At Home: A Short History of Private Life* (Transworld, 2010)

Fitch, Richard, 'Meat and Status. A Historical Look at Meat in the English Diet', *Cooking the Books* (2016), https://tudorcook.co.uk/blog/wp-content/uploads/2016/01/Meat-and-Status-R-Fitch-Final-V2.pdf

Freedman, Paul, *Out of the East: Spices and the Medieval Imagination* (Yale University Press, 2008)

Goodman, Ruth, *How to Be a Tudor: A Dawn-to-Dusk Guide to Everyday Life* (Penguin, 2015)

Myers, Daniel, 'Drummond's Rotten Meat: When Good Sources Go Bad', *Medieval Cookery* (undated), http://medievalcookery.com/notes/drummond.pdf

Newman, Paul B., *Daily Life in the Middle Ages* (McFarland, 2018)

71. Erin O'Keefe was eaten by mountain rats in 1876

Davidson, Levette Jay, 'The Pikes Prevaricator', *Colorado Magazine* 20 (November 1943)

Jessen, Kenneth Christian, *Eccentric Colorado: A Legacy of the Bizarre and Unusual* (Pruett, 1985)

72. Queen Elizabeth II threw food at poor people in Africa

Useful resources: Enfants annamites ramassant des sapèques devant la pagode des dames, photograph by Gabriel Veyre, 1899–1900, *Catalogue Lumière* (https://catalogue-lumiere.com/enfants-annamites-ramassant-des-sapeques)

73. In the 1930s, Marlene Dietrich was detained by the police for wearing trousers

Bach, Steven, *Marlene Dietrich: Life and Legend* (University of Minnesota Press, 2013)

Bard, Christine, *Une histoire politique du pantalon* (Seuil, 2010)

Spoto, Donald, *Blue Angel: The Life of Marlene Dietrich* (Cooper Square Press, 2000)

74. Two bullets collided at the battle of Gallipoli in 1915 – a billion-to-one chance

'1915 Seddülbahir Ahmet Uslu Müzesi', *Canakkale Otelleri* (undated), www.canakkaleotelleri.com/gezilecek-yerler/eceabat/1915-seddulbahir-ahmet-uslu-muzesi

Other helpful resources: Paul Walker, 7news Sydney, on Twitter (https://twitter.com/pdwnews)

75. These mysterious photos show an abandoned medieval village

Helpful resources: Alex Friedrich's website (https://alexfriedrich.de), Urbex Flickr collection (www.flickr.com/photos/3passa) and Props Flickr collection (www.flickr.com/photos/3passa); Studio Babelsberg (www.studiobabelsberg.com/en); Filmpark Babelsberg (www.filmpark-babelsberg.de)

76. Hugh Hefner's grandpa invented the Playboy Bunnies

Helpful resources: Steven Cook's *Alternity* series (www.steven-cook.com/Alternity)

77. This is the world's first Miss World

Lovegrove, Keith, *Pageant: The Beauty Contest* (Laurence King, 2002)

Stein, Elissa, *Beauty Queen: Here She Comes* (Chronicle, 2006)

78. This is the world's first robot

'Buffalo Soldiers Study', National Park Service (March 2019), www.nps.gov/chyo/getinvolved/buffalo-soldiers-study.htm

Guinan, Paul and Bennett, Anina, *Boilerplate: History's Mechanical Marvel* (Harry N. Abrams, 2009)

Mayor, Adrienne, *Gods and Robots: Myths, Machines, and Ancient Dreams of Technology* (Princeton University Press, 2020)

79. The pyramids were built by slaves

Lehner, Mark, *The Complete Pyramids* (Thames & Hudson, 2008)

Thompson, Stephen E., *Ancient Egypt: Facts and Fictions* (ABC-CLIO, 2018)

80. This is a photo of Bill the Butcher, the infamous nineteenth-century street-gang leader

Boissoneault, Lorraine, 'How the 19th-Century Know Nothing Party Reshaped American Politics', *Smithsonian* (26 January 2017), www.smith sonianmag.com/history/immigrants-conspiracies-and-secret-society-launched-american-nativism-180961915

Norton, Richard Arthur, 'William Poole bibliography' (2006), https://web. archive.org/web/20090628101111/http://richard.arthur.norton.goog lepages.com/williampoole

Other helpful resources: New York Times Article Archive (https://help.nytimes. com/hc/en-us/articles/115014772767-New-York-Times-Archived-Articles-and-TimesMachine-)

81. The world's first computer virus was a universal message of peace

'A Brief History of Computer Viruses & What the Future Holds', Kaspersky (undated), www.kaspersky.com/resource-center/threats/ a-brief-history-of-computer-viruses-and-what-the-future-holds

Spencer, Sean, 'Timeline of Computer Viruses', Mapcon (undated), www. mapcon.com/us-en/timeline-of-computer-viruses

Other helpful resources: Virus Encyclopedia (http://virus.wikidot.com)

82. Europeans built a bridge in Ethiopia but locals couldn't repair it and crossed the river with ropes

Pankhurst, Richard, *An Introduction to the Economic History of Ethiopia from Early Times to 1800* (Lalibela House, 1961)

Snailham, Richard, *The Blue Nile Revealed: The Story of the Great Abbai Expedition, 1968* (Signal Books, 2005)

83. In Victorian times, Dr Batty's Asthma Cigarettes were advertised as good for your health

'Driving me (Dr.) Batty', Ask MetaFilter (17 July 2010), https://ask.meta-filter.com/159771/Driving-me-Dr-Batty

Reames, O.K., *History of Zanesfield and Sketches of the Interesting and Historical Places of Logan County, Ohio* (Zanesfield Area Bicentennial Committee, 1976)

Other helpful resources: Jessica D. Griffin's website, *Old Main Artifacts*, (https://oldmainartifacts.wordpress.com/about)

84. This massive device was the world's first camera

Wade, John, *The Ingenious Victorians: Weird and Wonderful Ideas from the Age of Innovation* (Pen & Sword, 2016)

Other helpful resources: 'The Largest Photograph in the World of the Handsomest Train in the World', photograph, *c.* 1900, Indiana Historical Society (https://images.indianahistory.org/digital/collection/dc013/id/1177); Musée Nicéphore Niépce (www.museeniepce.com)

85. This is the first cat photo ever taken

Helpful resources: David Simkin's *Sussex Photo History* website (www.photohistory-sussex.co.uk); 'Portrait of a Family of Eight and a Cat', photograph, *c.* 1846, Getty Museum Collection (www.getty.edu/art/collection/object/104F1H)

86. This is the first dog photo ever taken

Chevelle, Chelle, 'The World's Oldest Photos of Animals', *Medium* (17 September 2020), https://thefundamentalsofphotography.medium.com/15-of-the-oldest-photos-of-animals-75a257dc68e4

The Daily Dish, 'The Photos of Pets', *Atlantic* (21 March 2009), www.theatlantic.com/daily-dish/archive/2009/03/the-photos-of-pets/204201/

Maurillier, Paul, 'Daguerre, Claudette, Lerebours: their early use of 'instantaneous daguerrotypes', *Collodions and Clopinettes* (1999), http://collodion.claude-marillier.net/PM/instantaneEN.html

87. The Victorians covered furniture legs because they were too arousing

Frost, Ginger S., *The Victorian World: Facts and Fictions* (ABC-CLIO, 2018)

Sweet, Matthew, *Inventing the Victorians: What we think we know about them and why we're wrong* (Faber & Faber, 2002)

88. During the Middle Ages, there were torches everywhere

Crane, Eva, *The World History of Beekeeping and Honey Hunting* (Taylor & Francis, 1999)

Sapoznik, Alexandra, 'Bees in the Medieval Economy: Religious Observance and the Production, Trade, and Consumption of Wax in England, *c.* 1300–1555', *Economic History Review* 72/4 (November 2019): 1152–74

Wisniak, Jaime, 'Candle: A Light into the Past', *Indian Journal of Chemical Technology* 7/7 (July 2001): 319–26

89. Beethoven was Black

Begg, Tristan et al., 'Genomic analyses of hair from Ludwig van Beethoven', *Current Biology* (2022): https://doi.org/10.1016/j.cub.2023.02.041

Comini, Alessandra, *The Changing Image of Beethoven: a Study in Mythmaking* (Random House, 1987)

Lerma, Dominique-René de, 'Beethoven as a Black Composer', *Black Music Research Journal* 10/1 (1990): 118–22

Rinehart, Nicholas T., 'Black Beethoven and the Racial Politics of Music History', *Transition* 112 (*Django Unpacked*, 2013): 117–30

Thurman, Dr Kira, Twitter (18 June 2020), https://web.archive. org/web/20220209001707/https://twitter.com/kira_thurman/ status/1273662957579272193

Wheelock Thayer, Alexander, *The Life of Ludwig van Beethoven*, trans. Henry Edward Krehbiel (Beethoven Association in New York, 1921)

90. These women in China in 1922 are being punished for the crime of witchcraft

Saunders, William Thomas, 'Portfolio of Sketches of Chinese Life and Character' (1871), https://hpcbristol.net/photographer/ saunders-william

Thiriez, Régine, 'Creating a user's guide on early photography in China' (30 January 2015), www.yumpu.com/en/document/view/36554919/ creating-a-users-guide-on-early-photography-in-china-regine-

Other helpful resources: 'ASIA 1. Album of prints (some coloured) of Singapore, Java, Indo-China, Hong Kong, Shanghai, Japan and the Suez Canal', late nineteenth century, The National Archives, Kew, CO 1069/416

91. Thumb down meant death for the gladiators of ancient Rome

Bontty, Monica M., *Ancient Rome: Facts and Fictions* (ABC-CLIO, 2020)

Carter, M.J., 'Gladiatorial Combat: The Rules of Engagement', *Classical Journal* 102/2 (December–January 2006/7): 97–114

Corbeill, Anthony, *Nature Embodied: Gesture in Ancient Rome* (Princeton University Press, 2004)

Corbeill, Anthony, 'Thumbs in Ancient Rome: "Pollex" as Index', *Memoirs of the American Academy in Rome* 42 (1997): 1–21

Gladiators: The Brutal Truth, presented by Terry Jones, dir. Alan Eirea, BBC (1999), www.youtube.com/watch?v=MyyuyKLO330

Morris, Desmond et al., *Gestures: Their Origin and Meanings* (Jonathan Cape, 1979)

Winkler, Martin M., *The Roman Salute: Cinema, History, Ideology* (Ohio State University Press, 2009)

92. This horrifying photo shows serial killer Leonarda Cianciulli making soap out of humans

'Leonarda Cianciulli', Murderpedia (undated), https://murderpedia.org/female.C/c/cianciulli-leonarda.htm

'Omicidi: caso Cianciulli', Museo Criminologico (undated), www.museocriminologico.it/index.php/2-non-categorizzato/120-omicidi-caso-cianciulli2

Other helpful resources: Lilly Library, Indiana University Bloomington (https://libraries.indiana.edu/lilly-library)

93. These girls are saying a sad goodbye to sailors during the Second World War

Volpe, Giorgio, 'In the Caribbean with Vespucci in 1963', *Apnea Magazine* (28 August 2014), www.apneamagazine.com/pesca-sub-caraibi-vespucci-17279?amp

Other helpful resources: Italian Ministry of Defence (www.difesa.it/Pagine/default.aspx); Marina Militare (www.marina.difesa.it/en/Pagine/default.aspx); Italian Navy Historical Office (www.icmh-cihm.org/en/what-we-do/military-archives/76-italian-navy-archives); Congedati Vespucci (www.congedativespucci.it)

94. Secret agents used amazing walking-backwards spy shoes to confuse the Nazis

Horn, Bernd, *A Most Ungentlemanly Way of War: The SOE and the Canadian Connection* (Dundurn, 2016)

Other helpful resources: Imperial War Museum (www.iwm.org.uk); Deutsches Schuhmuseum Hauenstein (https://museum-hauenstein.de/de/home/1/home.html)

95. The Iron Maiden and the Pear of Anguish were brutal medieval torture devices

Bishop, Chris, 'The Pear of Anguish: Torture, Truth and Dark Medievalism', *International Journal of Cultural Studies* 17/6 (2014): 591–602

Other helpful resources: Medieval Crime Museum Rothenburg (www. rothenburg-tourismus.de/en/discover/the-highlights-of-rothenburg-ob-der-tauber-top1o-sights/medieval-crime-and-justice-museum); Rijksmuseum de Gevangenpoort (www.gevangenpoort.nl)

96. During the Middle Ages, people drank beer instead of water

Angelakis, Andreas N. and Rose, Joan B. (eds), *Evolution of Sanitation and Wastewater Technologies Through the Centuries* (IWA Publishing, 2014)

Bennett, Judith M., *Ale, Beer, and Brewsters in England: Women's Work in a Changing World, 1300–1600* (Oxford University Press, 1999)

Chevallier, Jim, 'The Great Medieval Water Myth', *Les Leftovers* (2013), https://leslefts.blogspot.com/2013/11/the-great-medieval-water-myth.html

Did Medieval People Drink Water?, presented by Jimmy Johnson, The Welsh Viking (2020), www.youtube.com/watch?v=Ne2SkObB6Zw

Harris, Stephen J. and Grigsby, Bryon L., *Misconceptions About the Middle Ages* (Routledge, 2009)

Jong, Henk 't, 'De mythe van de vuilnisbelt' (2008), www.academia. edu/1009200/Mythe_van_de_vuilnisbelt

Mortimer, Ian, *The Time Traveller's Guide to Medieval England: A Handbook for Visitors to the Fourteenth Century* (Random House, 2012)

Placeway, Paul, 'Recreating Medieval English Ales', Carnegie Mellon University – School of Computer Science (1998), www.cs.cmu. edu/~pwp/tofi/medieval_english_ale.html

Squatriti, Paolo, *Water and Society in Early Medieval Italy* (Cambridge University Press, 1998)

Tilburg, Cornelis van., 'Greek and Roman ideas about healthy drinking-water in theory and practice', *eä Journal* 5/1 (June 2013)

Unger, Richard W., *Beer in the Middle Ages and the Renaissance* (University of Pennsylvania Press, 2007)

Woolgar, C.M., Serjeantson, D. and Waldron, T. (eds), *Food in Medieval England: Diet and Nutrition (Medieval History and Archaeology)* (Oxford University Press, 2009)

97. Hitler invented the motorway

Matzke, Michael, 'Die Straßen Adolf Hitlers, Reichsautobahnen 1933– 1941', diploma thesis (University of Vienna, 2008)

Voth, Hans-Joachim and Voigtländer, Nico, 'Nazi pork and popularity: How Hitler's roads won German hearts and minds', Centre for Economic Policy Research (2014), https://cepr.org/voxeu/columns/nazi-pork-and-popularity-how-hitlers-roads-won-german-hearts-and-minds

Zeller, Thomas, *Driving Germany: The Landscape of the German Autobahn, 1930–1970* (Berghahn Books, 2007)

98. When knights went on crusade they put chastity belts on their wives

Classen, A., *The Medieval Chastity Belt: A Myth-Making Process* (Palgrave Macmillan, 2007)

Harris, Stephen J. and Grigsby, Bryon L., *Misconceptions About the Middle Ages* (Routledge, 2009)

Smith, Lesley, 'Chastity belts and birthing girdles', *Journal of Family Planning and Reproductive Health Care* 33/4 (2007): 285–6

99. The flush toilet was invented by Thomas Crapper

Hart-Davis, Adam, *Thunder, Flush and Thomas Crapper: An Encycloopedia* (Michael O'Mara, 1997)

Reyburn, Wallace, *Flushed with Pride: The Story of Thomas Crapper* (Prentice-Hall, 1971)

Other helpful resources: Bob Cromwell's blog, *The Toilet Guru* (https://toilet-guru.com/blog/1.html)

100. A baby falling out of a window was rescued by the same man twice

'Miscellany', *TIME* (17 October 1938), https://content.time.com/time/subscriber/article/0,33009,848363,00.html

'Street Worker Hit in Plunge of Child', *Detroit Free Press* (28 September 1938)

101. This is an amazing Art Nouveau villa in Bucharest

Helpful resource: Thierry Lechanteur's website (www.lechanteur.be/category/exposition)

An Unconventional Index

Conventional indexes refer to page numbers. This one refers to chapters, and is organised by People, Eras, Places and Miscellaneous Themes.

Illustration Credits

p. 5 'Profil de la tête colossale du Sphinx' in Frédéric Louis Norden's *Voyage d'Égypte et de Nubie* (1795). Wikimedia Commons, public domain

p. 9 'Organisationsbuch der Nsdap 1937: Tafel 47 Dienst-und Paradean-zug der Allgem' in Robert Ley's 'Nationalsozialistische Deutsche Arbeiter-Partei, Reichsorganisationsamt' (1937). Wikimedia Commons under Creative Commons Attribution-Share Alike 4.0 International license, public domain

p. 33 'Actors "Sleeping" Draped Over Ropes' © Bettmann/Getty

p. 38 'Puck Christmas 1902' by Frank A. Nankivell in *Puck* vol. 52, no. 134. © 1902 by Keppler & Schwarzmann. Held by the Library of Congress, public domain

p. 43 'Mosteiro de Alcobaça', 19 April 2008, uploaded by Karstenkas-cais; edit by Waugsberg, Wikimedia Commons under Creative Commons Attribution-Share Alike 3.0 Unported, public domain

p. 53 'Clara Bow (1905-1965) US silent film actress about 1932' © Pictorial Press Ltd/Alamy Stock Photo

p. 56 Photograph by Scott van Looy; original artist unknown

p. 59 'Pep the Dog' (1924), Eastern State Penitentiary image library, gift of Joseph Brierley; photographer unknown

p. 63 Photographer unknown

p. 67 'East Zone, West Zone' © Jung/Stringer

p. 70 'Plague Doctor, 17th Century' © Science History Images/Alamy Stock Photo

p. 74 © Richard Tanton

p. 78 'François Bertillon, 23 months' by Alphonse Bertillion, 1893. Digital image, courtesy of The Museum of Modern Art, New York/Scala, Florence. Suzanne Winsberg Collection. Gift of Suzanne Winsberg

p. 81 With kind permission from GS Pshenichny Central State Film and Photo Archive of Ukraine; photographer unknown

p. 84 'The Lord Appearing to Saint Thomas and the Apostles', wooden panel in the Coptic Museum, Cairo, 18th century (AD), Greek style, artist unknown; photograph by Su Bayfield

p. 96 'Via Santo Spirito, Buchetta Vino', 17 July 2007, uploaded by Sailko, Wikimedia Commons under Creative Commons Attribution-Share Alike 3.0 Unported license, public domain

p. 98 Lutie A. Lytle: illustration in *Occupations for Women* by Frances Elizabeth Willard, published by The Success Company, New York, 1897. Wikimedia, public domain. Marian Anderson: photograph ca. late 1920s © Everett Collection Inc/Alamy Stock Photo. Sadie Alexander: University Archives and Records Center, University of Pennsylvania

p. 104 French house photograph by François Boscher, taken for Ouest-France

p. 146 'Jacques-Louis David – Oath of the Horatii' © The Artchives/Alamy Stock Photo

p. 153 Detail of the Bayeux Tapestry courtesy of the Bayeux Museum

p. 157 'Flooding of the Seine (31 January 1910), rue Jacob', Clark Art Institute, Lent by The Troob Family Foundation, TR TR2001.44.3

p. 166 'Bertha Benz' courtesy of Mercedes-Benz Classic

p. 183 Illustration from *Narrenschiff* by Sebastian Brant (1457–1521), Basel, Scan einer Kopie des in Basel Liegenden Orginals von 1499, Wikimedia Commons, public domain

p. 198 'Hans Langseth portrait' by Nils C. Jorgenson, courtesy of Institute for Regional Studies, North Dakota State University, Fargo (Folio 13.1)

p. 201 'Ethiopia Essay: Haile Selassie' © Alfred Eisenstaedt/The LIFE Picture Collection/Shutterstock

p. 210 'Women in shorts "cause" car to crash into pole', Fonds 1257, Series 1057, Item 4766, courtesy of the City of Toronto Archives; public domain

p. 213 'Mr Warren helmet testing' by Ullstein Bild © Flight Collection/TopFoto

p. 217 'Self-portrait' by Robert Cornelius, 1839 © World History Archive/Alamy Stock Photo

p. 219 Hippolyte Bayard portrait, courtesy of the Société française de photographie collection (coll. SFP), Paris

p. 220 Original: 'Pfc. Leo J. Powers – Unlikely Medal of Honor Recipient During Battle of Monte Cassino' Bundesarchive photo, DefenseMediaNetwork, February 3, 2014 https://www.defensemedianetwork.com/stories/pfc-leo-s-powers-unsung-medal-of-honor-recipient/; Wikimedia Commons, German Federal Archive. Photoshopped version: Filmakademie Baden-Württemberg GmbH

p. 224 'Madame Tussauds - Original Guillotine Blade that Beheaded Marie Antoinette' © Danie van der Merwe

p. 228 Courtesy of The National Museum of the Royal Navy

p. 231 'The President's House' by George Munger (between circa 1814 and circa 1815), The White House Historical Association, Wikimedia Commons, public domain (PD-US-expired)

p. 237 Denver Public Library Special Collections, C Photo Collection 516

p. 240 'Vietnamese Children (1900, French Indochina) - by Gabriel Veyre', YouTube, Gabriel Veyre (between April 1899 and March 1900), Film #1274 in the Lumiere Catalogue, https://www.youtube.com/watch?v= WE9vxl9VQoU

p. 244 'Marlene Dietrich', 1930 © Ullstein Bild Dtl./Getty

p. 249 © Paul Walker

p. 253 'The Dark Ages' © Alex Friedrich

p. 257 Original photograph: photographer unknown. Photoshopped image: 'Grandpa Hefner's Jack Rabbit Club', 2011, © Steve Cook / ARS, NY & DACS London, 2023

p. 260 'Cléo de Mérode portrait', 1903, by Anton Blomberg, uploaded by Swedish Performing Arts Agency, Stockholm, Wikimedia Commons, public domain

p. 263 Original image: '10th Cavalry Escort to General Merritt's Party, St Mary, Montana' by A. B. Coe, 1894–08, sourced from the Montana State Library Montana History Portal, https://mtmemory.recollectcms.com/ nodes/view/75309. Photoshopped version: Paul Guinan

p. 270 International Center of Photography, Gift of Steven Kasher, 2007; photographer unknown

p. 273 '1988-03 Universal Peace virus', Mike Evangelist (2 March 1998), Wikimedia Commons under Creative Commons Attribution-Share Alike 3.0 Unported license

p. 276 'Sebara Dildiy Bridge', uploaded by Kenneth Frantz (10 October 2011), Wikimedia Commons under Creative Commons Attribution-Share Alike 3.0 Unported license, public domain

p. 280 © Aaron B Howe

p. 284 'A very large camera designed by George R. Lawrence – 1900' © Photo-Fox/Alamy Stock Photo

p. 288 'Victorian Persian cat' (est. 1880), photographer unknown, sourced from PetDarling, Wikimedia Commons, public domain

p. 290 'A portrait of the Brighton photographer Harry Pointer with three of his cats' © The Picture Art Collection/Alamy Stock Photo

p. 292 'Poodle With Bow on Table', photographer unknown, est. 1850. Courtesy of Sotheby's

p. 294 'Dog' by Louis-Auguste Bisson (1841–1849), Gilman Collection, Purchase, Jennifer and Joseph Duke Gift, 2005. Held by The Met, public domain

p. 295 Courtesy of Claude Marillier. Provenance uncertain, believed to be 'Médor' by Louis Daguerre; date unknown

p. 309 'Female Prisoners in the Cangue' by William Saunders (est. 1870-1880), The National Archives, Kew, ref. WO 169/24904 © 2008 SOAS

p. 312 *Pollice Verso'* by Jean-Léon Gérôme, (1872), Collection of Phoenix Art Museum, Museum purchase, 1968.52; photograph by Mike Lundgren, Wikimedia Commons, public domain

p. 317 'Old lady making soap' (1925) from the Frank M. Hohenberger Photograph Collection. Courtesy of The Lilly Library, Indiana University, Bloomington, Indiana

p. 321 Courtesy of the Italian Navy Historical Office; photograph by Roberto Borra, 1963

p. 324 © Deutsches Schuhmumem Hauenstein; photographer unknown

p. 329 First: 'Les Poires D'Angoisse' in *La Science Illustrée* No. 549, uploaded by Inconue (4 June 1898), Wikimedia Commons, public domain

p. 331 Etching, 43421i, Welcome Collection, public domain

p. 350 © Thierry Lechanteur